Memories of a
MUNCHKIN

Memories of a MUNCHKIN

An Illustrated Walk Down the Yellow Brick Road

Meinhardt Raabe
with Lieutenant Daniel Kinske, USN

Foreword by
Mickey Rooney

Back Stage Books
New York

To the memory of Marie Raabe, beloved wife
—M.R.

To my dad, the "nice big guy"—
Chief Petty Officer Daniel Leonard Kinske, U.S.N.
—D.K.

First published in 2005 by Back Stage Books,
An imprint of Watson-Guptill Publications,
A division of VNU Business Media, Inc.,
770 Broadway, New York, NY 10003
www.watsonguptill.com

Library of Congress Cataloging-in-Publication Data
Raabe, Meinhardt, 1915-
    Memories of a Munchkin / by Meinhardt Raabe with Daniel Kinske ; foreword by
Mickey Rooney.
        p.   cm.
    Includes bibliographical references and index.
    ISBN 0-8230-9193-7
    1. Raabe, Meinhardt, 1915– 2. Motion picture actors and actresses—United States—
Biography. 3. Wizard of Oz (Motion picture) 4. Dwarfs in motion pictures. I. Kinske,
Daniel. II. Title.
    PN2287.R214A3 2005
    791.4302'8'092—dc22   2005000543

Manufactured in U.S.A.

First printing 2005

1 2 3 4 5 6 7 8 9 / 12 11 10 09 08 07 06 05 04 03 02

Senior Acquisitions Editor: Mark Glubke
Edited by Laaren Brown
Designed by Jay Anning, Thumb Print
Graphic production by Ellen Greene

Contents

Foreword

"CALM DOWN, AND IT WILL ALL WORK OUT SOMEHOW. PEOPLE WILL love it." That is what I told Judy Garland sixty-five years ago when we opened *The Wizard of Oz* on its initial release at the Capitol Theatre in New York City. She was very young and was understandably worried about whether the film would be a success. I knew it was going to be big, and Judy felt relieved because she always relied on my advice.

I also think people will love Meinhardt's wonderfully humorous and insightful autobiography. It has been long overdue for one of the film's real Munchkins to finally tell his story. This has been no small "undertaking"... even for one who played the Munchkin Coroner!

Meinhardt worked with most of the future Munchkins years before the film, in various world's fairs and expositions, and had firsthand experience concerning the people and personalities who shaped the impish inhabitants of Munchkinland and touched the hearts and minds of millions.

This book is a special treat for *Wizard of Oz* fans, with its exquisitely detailed insight into the day-to-day filming and Meinhardt's rare personal movie memorabilia and unpublished photographs of the set and cast.

Everyone will enjoy this book, which, like the film, inspires and gives hope to each of us as we continue to follow our own yellow brick roads in search of what lies over the rainbow.

—MICKEY ROONEY

Preface

IF ANYONE HAD TOLD ME IN MY YOUNGER DAYS—THOSE DAYS that feel like yesterday—that I would ultimately be known worldwide as a cordial yet slightly diminutive coroner, I would have asked politely for a liberal sip of whatever libation was presently being enjoyed.

Actually I don't drink, but even the sober truth is stranger than fiction, and it will be my distinct pleasure to share how this fame came to be.

For nearly ninety years now, I have been walking down my own personal yellow brick road of life. Lately, pausing at the most recent bend to share my life story has seemed to be a good idea.

This tale is not all mine to tell, though. It is the story of all people, big and small, "normal" and challenged. Many have been told at some time that they were "different" in some insignificant way and so would never amount to anything. This is the classic parable of being the underdog who overcomes overwhelming odds. I just happen to be the spokesman for this particular story (although, admittedly, a rare spokesman—who can still walk under a dog himself!).

Many fine books have been written through the years about *The Wizard of Oz* film, and I have enjoyed reading and recommending a number of these. My intention is not to compete with their wonderful authors. But until now the story of the movie has never been told entirely from the point of view of any of the 124 little people who worked on it—except for a few anecdotes and interview excerpts here or there.

I felt I could contribute more insight into the film than was revealed by the few interviews that I have done in the past. So I took up a fresh scroll, intent on shedding some new light on the subject. As one who was present during the production of this truly American classic, I have always revered it and all of the personalities who played a part, however small, in its creation.

I hope that all of you will enjoy my attempt to chronicle the events of my past.

—MEINHARDT RAABE
The Munchkin Coroner
Penney Farms, Florida

Here I am with my coauthor, Lieutenant Daniel Kinske, and the great caricaturist Al Hirschfeld, who contributed the cover art of this book. Amazingly, he was one of the original artists on promotional materials for The Wizard of Oz.

Introduction

MEINHARDT RAABE IS A ONE-OF-A-KIND PERSON and is just as big an American as anyone else. His beginnings are similar to Dorothy Gale's in the MGM film adaptation of L. Frank Baum's classic children's story *The Wonderful Wizard of Oz*. Meinhardt grew up on a dairy farm in Farmington, Wisconsin, and although diminutive in stature, he worked very hard to better himself and succeed in a world driven by size.

He was magically transported to the wonderful world of Hollywoodland and made an indelible contribution to what has indisputably become the most popular classic family film ever made in America. His proclamation of death for the Wicked Witch of the East is one of the most oft-quoted and best-recognized lines in cinema.

Much more than meets the eye exists in this man who champions the causes and successes of all little people, past and present. Nothing has come easily to Meinhardt, who set out to make his living during the Great Depression and whose stubbornness and tenacity overcame almost any adversity. He was Oscar Mayer's spokesman, "Little Oscar," for more than thirty years and rode around in the very first Wienermobile. He is an accomplished pilot who flew every type of single-engine plane in existence during the 1940s. He also did his part during World War II by joining the Civil Air Patrol, rising to the rank of ground instructor. He taught aeronautics to young draftees, enabling them to enter the army's elite air corps instead of going straight to the infantry. And he performed actual rescue missions with his Civil Air Patrol unit—silently, but proudly, becoming the smallest pilot in uniform during the war.

If it weren't for my mother, Patricia Kinske, this book would have never gotten off the ground. She met Meinhardt and got to know him very well on a cruise ship that sailed out of Fort Lauderdale early in the spring of 2002. This was the second annual Munchkin-themed cruise, and thirty participants were able to spend time with the four Munchkin celebrity guests. On the final evening, my mother and Meinhardt were paired together. They had a great time, and once she found out how close he lived to me in Florida, she had the foresight to ask if I might visit him someday. A few days later, she and I did just that.

Like everyone who meets Meinhardt, I was mesmerized by his charm and charisma. Instantly I realized that there was much more to this man's life than having been a Munchkin, and I could not believe that he had not written a book about his fascinating life. But he has the humility that is prevalent in our World War II (and prior) generation, and he did not think that his story was interesting, or special, enough to be told.

I wrote Meinhardt several times to pitch this project, and finally he relented. We were not long into the process of interviews and trips together before we realized that this unlikely pairing of a Munchkin and a naval lieutenant with sixty years' age difference somehow created the perfect chemistry to complete what would ultimately develop into a three-year project.

Becoming better acquainted with this venerable gentleman, as he has shared his life with me during the writing of this book, has been a pleasure. Now, at eighty-nine, Meinhardt is the eldest of the nine surviving Munchkins—yet he has not shown any signs of slowing down. He continues to travel across the nation, attending various *Wizard of Oz* festivals and countless public appearances and assisting charity organizations.

In reading this book, you will gain an understanding of why I always have, and always will, look up to Meinhardt Raabe—the Munchkin Coroner.

—LIEUTENANT DANIEL KINSKE, USN
Benzonia, Michigan

This scale model of Dorothy's house was made for a national television commercial. Mr. Raabe was pleased to revisit the Wicked Witch's official cause of death.

CHAPTER ONE

Wisconsin, He Said, Was the Name of His Star

GREAT STATE OF Wisconsin is where my story began. On September 2, 1915, I was born into a family of German dairy farmers in Watertown, Wisconsin. This is in the southeastern portion of the state, about fifty miles northwest of Milwaukee as the witch flies. Actually, we lived in the small town of Farmington, in Jefferson County, and the city of Johnson Creek was used for the post office address. However, the nearest big city was Watertown, and it was our family's closest connection to the outside world in those days.

As I look back now, the similarities between the farms where Dorothy Gale and I grew up—well, where I grew *a bit*, anyway—are striking. One pleasing difference, though, was that our farm was much larger than hers.

A dusty two-lane dirt road peeled off our nearest paved road to meander past our farm. This stretch of dirt road was empty most of the time, and the rare car or wagon passing by would leave a winding trail of dust in its wake. Other than these occasional plumes, our farm was as serene as any Grandma Moses painting.

Our white farmhouse consisted of two big stories and an attic. The large, heavy, dark-stained oak door was usually left ajar, and the self-closing screen door took most of the abuse. That screen door seemed to squeak no matter how much it was oiled, and my parents heard its complaint many times.

A brick (brown, not yellow) path, about a hundred feet long, led from the house to the dirt road. Flanking the driveway were two mammoth oak trees that had existed long before the house was built in the late 1880s. Numerous maple

In this family portrait, I'm sitting on the hood of our Model A Ford touring car. My father taught me to drive in this car.

13

My parents, Henry and Eleonora Raabe.
This is their wedding picture, taken in 1911.

trees also shaded the house, but it was the oaks that always stood out in my mind, like two unmovable and indomitable guardians of our humble home.

Wood was abundant and our large house, typical for the area, was solidly built with pine and hardwood. Frank Lloyd Wright himself would have admired the way the natural materials of the area were used in the dwelling! On the front of the house was a concrete portico with stalwart square pillars and gingerbread trim. A large wooden porch swing, hand carved from hickory by one of my uncles, hung from the ceiling. It had been given to my parents as a wedding present, and their names were inscribed in the center: Henry and Eleonora Raabe (pronounced "Rah-bee").

My paternal grandfather, Herman Raabe, had emigrated from Germany to America in the late nineteenth century, while in his early twenties. My father, Henry Herman Raabe, was the youngest of four sons—a first-generation American,

born in Wisconsin. My mother, Eleonora Rummler, and her parents, August and Mathilda, were all born in the United States, so my mother was a second-generation American.

As a German immigrant, Grandpa Herman had to work as a laborer until he was able to earn enough money to start a farm. He bought a slightly dilapidated farmhouse in Watertown, set on about ten acres of land, and spent two years repairing and renovating the place, where he established a successful dairy farm. Over the years, he was able to accumulate several farms, and as his sons started families of their own, each took one of the farms and continued to work the land. The name Raabe became firmly established in Watertown.

My grandfather was a semi-invalid when my father, as the youngest child, became responsible for running the family farm and caring for his parents. Grandpa Herman's mode of transportation was utilitarian: My dad simply attached casters to the bottom of a kitchen chair. This jury-rigged wheelchair allowed Grandpa Herman to navigate through the house, but of course he couldn't go up and down steps, nor did he go outside in the chair.

Running water and electricity were nonexistent. In fact, we had no electricity in the house until after I left for college. For readers surrounded by today's modern conveniences, this might be hard to imagine, but it seemed quite normal at the time, and we were very comfortable in our solid wooden fortress during even the harshest Wisconsin winters.

Grandpa Herman was mentally very sharp, and very affectionate toward me. He always seemed to enjoy my company, and his health problems actually benefited me—I was able to spend many happy, quiet hours with him. Since he was very anxious that I should learn to speak proper German, I became his proton-sized protégé. With his guidance, I had finished the entire German primer by the time I was four years old, in 1919.

My younger sister, Marion, was only a baby when Grandpa Herman died in March of 1919, so she never got to know him or to learn German. This was unfortunate, because I feel that the ability to speak more than one language gives a person a much broader understanding of the world. In those days I had no idea of the life-changing advantages it would afford me, but I was happy being bilingual.

Work on a farm was perpetual, and my father frequently enlisted my mother's help just to keep the place running. When it was time to harvest the hay, she drove the horses hitched to the long trailer as my dad loaded all the bales. When I think about how he returned from a day's work covered with hay poking out of his shirt and sticking in his hair, I chuckle at the memory and liken it to that of Ray Bolger as the Scarecrow. Upon seeing this image, I imagine my grandfather would have referenced Fred Stone, who was the first actor to play the Scarecrow, in the very successful musical-comedy stage version of *The Wizard of Oz*, which opened in 1902.

My dad had a healthy sense of humor, but he was rather somber most of the time, for his responsibilities were many back then. Taking care of a family that included his parents was hard enough. Carrying these obligations during the Great Depression was even more of a challenge. But at that time farming was probably one of the better ways to sup-

port a large family. We always had plenty of fresh food to eat, and we were very fortunate for that.

Along with the dairy farm, we maintained many acres of pastureland and raised a variety of livestock. Part of the land was used for growing grain and corn to feed the cattle, hogs, and chickens.

I relished the time spent with my father when I was younger—probably, in part, because he was always very busy with his duties. When time permitted, and the weather was pleasant, he took me fishing and hunting in the woods.

Marion has always looked up to her "big brother."

He hunted often in the fall, and a good portion of our menu consisted of wild rabbits and chickens, which he skinned or dressed so that Mother could roast them for our dinner.

When I was very young, my parents realized that I was not growing normally. Very concerned, they took me to various doctors to see what could be done. None of the doctors was able to make a specific diagnosis for my condition, and all of them kept saying that I was just slow to grow. My parents were told to give me only the most nutritious and natural foods available and to avoid such stimulants as coffee and tea. This was long before today's scientific breakthroughs in the field of endocrinology; at that time, the study of glands was not part of the standard medical curriculum.

Of course it was quite evident that I was extremely small for my age, but no one in our area had even seen a midget, much less realized that I was one of them. We didn't know that no amount of food, natural or otherwise, was going to accelerate my growth.

My confirmation picture, taken when I was 12 years old.

Marion was of normal size. Despite our four-year age gap, by her fourth birthday she had reached my height and we were wearing clothes that were the same size, sewn by our mother. Marion is a sweet and kind woman who has always looked up to me in many ways, but physically she has had to look down at me since she turned six.

At one point my parents took me to a prominent physician in Milwaukee, but his advice was much the same as the other doctors' regarding natural foods. He prescribed a pill that was really just a yeast tablet. I took that pill religiously, every day for nearly four years, but it had no noticeable effect.

I knew it was common for parents to closely monitor and praise their children's growth, so it did not strike me as abnormal to be measured often. My dad was always anxious to record my growth, and he marked my height on the wall every few months. From the age of fourteen to twenty-one, I grew only one-quarter of an inch per year—let's just say the numerous chalk lines merged into a single fat line. I was less than four feet tall throughout my school years and well into early adulthood.

Today it seems very obvious that I was a midget, but sometimes in the absence of other tangible evidence it really takes one midget to recognize another. Times were different then: There were no computers or websites for finding information, no cheap long-distance telephone services to call any specialist in the country. Besides, in the 1920s the medical community was still unraveling the mysteries of my growth deficiency, which stemmed from the underdevelopment of my pituitary gland.

So I continued to spend my childhood being just kind of known as a little squirt. Not until my trip to the Chicago World's Fair Midget Village in 1933, at the age of seventeen, did I realize that "midget" was the commonly used term for my genetic predisposition, and that this name, like the condition, was permanent: I would remain small for the rest of my life.

My mother insisted that Marion and I help her as part of our daily routine. Before I was ten years old I had learned the basics of horticulture while working alongside Mother in her garden. More importantly, I had gained an appreciation of and love for this science—we may have been tending vegetables, but they were our bread and butter during the Depression.

Mother instructed me by explaining, "This row is going to be beets, and this row is going to be radishes." She gently teased me, "You are closer to the ground than I am, so you will have the fun job of pulling the weeds." Since I always remained closer to the ground than anyone else in my family, I had the weed-pulling duties for quite some time!

Many midgets describe the rigors they had to endure living in a world where things were built for someone twice their size, but I never really thought about that too much. I always had a full-sized bed, and I just got used to having to hop in and out of it each day. Other impediments were overcome quickly; it became second nature to stand on my tiptoes to reach the kitchen sink, or to stand on a chair to reach into an upper cupboard.

We had a nice family. Dad had two older brothers, Emil and Robert, and a sister, Millie. One trip each summer was made to Emil's house in Rio, Wisconsin. Robert lived much closer, in Rome, Wisconsin, and we visited him more often, on Sunday afternoon trips (although we did not always do what he and the other "Romans" did).

Summertime also meant visiting other relatives and friends. Some of my father's relatives lived in Milwaukee, and sometimes they would inform my mother when a "big sale" was going to be held and at which downtown store. Then we'd all pile into our old family Ford for the day trip, if Dad could get away from farmwork.

Dad's sister, Millie, lived closest to us, near Johnson Creek. Dad's brothers' children were older than we were, and some were even married. But Millie had a boy my age, named Raymond, and a girl Marion's age, named Ruth (who still resides in Watertown, near my sister). Marion and I liked going to their home in the summer because they lived on the Rock River, where we all loved to fish and swim.

For some reason, the cousins and my sister got a kick out of throwing me into the river. They'd all give me the heave-ho and see how far they could toss me. I pretended that bothered me somewhat, but in truth I had fun. It was like flying through the air—and it was free!

My biggest thrill, at any time of the year, was to glimpse an airplane in the sky. Airplanes were rare at that time—less than twenty years after the Wright Brothers' historic first flight at Kitty Hawk, North Carolina. I don't remember the first plane I saw, but I dreamed of seeing them up close—and of actually flying them. Who knew that these boyhood fantasies would become a reality during World War II? Though the main branches of the military would doubt my aviator abilities, the Civil Air Patrol certainly thought I had the "Wright" stuff!

Oz on Stage

Author L. Frank Baum and illustrator William Wallace Denslow began working on their second book together, *The Wonderful Wizard of Oz*, at the turn of the last century in 1899; the book was published in May of 1900. It was a runaway hit, selling out its first printing in just two weeks. It was the best-selling children's book of 1900.

Baum and Denslow were approached with many offers to capitalize on the success of their creation. In 1902, Fred A. Hamlin, business manager of the Chicago Grand Opera House, made an offer that intrigued them both. Hamlin thought the Oz story would make a great musical show and wanted to produce it. Veteran stage director Julian Mitchell agreed to direct the play, and it opened on June 16, 1902. Like the book, the musical became an overnight sensation—with a run that lasted a decade.

A big factor in the play's success was the dynamic synergy created by former acrobat Fred Stone as the Scarecrow and David Montgomery as the Tin Woodman. These two had previously been a successful comedy team in vaudeville; with their four-year run in the musical of *The Wizard of Oz*, their great feats of physical showmanship made them revered by the public. Arthur Hill, a pantomime star, was also a former acrobat; he breathed life into the Cowardly Lion, inside a cumbersome eighty-pound costume.

In 1925, former vaudeville comedian Larry Semon directed a silent-movie version of *The Wizard of Oz* featuring Oliver Hardy as the Tin Woodman. Just a few years later, Hardy would join Stan Laurel to form a famous comedy duo.

The twentieth century saw many, many other stage and screen versions of *The Wonderful Wizard of Oz*, ranging from countless children's theater adaptations to *The Wiz*, the Broadway musical that ran for most of the 1970s and was later made into a movie.

This three-sheet poster, unseen since the first run of the first musical of The Wizard of Oz, *shows Fred A. Stone as the Scarecrow—a national sensation!*

The Cowardly Lion stars on this ultrarare half-sheet poster. In 1902, The New York American & Journal gave away sheet music for the Wizard of Oz hit "When the Circus Comes to Town" with every copy of the Sunday newspaper.

In the 1902 musical, Dorothy and her battered house meet the Munchkins—all played by women! The Good Witch of the North (holding the rod) was played by Edith Hutchins.

The 1925 silent movie of *The Wizard of Oz* was directed by and starred the vaudeville clown Larry Semon. Dorothy was played by silent-film star Dorothy Dwan, who married Semon just before the movie's release.

This scene card shows the cast of the 1925 silent movie: Spencer Bell as the Cowardly Lion, Oliver Hardy as the Tin Woodman, Charles Murray as the Wizard, and Larry Semon as the Scarecrow.

In October of 2003—more than one hundred years after *The Wizard of Oz* musical's success—the Broadway musical *Wicked* opened. *Wicked*, based on the book of the same name by Gregory Maguire, is a prequel to the book *The Wonderful Wizard of Oz*. Its story, an entertaining reflection on the nature of good and evil, reveals that the Wicked Witch of the West, Elphaba, and the Good Witch of the North, Glinda, were friends before things changed in Oz.

Meinhardt Raabe attended the show at the Gershwin Theater in New York City soon after it opened. He was amazed to see the Winged Monkeys flying right above his head during the performance. Even the Wicked Witch of the West sailed high into the rafters—not unlike her soaring voice!

After the show, Meinhardt was invited backstage to greet the cast. There he stole the spotlight as he traded quips with theater veterans Joel Grey (the Wizard) and Carole Shelley (as Madame Morrible) and delightfully reminisced with the lovely Witches—Idina Menzel (Elphaba) and Kristin Chenoweth (Glinda). The Munchkin Coroner also enjoyed staring nearly eye-to-eye with the show's lead Munchkin, Boq, played by Christopher Fitzgerald, and Michelle Federer, who plays Nessarose, the Wicked Witch of the East.

Backstage with the cast of Wicked, Meinhardt Raabe meets Kristin Chenoweth, Joel Grey, and Idina Menzel. Mr. Raabe was the first and only Munchkin to meet the original cast.

Glinda, played by Kristin Chenoweth, meets Elphaba, the Wicked Witch of the West, played by Idina Menzel, in the Broadway musical Wicked.

SO MUCH HAPPENED BEFORE DOROTHY DROPPED IN.

A NEW MUSICAL
WICKED
THE UNTOLD STORY OF THE WITCHES OF OZ.

CHAPTER TWO

One-Room Schoolhouse
to One-Ring Circus

WITH REGARD TO MY EDUCATION, I am the product of a one-room country schoolhouse. These schools were ubiquitous back in the 1920s, but they are seldom seen today unless they have been converted into churches or museums. Our little Maple View School was built in the late nineteenth century by farmers. The plain structure was made of local pine that had been painted and repainted red many times, the trim edging done in black. An anonymous carpenter had added an ornate bell tower and gabled roof to lend a touch of character.

Five thick, rough-hewn wooden steps led up to the big double doors of the schoolhouse. (This is the kind of thing you remember when you are small.) The building consisted of one large room with a pitch-black potbelly wood stove in the center. Wood was stored in the adjoining shed, which was kept full by local farmers who allotted a certain portion from their wood lots to the school.

We sat in old-style wooden desks with metal frames, while the teacher had a large, rectangular desk made entirely of solid hardwood. Children of the first through eighth grade levels attended, to a maximum capacity of fifteen students; yet I don't think we ever had more than thirteen while Marion and I were there. In fact, only one other student was in my eighth-grade class. Her name was Luanda, and we were close friends while growing up together.

The school's library was no bigger than a single file cabinet drawer, but we still read the classics of that time. Unfortunately, *The Wonderful Wizard of Oz* was not among the sparse selection, and to this day I still have not read the book.

Yet even at an early age I was indirectly crossing brick roads with its author. One of my own most dog-eared volumes was *Denslow's One Ring Circus and Other Stories*, given to me in 1918 as a Christmas present by my parents.

It had been written in 1903 by the same W. W. Denslow who, three years before, had provided the illustrations for L. Frank Baum's *The Wonderful Wizard of Oz*.

Many years passed before I recognized the association— but I still have *One Ring Circus* today! So though I never experienced the magic of Baum's Oz book as a child, I *was* entertained and delighted by the whimsical drawings of W. W. Denslow.

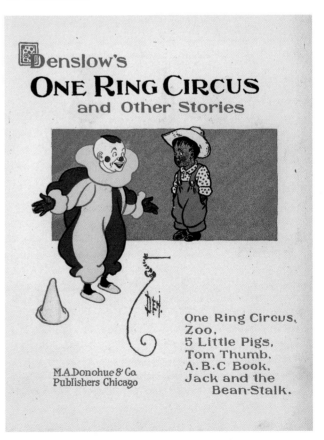

I read my cherished copy of Denslow's One Ring Circus and Other Stories *many, many times.*

Buster got me into trouble—just like Toto did!

The walk from our farmhouse to the schoolhouse was only a country mile. We were one of the closer farms to the school and my little legs were glad, although I was pretty agile back then. After my chore of milking our two cows was completed and my mom had made our breakfast, I walked with my sister to start the school day.

Our teacher was a stern and somewhat grisly looking woman. She was quite elderly and small in stature, but still imposing to all the children (and to some adults!). Her name was Miss Augusta Weber, and although she wasn't nearly as bad as Dorothy's Miss Gulch, she did admonish me on occasion, when I allowed my dog, Buster, and sometimes my duck, Ikey, to follow me to school.

Miss Weber was not a mean person; she just didn't have time to dawdle around with us very much. She had the prodigious task of teaching eight subjects to eight grades every day, and that didn't leave much time to correct disciplinary problems. Of course, she spoke sharply to the occasional overly rambunctious kid once in a while, but just a little bit of sternness on her part settled any problems, and we went on with our lessons without further ado.

When I started grade school, we didn't have such a thing as kindergarten or a Head Start program. Nevertheless, I was ahead of the game by being fluent in both German and English, and my language skills offset my more obvious physical shortcomings.

Our Christmas programs were the source of excitement for weeks on end. The yearly pageant was quite a big deal, and we rehearsed for weeks. Everyone not only had a part in the play, but contributed to making the sets or costumes. These productions provided my earliest foray into the world of show business.

Because of my small size and loud voice, I was invariably cast as Tiny Tim every time we decided to put on Charles Dickens's classic *A Christmas Carol*. (Who knew I would later pursue a vocation similar to bookkeeper Bob Cratchit's?) I could, and maybe *should*, have tired of playing the same part time after time—but it gave me my first taste of show business and the addictive applause of grown-up audiences.

A small ceremony at the one-room schoolhouse commemorated graduation from the eighth grade. I remember being happy that my grandmother attended mine, because she was in very bad health at this time; she would be gone just a few short months later. She gave me a handsome white boutonniere, and I had my graduation photo taken with it on my lapel.

Although in my childhood and early youth I didn't realize it, the years spent in the Maple View School were the proverbial calm before the upcoming storm of prejudice and ridicule that I would have to weather, like it or not. I didn't encounter problems or teasing in grade school, because we were all just kids from the same neighborhood and there were so few of us. My size was not an issue.

After a hardworking summer on the farm, I enrolled in Johnson Creek High School, about ten miles from home. I was able to catch a ride with a neighbor boy who was two grades ahead of me.

The principal of the school, who was also the basketball coach, immediately noticed my height. He sent me to the hospital of the University of Wisconsin (the school from which I would later graduate) for a thorough exam. Again, no significant findings were revealed, and he had no choice but to let me attend school. I got the feeling he might have been hoping that the doctors would give him a medical reason to exclude me.

Regrettably, the less-forgiving atmosphere in high school began to foreshadow the real-world prejudices that I would encounter time and time again. It was the beginning of my education in the way that most people would tend to treat me.

In the small country high school, the initial taunts started simply enough with the sports players. "Hey, Raabe," they jeered, "what are you going to amount to? You can't play football, you can't play basketball—so what are you good for?"

Suddenly, I was very aware of my abnormal lack of height, and I began trying to avoid activities that would expose me to ridicule. When we had gym class, I would end up alone doing push-ups or sit-ups while the other kids played basketball or did other group activities. It did dampen my spirits a little bit, but sometimes solitude was a better alternative than ridicule.

Regrettably, to avoid further taunting I did not attempt to date any of the normal-sized girls in our high school, even though there were a few I really liked. I was never exactly in the running for prom king at our school, but I did have one Cinderella moment when a girl from a nearby high school asked me to be her escort at her junior prom. It was just one evening but, although our ball ended even earlier than midnight, it gave me a taste of what my full-grown peers took for granted.

With the other kids towering over me as much as full-grown adults, I had to look for ways to mitigate my midget status. Academics gave me the opportunity to stand on an equal footing with, and in some instances to even surpass, my fellow classmates. So my new best friends and allies became English, history, and geometry.

My dad was very insistent that he wanted to have a musician in the family, and while I attended high school he gently coaxed me into joining the marching band. My fingers were not long enough to play a B-flat clarinet, so a C-melody clarinet—a midget clarinet, a perfectly scaled-down replica, kind of like me—was chosen.

Finding a clarinet I could finger and learn to play with a modicum of melody proved to be the easy part. Marching was definitely a new challenge for me, but my spirits were up and I was determined to please my father. I had to take at least two full steps to everyone else's single step, but I managed.

I continued to put one foot in front of another in all aspects of my high-school years, and before I realized it I was stepping up to receive my diploma. Whether the crowd was looking at me with approbation or disgust was never on my mind; the only picture I remember is of my family. Their approval was unconditional.

My family's support was an integral reason for my looking further into my own future. Even before the commencement speeches at my high-school graduation had ceased, my mind was drifting toward my dreams of college, flying, and my future. It was almost unheard of for a midget to attend college back in the '30s—so it was a good thing I still did not realize that I was one.

Resources were very limited back then, and money was essential not only for attending college, but for staying there.

For my eighth-grade graduation picture, I posed with feathered friends.

It was during my senior year of high school that I literally found the solution in my own backyard. I did what came naturally to me as a farm boy: I took care of farm animals. I began by raising rabbits, thinking it would be something I could handle in my spare time while, hopefully, turning a dime in the process. I took good care of them and gave them our best feed. Eventually I also raised ducks and chickens.

When the rabbits or birds were fully grown, I would take a few of them into Watertown to peddle to the local butchers. I got to know those butchers pretty well, and they were usually impressed with the plumpness of my stock, giving me ten cents per pound for rabbits plus generally a fifty-cent bonus. I saved every cent of profit, and this gave me just enough money to fund my entire first year of college at the former Northwestern College in Watertown.

CHAPTER THREE

I've a Feeling We're Not in Wisconsin Anymore

N AUGUST OF 1933, DURING THE SUMMER before I began my freshman year in college, a new opportunity arose—one that would change the course of my life.

I became interested in, then insatiably curious about, a tale recently told by family friends who had just returned from Chicago. "Raabe," they exclaimed, "there's a whole city teeming with only little people at the world's fair!" My mind raced at the thought of such a wonderful place, and it didn't take me long to make up my mind to travel there to see it for myself . . . no matter what. An aunt of my mother's whom she had not seen for years lived in Chicago, so under the guise of visiting her I coaxed my parents to take me to the Windy City.

Even though Chicago is less than 150 miles south of Watertown, it took a full day to get there in most cars—including our 1929 Model A Ford touring car. Marion, who was barely a teenager, wanted to go too, but she had to stay home with an aunt and uncle. Marion was rather precocious and seemed to understand how important—both physically and mentally—this journey would be for her "big brother."

Ticket prices for entrance to the fair were fifty cents for adults and two bits for children. Even though I was seventeen at the time, I entered by paying half price, due to my half size. At least my stature was starting to work for me instead of against me.

A ticket to the 1933 Chicago World's Fair was my ticket to a world of little people.

Strolling down the promenade with my parents was an exciting, eye-opening experience. The fair's entrance was along a bay of Lake Michigan. Huge, billowing banners lined the sidewalk on both sides, usually snapping back and forth in the breeze off the lake. The fair was divided into two main sections that were connected by a large bridge.

I left my parents to their own wanderings and made my way to the Midget Village alone. Pipe organ music and the chatter of the crowd filled my ears, and many of the attractions began to look identical, until I spotted a tower in the distance. At the top, in bold red letters, was written MIDGET VILLAGE. My heart started to pound and I bounded toward the entrance.

The word "midget" blared at me on innumerable signs outside the village and on the vividly colored lithographed posters boldly advertising the attractions inside. I saw images of a pretty little lady named Stella Royale, who was dubbed "The World's Most Beautiful Midget." I still did not know what a midget was, but if *she* was one then I was willing to learn more details.

Though a tiny town, the Midget Village boasted quite an imposing entrance. The entire village occupied just over a

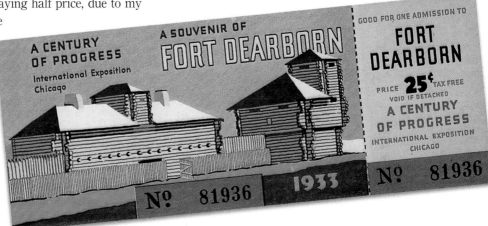

city block, and it was surrounded by a ten- to twelve-foot turreted wall, complete with towers. Giants well over seven feet tall guarded the city. The euphoria and wonderment I experienced as I walked through that stone archway for the first time is indescribable, but my feelings must have been similar to Dorothy's as she first walked through the doorway into the fantastical Land of Oz.

Beyond the wall I found a large public square with an ornate fountain centerpiece. Shops on all sides of the square were big enough for the public to enter, but had scaled-down furniture and facilities for the midgets who ran them. The three-story town hall was open to all visitors. It housed the working offices and quarters of the mayor, plus the police station, fire department, courtroom, and jail.

▲ *The Midget Village at the Chicago World's Fair of 1933 was very alluring—especially the advertisement for the beautiful Stella Royale, "The World's Most Beautiful Midget." A few years later, she went on to become a Munchkin Villager, along with her brother and sister.*

▶ *One of the giant guards, more than seven feet tall, talks with fairgoers outside the Midget Village.*

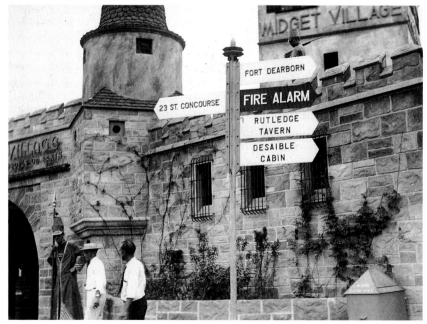

I had barely taken my first eager steps into the Midget Village when a little person in motley attire called to me. "Hey, buddy," he hailed. He was about my height but had a dark mustache and beard—and he looked me straight in the eye! "Are you looking for a job?" he asked, eagerly puffing on his cigar. He wanted to take me to his manager. Clearly, he was serious!

I was stunned by his instant acceptance. Someone was actually interested in me *because* I was small. *And this someone was like me!* This unexpected, alluring prospect left me speechless—but I had to decline. The fall semester at Northwestern College would begin in a couple of weeks, and I was determined to earn my degree despite this tempting opportunity.

The Midget Village even published its own newspaper. This rare example is from June 1933.

I spent all of my time in the Midget Village during that three-day visit to the fair. My parents left me to my own devices, entertaining themselves at the other exhibits and activities. Only about sixty midgets inhabited the village that year, but to me they seemed miraculously numberless. The existence of a community of people who were just like me was a stunning discovery.

Adults had used the term "midget" around me, but I had assumed that it was just another pejorative for my lack of height—not an actual classification. Children had the greatest variety of names for me in my youth: runt, pip-squeak, peanut, peewee, knee-high, and many more. Perhaps the adults considered "midget" a more polite euphemism; they had traveled enough to have seen or heard about real midgets living and working elsewhere in the country. But in Watertown, Wisconsin, I was unique and uninformed. I was a little person with a lot of names, and none of them made me feel good about myself.

These little people at the fair came from all over the world and were as different in background and experience as they were similar in stature. Some were married and had children,

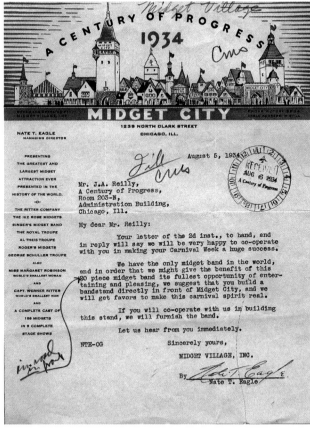

Nate Eagle, one of the managers of the Midget Village and Midget City, wrote to me and many others on this elegant letterhead.

some were longtime performers, and many even had regular jobs throughout the year. The most important revelation I had that first day at the fair, and one that echoed throughout the rest of my life, was that my being small would no longer be a handicap: A whole new world of opportunities awaited me. Though I was adamant about attending Northwestern College as a freshman in the fall, the visit to Midget Village was seared in my memory forever.

During that first year in school, though, it was always difficult to find new ways to finance my education. The pennies from the poultry, dimes from the ducks, and change from the chickens lasted just long enough to pay for my first full year of college. So I was always open to any opportunity that might help pay my tuition.

I was able to earn twenty dollars a month working for the school: serving food (or something that resembled food) in the cafeteria, assisting in the school library, or helping the professors. Although I aided a few teachers, I think I most enjoyed working with the physics professors in the laboratory. Using the Bunsen burners, Erlenmeyer flasks, chemicals, and scientific tools was fun—I had not been exposed to these things before—and the scientific approach appealed to me. This money helped, and I had some other side jobs.

Still, all of this wrangling and financial finagling only lasted so long; it became clear that the last of my education savings would be depleted by the end of my second semester at Northwestern. Memories of "Hey, buddy, are you looking for a job?" popped into my head, so I wrote to Mr. Nate Eagle, one of the managers of the Chicago World's Fair Midget Village, to ask what the chances were of securing a job for the coming summer.

He promptly replied with a simple letter: "Mr. Raabe, please send me a full-length picture and short résumé at your earliest convenience." He was just making sure that I was actually what he deemed a "midget"—that is, growth hormone deficient and hence a "perfectly scaled-down person"—rather than what was considered to be a dwarf. (Today, these little people are known to have achondroplastic dwarfism, a genetic condition not alleviated by modern synthetic growth hormone treatments. "Midgets" are now called proportional dwarfs, and in many cases, growth hormones do have an effect on their stature.)

In the early spring of 1934, I didn't have much time to ponder the deeper issues of this discrimination against achondroplastic dwarfs. The Great Depression was raging, and I was quick to try to snap up any kind of decent job. Times were hard for all Americans, and you did what was needed to survive.

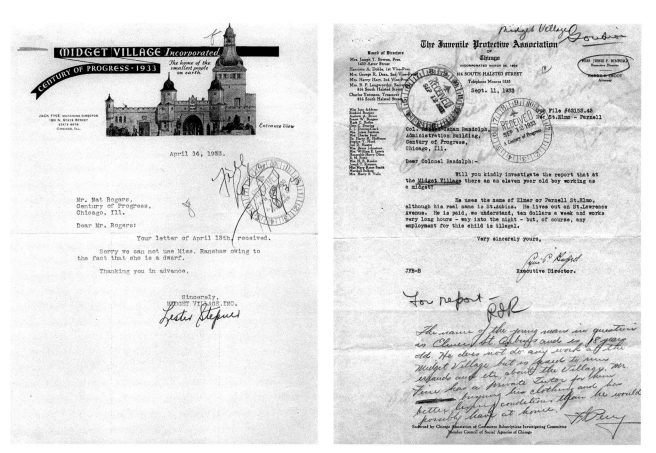

In 1934, achondroplastic dwarfs were even more discriminated against than midgets.

The handwritten note says that Pernell Elmer St. Aubin was eighteen years old; but he was born on December 22, 1922, and would have been only ten when this letter was written. "Little Elmer" was one of only five achondroplastic dwarfs featured in The Wizard of Oz.

After he had received my picture, Mr. Eagle sent another letter: "We will hire you, Mr. Raabe, provided you can be here the day the fair opens." This was a bittersweet acceptance, because opening day was the 26th of May, a few weeks before the spring semester ended.

The news was disheartening, but I returned to my room and started making calculations about my options. After listing the requirements I would need to fulfill in order to finish the semester early, I decided to take my tentative game plan to my professors. They didn't seem too receptive to an early finish but said it would be fine with them as long as the college president gave me the nod.

I went to the president's office to make my appointment to see him. His secretary was quite young and was especially nice to me. When I came back for my meeting, she made me very comfortable but seemed to be turning into a kind of mother hen.

My stature and lack of growth hormones made me look more like a grade-school student than my internal image of big man on campus. Looking much younger than I really was came with its ups and downs, but on the whole I would have preferred to be treated like everyone else. My youthful look confused people—such as the secretary, who was not surprised when I readily accepted her cookies but was more than a little perplexed when I washed them down with black coffee.

I entered the office of the president, then explained my predicament. I said that I greatly wished for his permission to take my exams early, adding, "I have all my reports and papers in for the year. I am also ready to take my chances on the finals."

"So, you are going into the show business?" he replied. "Well, you will never come back here." Northwestern was grounded in theology and didn't hold much regard for theatrical occupations, or for the field in general. He was sure that once I had lived the wild life, I would be lost forever.

Undaunted, I countered, "Sir, if I do not take this job, I will not be coming back anyway, as I will not be able to afford the next year's tuition."

FAMOUS CITIZENS AN[D]
IN MIDGET C[ITY]

MAYOR JAMES DOYLE
PRESIDENT OF MIDGET R.R.

IKE OF THE FAMOUS
IKE & MIKE TEAM

CAPT. WERNER
SMALLEST MAN IN
THE WORLD, AND
NATE EAGLE, *City*
Manager

MIDGET CITIZENS RESTING
IN MIDGET CITY PARK

RITTER MIDGETS, EUROPEAN
STARS MAKING FIRST
APPEARANCE IN AMERICA

STREET SCENE

SADIE
WILLIAMS

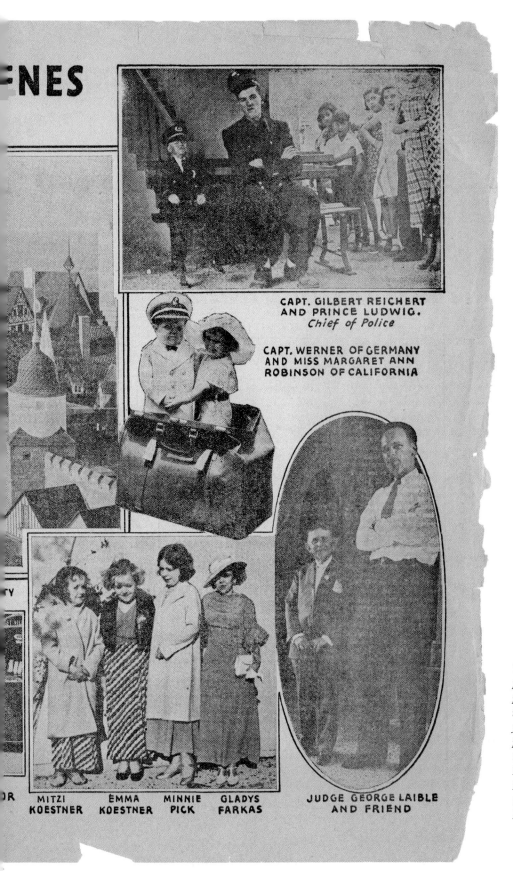

CAPT. GILBERT REICHERT
AND PRINCE LUDWIG.
Chief of Police

CAPT. WERNER OF GERMANY
AND MISS MARGARET ANN
ROBINSON OF CALIFORNIA

MITZI
KOESTNER   EMMA
KOESTNER   MINNIE
PICK   GLADYS
FARKAS

JUDGE GEORGE LAIBLE
AND FRIEND

The Midget City News *printed news stories and pictures—pictures that inevitably featured many future Munchkins. On these pages, not seen in more than seven decades, are Prince Ludwig, Emma and Mitzi Koestner, Ike Matina (of Ike and Mike), and Major James Doyle.*

On this postcard, a large group of "residents" pose outside Midget City in 1934.

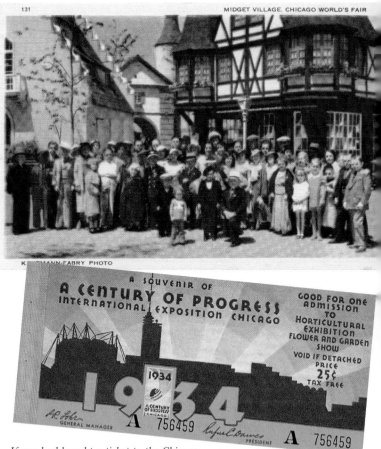

If you had bought a ticket to the Chicago World's Fair in 1934, you could have seen me—and 157 other employees of Midget City.

He seemed incredulous at my unflappable, and unflagging, stance on the matter, but he finally gave in. "I see you have made up your mind, but I am just afraid we will never see you again," he said. He signed my permission letter and shook my hand. The professors gave me the final exams, and I passed them all. Some of the grades were not what I would have liked to have received, but the trade-off was acceptable, and it was the best alternative I had to continue my education at that time.

My taxi driver dropped me off at one of the Chicago fair's main entrances on May 24, 1934. Slowly and excitedly I worked my way back to the Midget Village that I had seen the previous summer. Plenty of people—both midget and average sized—were there, making final preparations. I found out that the Midget Village was now called the Midget City. The size of the attraction had increased in both popularity and the number of diversions offered within its gates. Its population of little people had exploded to a final tally of 158—nearly tripling that of 1933—which was

twenty-four more than would work on *The Wizard of Oz* film just four years later.

I reported to Mr. Eagle, who set me up with my lodgings and my employment in general. All of the midgets were housed off the fairgrounds in a Chicago tenement. Most of us had roommates; mine was Elmer Spangler, a veteran performer who had worked at the village the previous summer as the conductor of the midget band.

Elmer was an amiable fellow and made me feel right at home. An accomplished musician and conductor, he was pleased to learn that I knew how to play an instrument. Along with loving music, Elmer enjoyed watching the fan dancers at the other attractions and had quite an infatuation with one in particular.

Elmer and I met up again later, when we both played Munchkins in *The Wizard of Oz*. I cannot remember all of the midgets from the fair who later became Munchkins— but at least thirty of the little people in *Oz* worked in the Midget City during the summers of 1933 and 1934.

The Midget City was on the east side of the fairgrounds, tucked away on the street that contained the foreign villages. This area was labeled "A Trip Around the World" and included such themed villages as The Oasis, Black Forest, English, Colonial, Spanish, and German. The fairground layout itself closely resembled the previous summer's, and I had little trouble finding my way around.

A very popular attraction in another area of the fair was the Sinclair Gas exhibit, designed to entice visitors to learn more about the company's products. The exhibit's mascot was "Dino," a large green brontosaurus, and numerous other dinosaurs were featured as well. Dino craned his neck back and forth, while the *Tyrannosaurus rex* opened and closed its massive maw. These were not the animatronic wonders of today's high-technology theme parks, but at the time they were far ahead of anything that the general public had ever seen. This was our thirties version of director Steven Spielberg's *Jurassic Park*.

Though I was technically employed at the fair, "working" felt different there than it had on any of my previous jobs, thanks to the wonderful interactions I had with the other midgets. Over the course of the summer I made many acquaintances—a few of whom I still have today, some seventy years later.

I remember meeting many interesting midgets—or "little people," as we prefer to be called today—at the fair. Most of them were on their own, like me, but a few families did work in the Midget City. Among these were the Cliftons: Mr. and Mrs. John Clifton and their daughter, Myrna Mearl. All three were little people. Myrna was only about eight years old at the time and was just as nice as could be. She enjoyed helping out her parents and was very polite to me, with her southern charm and Texas accent.

Years later, Myrna Mearl would marry a friend of mine, Clarence Swensen, who would play one of the Munchkin Soldiers in *The Wizard of Oz*. Myrna and Clarence are still my good friends, and we occasionally see each other at various annual *Wizard of Oz*-themed conventions.

Mr. Clifton, a very congenial man, told me that he had previously been employed as one of the original Buster Brown salesmen for the Brown Shoe Company. "Little Buster" originated as a popular cartoon character created by Richard Outcalt. Buster's mischievous antics with his little dog, Tige, and sister, Mary Jane, were a funny-paper favorite among children at the turn of the twentieth century.

A young executive from the Brown Shoe Company serendipitously met the cartoonist at the 1904 St. Louis World's Fair and bought the character's name from him. The Brown Shoe Company then created an ingenious and

Future Munchkin Charles Royale (brother of the beautiful Stella) sits on a life-sized triceratops at the Sinclair Gas Company exhibit.

innovative marketing strategy centering on this early—and soon immediately recognizable—mascot. Three midget men were employed to tour separately on the road. Each wore a Buster Brown costume and was accompanied by a trained boxer dog—named, of course, Tige. These three Busters toured the entire country from 1904 to 1930, selling and promoting Brown shoes at theaters and department stores.

John Clifton was only the second little person to portray Buster Brown, from 1912 until 1925. He met his wife, Selecta, in 1923, while in costume—I guess he must have looked pretty dapper in his blond wig, red beret, knickers, and Lord Fauntleroy jacket! John retired in 1926, when his first, and only, daughter was born. He then decided to settle down and take care of Myrna, Selecta—and his little dog, Tige, too!

John enjoyed his time as Buster Brown and related many exciting stories to me about his life on the road. A few years later I would be reminded of his experiences when I decided

The three Buster Browns traveled the country selling shoes. They were among the first midget salesmen—a tradition I would later follow.

John Clifton looked dapper in his Buster Brown costume.

to carry on the midget mascot tradition by working as "Little Oscar"—coincidentally, also number two—for the Oscar Mayer meat company. My Wienermobile, however, would be a far cry from John's horse and buggy. "Traveling was harder on Mr. Clifton's dogs than it was on him," Selecta told me. "He went through three Tiges."

George and Anna Laible were the oldest married couple at the Midget City and celebrated their fortieth wedding anniversary during the summer I worked with them. They had been on stage since childhood—when President Grant was in office—and had many wonderful stories about their married years, including a marine adventure. Anna recalled their crossing the Atlantic Ocean on a steamship named *The City of Paris* not long after the Spanish-American War had been declared. Their vessel narrowly escaped capture by Spanish warships as they departed England in 1898. Although they made it back to the United States safely, Anna reported, "We have never left the country since!"

I first saw George when he was presiding as judge over the little courtroom in the Midget Village in 1933. He played his part remarkably well and was quite believable. George performed several roles during his tenure at the fair, but the judge was his personal favorite. He was quick to note, however, that the courting he was proudest of concluded when his beloved Anna said yes to his marriage proposal, in 1895.

George had worked at the 1893 Chicago World's Fair at the age of twenty-four, some forty years prior to the Chicago fair. Called the World's Columbian Exposition, the 1893 event was the last great fair of the nineteenth century. George was working there when Grover Cleveland, then the sitting president, introduced a new technology at the auspicious opening ceremony by flipping a switch to turn on the electric lights via alternating current.

Although George did not mention seeing the president, he did recall viewing another famous statesman: "I saw a black man with a large entourage of white men—an uncommon

More news from Midget City! These pages show Jack Glicken,
a future Munchkin, as a police lieutenant in the city.

sight at the time—who was one of the most dignified-looking gentlemen I had ever seen. He had on a dark suit and had a large gray beard. You just knew he was a great man by the number of people following him around." George learned in the following day's paper that this distinguished gentleman was famed abolitionist Frederick Douglass.

George seemed to enjoy our Chicago fair more than 1893's, but he fondly remembered his earlier job. He even gave me a few personal items from that fair for my own collection of memorabilia. I still have one of his Columbian Exposition tickets and some unused postcards.

Another future Munchkin, Major James Douglas Doyle, was the mayor of Midget City. (He did not play the Munchkin Mayor, though—that was Charles Becker, who wasn't in Chicago.) Major Doyle told me that when he was born, in 1869, he was so tiny that the nurse tucked him into a child's woolen stocking for warmth.

James's "Major" was honorary, and it was not unusual for midgets to boast similar titles. In fact, *The Wizard of Oz* had at least two Majors, two Princes, a Princess, a Duchess, and a Lord!

My friend George Laible had worked at the World's
Columbian Exposition in 1893, forty years before I
met him in Chicago. He gave me these souvenirs of
the earlier exhibit.

Even the "residents" of Midget City read "the world's smallest newspaper," though it was mainly a promotion gimmick.

Captain Werner Ritter and Miss Margaret Robinson were touted as the smallest man and woman in the world. It wasn't hard to believe, because I'm just over forty-eight inches here, and I tower over Captain Ritter, twenty-six inches, and Miss Robinson, twenty-eight inches.

I had first met Bela and Matjus Matina—the midget twins better know as Mike and Ike—at the fair in 1933. Their behavior would later become infamous in *Oz* film lore, but although I saw them quite frequently during the summer of '34, I was not a witness to their night forays in Chicago, since I was kind of a tiny teetotaler.

The twins were born in Budapest, Hungary, in 1903, and emigrated to the United States in 1916 with their older brother, Lajos, or Leo, who was also a midget. Mike and Ike enjoyed fooling their fellow townspeople at the fair—which one was Mike and which one was Ike? The two had various roles while working in the Midget Village and City. I best remember when they were paired up in the boxing ring. People didn't know whether to laugh harder at the sight of the puny pugilists pounding on each other or at the fact that they couldn't be told apart—except that one wore white trunks and the other black.

Mike and Ike were also known by the last name of Rogers, the surname of the woman who had adopted them: Mrs. Sybilla D. Rogers. She had been the smallest in a family of twelve that included a midget sister and brother. Now a sixty-two-year-old mother and grandmother, she was thirty-six inches in height (two inches shorter than Mike and Ike) and the wife of an average-sized husband and showman named Tom Rogers. They had two average-sized sons, Manson and Mervin, and a daughter, Mrs. Lilly Smith, who was a little person.

Mrs. Rogers had adopted two other midgets, as well: a forty-inch contortionist named Princess Mariska and a thirty-nine-inch dancer named Princess Suzanna. (Two more titles!) They all lived with Mrs. Rogers in her home in Philadelphia when not performing on the road. Her husband had passed away in the late 1920s, yet her family continued to grow.

Sybilla was hailed as "The Smallest Grandmother in the World" in the 1933 and 1934 Chicago World's Fairs. She fit the part to the tee with her genuine, and unconditional, sweet, kind nature. I think she would have adopted me had I not vehemently protested that I already had two parents!

Mrs. Rogers may have been a grandmother, but the real Grand Old Lady title went to Miss Jennie Quigley. She was a forty-inch midget born August 20, 1850, in Glasgow, Scotland, who had arrived here at age thirteen—in 1863, when the country was still embroiled in its bitter Civil War. She vividly remembered hearing that John Wilkes Booth, an actor loyal to the South, had shot President Lincoln. "It was anything but a Good Friday that year of 1865," she recalled. "That great man held on as long as he could."

Miss Quigley had started out with her parents in New York City, but her first visit to the Windy City, in 1871, changed that. The Great Fire had recently been extinguished and the city was still smoldering. "Everything was leveled but the water tower," she remembered. "Everywhere, people could be seen dragging out singed safes of all sizes and shapes. Some items remained intact, but many valuables, such as paper money and stock certificates, were burned beyond recognition. It was a sad time, but the city's 'still here' attitude prevailed." The spirit of the Chicagoans had impressed her, and she called that town home forever after.

Miss Quigley and George Laible were the only two people I met who had worked at both Chicago World's Fairs *and* had met both Charles Stratton—"Tom Thumb"—and his wife, Lavinia Warren. Miss Quigley had enjoyed hearing the famous couple's tale of meeting President Lincoln.

The marriage of Charles and Lavinia, in New York City, in 1863, was orchestrated by the great showman P. T. Barnum. It had created so much fanfare that it had displaced the Civil War as the news headline. The couple was later invited to the White House for a private meeting with the president. "It was an honor to meet him," the forty-inch-high Tom Thumb recounted to Miss Quigley—"but he did have to be the tallest president we've ever had!"

Miss Quigley could always be found chatting with fairgoers who visited her at her post in the Midget City's hotel. She was a wealth of knowledge, and I would say hello to her whenever possible, just to hear her ever-polite responses in that fantastic Scottish accent of hers. It was unfortunate that she missed out on being immortalized in *The Wizard of Oz*, but she passed away on March 11, 1935—so this humble tribute will have to do.

A group of syncopates, Singer's Midget Band, performed in the Midget City's open-air theater as part of the Wee Revue show, and that's the first time I heard the name Leo Singer. Singer was an average-sized man whose troupe comprised fifteen midget musicians and entertainers. The troupe had been known internationally for more than twenty-five years, since 1908, and by 1938 its popularity still had not waned. Singer's thirty years' experience, in part, led MGM to award him the master contract for acquiring midgets to play Munchkins in *The Wizard of Oz*. At least two midgets from Singer's band act became Munchkins a few years later: my roommate—the band's conductor—Elmer Spangler, and Jimmie Rosen, the master of ceremonies.

I remember another act, called the Floradora Sextette, made up of twelve "residents" of Midget City. Some came

"Midget acts" were common in the 1930s. The Ritter Music Troupe was one of several at the fair in 1934.

THE RITTER MIDGETS AT THE 1934 CENTURY OF PROGRESS, CHICAGO, ILL.

from Singer's troupe, some were independent performers. Eight of them later became Munchkins and danced their way to *Oz*: Helen Hoy, Elmer Spangler, Helen Royale, Charlie Royale, Stella Royale, Prince Ludwig, Anna Leslie, and Marguerite Hoy. Paired off into six couples, the twelve performed their numbers in the Midget City's open-air theater, dressed to the nines—the men wearing tuxedos and top hats, the ladies in elegant silk dresses and feathered hats.

I would occasionally watch them dance just to see my roommate in action. Elmer was not a bad dancer but was probably better at conducting his band than he was at being a half-pint hoofer. His penchant for viewing the average-sized fan dancers in other exhibits resulted in his most exciting revelation to me: He had seen Sally Rand, the most famous fan dancer of them all, performing at the Old Mexico nightclub.

My job was not as glamorous as some of the others, for I was more involved in the business of the fair than the entertainment. That made sense as well as cents, because my curriculum at Northwestern was heavy on business courses (and I had learned a few things from those rabbits and ducks).

Numerous vendor booths lined the Midget City, and I was a barker for one of the owners, who sold various trinkets, bric-a-brac, and paper flowers. He was a Japanese man, and his English was not very good. Although I could understand him after a while, he wasn't able to talk to the public well enough to sell his items. This was my first sales job, and it allowed me to stretch my fast-talking skills. Along with

Stella Royale, Charles Royale, Johnny Leal, and Elmer Spangler danced and sang in the Floradora Sextette. Later all four would dance down the yellow brick road!

The Old Mexico nightclub at the fair attracted some of the biggest stars of the day—and some who would be the biggest stars of the future. The Gumm Sisters are featured in this ad. The youngest Gumm Sister, Frances, would later change her name and become . . . none other than the immortal Judy Garland.

The Midget Band, headed by my roommate, friend, and fellow Munchkin Elmer Spangler, appeared in the Midget Village News, *along with Stella Royale and her sister and Major Doyle.*

Like most of the little people in Midget City, I was interviewed at the fair's Science Hall by Dr. Wesley Dupertuis, who taught at Harvard University. He took measurements for use in his anthropometric studies at Cambridge.

providing an income, this experience allowed me to gain confidence in my ability to deal with people successfully.

Ostensibly, I was the operator of the booth and he was the cashier. It worked this way with most of the booths at the fair: The midget was the "front man" and appeared to be the operator, but really the owner (in this case, the Japanese gentleman) was always in charge.

As the crowds came through, I became adept at making snap judgments as to what might appeal to each person. From inside the booth, I played the barker, using a quick sales pitch to bring fairgoers to the booth to view the merchandise. It was best to entice one group to stop for a look, and then quickly lure another. If you could get a little crowd assembled, it would rapidly increase in size because everyone was naturally curious to see what all the fuss was about.

Once a large crowd had stopped, I really laid on the pitch, and usually someone bought one or two items. Sometimes this backfired: One person would break off from the corner and the rest would follow his or her lead, like a falling house of cards.

Many times after a good turnout, the Japanese gentleman gave me an extra half a buck for my efforts. It wasn't much of a job, but I was happy not to be dancing around with a top hat and cane, like Elmer, or boxing in the ring, like Mike (or was it Ike?), for the public's enjoyment.

Even though my experience at the Chicago World's Fair was a positive one, we as midgets were still considered oddities. It was probably not a coincidence that Ripley's Odditorium was directly across the street from the Midget City. That exhibit featured actual sideshow performers.

We were not considered to be even second-class citizens in those days, but oddities, curiosities, or freaks. Indeed, the film *Freaks* cast midgets as well as physically deformed sideshow performers. It had been released just two years previously by famed *Dracula* director Tod Browning, and two friends of mine were its midget stars: siblings Harry and Daisy Doll.

The film was about a full-grown woman who finds out that Hans (Harry Doll, then called Harry Earles) is the heir to a fortune, so wants to marry him for his money. One of

Sideshow performers were featured in Ripley's Odditorium, just across the street from Midget City.

Freaks asked, "Can a full-grown woman really love a midget?" The answer is yes—but not in the early 1930s. Although Harry Doll (who was first known as Harry Earles) was a star of Freaks, he seldom appeared in advertising for the movie. This scene card is a rare exception.

Harry Doll, the star of Freaks, and his average-sized costar, Olga Baclanova, were visited on the set by Harry's sisters, Tiny Doll and Daisy Doll. All three Dolls were later Munchkins.

the taglines plastered on the theatrical posters for the film was, "Can a full-grown woman really love a midget?" Well, the answer is yes, but this subject was taboo in the early 1930s. Little people were considered abnormal, and at this time no human rights organization existed to speak out against the way the film portrayed us as a group.

Harry himself was certainly not outspoken—his speech was unusually droll, very clear, and calm. He would have been perfectly polite and collected in the midst of an earthquake. *Freaks*, however, spoke graphically for itself; its depiction of extreme deformities revolted many moviegoers, and it was even banned in England for decades. *Freaks'* dark view of midgets was at the other end of the rainbow from the joyful, welcoming inhabitants of Munchkinland. *The Wizard of Oz* it was not—but *The Wizard of Oz* was still six years down the road.

I believe that films such as *Freaks* can affect the way people view a certain group—especially if a single film is the public's only exposure to that group. I witnessed an example of this early 1930s' public mind-set at the fair: I was talking to one of the gate guards, Gilbert Reichert (who was from Germany), when an elderly woman approached this seven-foot-six inch giant to ask, in all seriousness, "Are you really the father of all these midgets?"

Gilbert was a little slow, but he had a good sense of humor and just smiled when confronted with such outrageous, yet innocent, questions. I was asked many similarly inane—yet innocent—questions, such as "What do you eat?" and "Do you live here in the Midget City year-round?" But they never really bothered me. We were employees, and it was our job to be polite. By calmly answering the queries of the curious, we helped them to realize that we were just like them.

Gilbert was co-chief of the Midget City police force. His partner was Charlie Ludwig, an elderly and soft-spoken midget. One of their ruses was to have Charlie, dressed in his police officer uniform, pretend to give a male fairgoer a hard time about something or other. When Charlie had baited the man to the point where he was upset, Gilbert would creep up behind him and ask what the problem was. These amiable David-and-Goliath pals always enjoyed their games—and as long as the customers were entertained and kept coming into our city, the managers were content to let these midgets and giants run amok.

In late August of 1934, I returned to Watertown, with about a week to spare before school started up again. I recounted my latest exploits for my parents and sister. When I showed up at school, the president shook his head in disbelief. "Hello, Mr. Raabe," he said incredulously. "I never thought I would see you again!"

Meinhardt Raabe, 18, 'the Northwestern college Midget', is a member of the midget village at a Century of Progress exposition. Meinhardt, whose home is near Johnson Creek, has been with the little folks since the opening of the fair for the 1934 season.

Back at Northwestern, I made the news with Mr. Giedona, the tallest student at the school, in an article about my Chicago World's Fair exploits.

Because he was so impressed that I had returned against the odds, the following summer it was much easier to go to him with my proposition to work at the 1935 San Diego World's Fair (officially the California Pacific International Exposition). Realizing how sincere I was about funding my education, he gave me a simple wave of the hand for permission—and another wave the following year, when I worked at both the Texas Centennial Exposition and Cleveland's Centennial Great Lakes Exposition.

The San Diego fair hired less than half as many little people as the more prodigious '34 Chicago fair, but it was still a popular event. We had a Midget Farm at the exposition, and since I came from a farm and knew how to deal with the animals, I was perfectly suited for the job.

The management had picked up the sponsorship of a local dairy, so each of us was required to wear a white dairy uniform with a cap, and the company's name was on everything. There were stunted cows and ponies, but generally the Midget Farm was just a regular petting zoo that was run by midgets.

Every morning I saddled and rode each of the five ponies up and down the road, calming them before any visiting children rode them. Then I helped the children climb onto

In San Diego, my farm boy background helped me at Midget Farm, a petting zoo.

At the Texas Centennial Exposition, I played my clarinet in the band—and almost melted like the Witch, from the heat! The Midget City in Dallas reunited me with Victor Bump and introduced me to Clarence Swensen.

the horses and into the saddles. The horses followed a certain path instinctively, and that gave the children the illusion that they were riding all by themselves—though I always walked beside them, holding the reins.

When I began the job, I didn't know that this pony quintet had worked in a circus and had been trained to do certain tricks—but they quickly educated me. One morning, taking one of them for his customary constitutional, I must have patted him in the wrong place, because he jumped over a fence; I was thrown off and became entangled in a tree!

In San Diego my roommate was Jack Glickstein, who later changed his surname to Glicken. He would go on to play one of the Munchkin Elders in *The Wizard of Oz*, providing part of the humorous dialogue that prefaced my entrance. It is Jack who says "Physically, morally," asking me for assurance that the Witch is verifiably dead. Jack is pictured with me in many of the Munchkinland publicity stills—most notably in the film's only Munchkin lobby card.

Jack had gained some notoriety—which happened to little people back then when they did anything mildly significant—with his marriage to Miss Mildred Monti. It was highly publicized because of their difference in size. He was only forty inches high and couldn't have weighed more than sixty pounds, whereas the "little woman" measured five feet eight inches and tipped the scales at more than four hundred pounds. She was a twenty-one-year-old theater performer, and he was thirty-five at the time. Jack stood on a table while the justice of the peace read the sacred vows. A dutiful husband, Jack loved Mildred very much. Theirs was just one of those strange pairings that occur in *amour*—unfortunately, the press had a field day with some not-very-flattering headlines.

In 1936, I began my final summer working for the fairs by heading down to the Texas Centennial on a train. Fifteen other little people and I spent two weeks in Dallas as part of a newly formed midget band. I had been contacted about this opportunity while in school and was able to accept the contract because the fair—like Chicago's—was mostly held during the summer recess after my junior year at Northwestern.

The Dallas fair is where I met Clarence Swensen, born and raised in Texas.

Clarence played the saxophone in the band; I played the clarinet; and Victor Bump, my friend from the Chicago World's Fair (where he'd sold Good Humor ice-cream products, dressed in that company's trademark white uniform) played the cornet. If I had been clairvoyant I would have skipped the Texas engagement altogether. It was so hot there that our thick wool band uniforms were drenched after each day's performance. When the Midget Band managers contracted to move us up to the Cleveland Centennial after only a fortnight, it was music to my ears.

Our band was now employed in Cleveland's Centennial Great Lakes Exposition's Midget Circus. It boasted various midget acrobatic acts, and our job was to play circus music before, during, and after the show.

The exposition was on the shore of Lake Erie, and the cool breezes off the water were a welcome change from the Texas heat. Sometimes, however, it became extremely windy, and the main circus tent—the "big top"—literally began to levitate. The audience sat on rows of benches in the back of the tent, on the outskirts of the performing area, or "ring" (hence the term "one-ring circus"). The performers prepared for their entrances in two smaller tents that were connected to the big top.

The lake winds could be dangerous. On one particularly windy day, a woman in the audience was sitting by herself near a huge tent pole. A heavy gust lifted it up, then dropped it down just inches from where she sat. Had the pole hit the bench, it would have shattered; at the very least, the woman would have been thrown into the lake.

At such precarious times other circuses might have sent in the clowns to calm the crowd—but we sent in the elephants to hold down the tent. When the winds picked up tremendously, a trainer brought the four humongous African elephants to the center of the big top and had them wrap their trunks around the two main tent poles: instant animal anchors!

In Cleveland I was in a real one-ring circus!

45

Our band played very close to where the elephants were kept when the animals were not performing or holding down the roof, and to us they looked enormous. They were usually tethered to the pole or to a heavy block on the ground, but they could still move around a bit, and still inside the big top. Standing closest to them was our bass drummer.

If our tempo slowed down too much to suit their taste, the elephants began to swing their trunks at us. On one occasion our drummer was actually picked up and thrown into the audience benches by a protesting pachyderm! From that day forward, the drummer always kept an eye out to make sure the elephants were not too close.

Working at the Midget Circus was my last job with the fairs. However, I did not return to Northwestern College in the fall. I transferred to the University of Wisconsin in Madison. Northwestern was primarily a theological school that prepared students to become priests. I had thought of it as a kind of community college and had attended as a commercial student. This meant that I could take the core-curriculum classes, but would not be able to obtain a degree.

Whenever I returned home, the local Rotary Club invited me to speak to the group. They especially enjoyed hearing about my exploits at the world's fair and grew fond of those tales. When I told them in 1936 that I was transferring to the University of Wisconsin for my senior year, they wanted to help me out. The secretary at the Rotary Club knew one of the secretaries at the Madison Rotary, and that group found me a job as a pageboy at the Loraine Hotel.

I wore a red bellhop-style costume that made me look something like the famed Philip Morris Company mascot, "Little Johnny." During the early 1930s and 1940s, Johnny could be seen in newspapers and heard on the radio, loudly paging, "Call for Philip Morris!" and boosting company sales. He was portrayed by a four-foot midget bellboy named Johnny Roventini.

I worked at the hotel after class, from 5 P.M. to 8 P.M., throughout my senior year, and found it to be a great job with some fringe benefits. One of these was that my meals there were paid for; the other was that the route to the hotel, which was fraught with hills, provided my exercise for the day.

I do not remember what my weekly salary was, but I do remember that tips were just a nickel. Sometimes during the football season, the guests who were in town for the games at the university stadium gave a generous tip of a quarter when the Badgers won the game. This gave me reason to celebrate, and my appreciation for the sport—and its tipping (and sometimes tipsy) fans—grew.

My college graduation from the University of Wisconsin in June of 1937 was the first in the Raabe family, and many family members attended. They were very proud of me that day, and I was happy not only to prove to them what I could do by applying myself, but to provide a positive example for my little sister. When graduating from Johnson Creek High School the month before, she had mentioned "looking up" to me in her valedictory speech.

Call for the Loraine Hotel!

Wisconsin governor Philip Fox La Follette, son of the legendary United States senator Robert Marion La Follette, was the guest speaker at my commencement. As I stepped up to the podium to receive my degree, he spontaneously picked me up off the stage and held me in front of the crowd, declaring, "Folks, I want you to take a look at our smallest graduate ever!" This "politically incorrect" acknowledgment would never occur today, but at the time I did not mind. I finally stood—with the help of the governor of the great state of Wisconsin—head and shoulders above my peers.

At both universities I hadn't minded people mistaking me for a child, only to be shocked by what came out of my mouth—not that I spouted profanities. Rather, I seemed inordinately literate for someone they thought was a youngster.

This was funny, but I worried about not being taken seriously as an accountant. Before the glow of the graduation ceremony had begun to fade, my worries would be confirmed.

That afternoon, recruiters were talking to my fellow students about vocations. I was not approached by any of these visitors, so I boldly marched up to them to see what my chances were of obtaining a job. They simply shook their heads dismissively. "You've got no business here with us, young man. You belong in a carnival," they told me. That hurt. One of them was honest enough to explain. "Understand, see, we're out here doing a job," he said. "We are not the bosses. We are only here to find prospects. If I came back with you, the boss would take one look at you, and then we'd both be out of jobs.

Meinhardt Raabe, Watertown, (above), the smallest student in the university, posed in cap and gown for the camera man just before he led the graduating seniors of the commerce school across the platform to receive his diploma from Pres. Clarence Dykstra.   —Photo by Reierson Studio

Graduation day! I led the class into the commencement ceremony—and made the local paper.

CHAPTER FOUR

In the Name of
the Wiener Guild

ZEROING IN ON MY LACK OF SIZE occurred often in my earliest years, but I tended to thrive on adversity and quickly developed persistence and tenacity. The Oscar Mayer Company had a plant right in Madison, so I decided to give it a shot. The company produced "fine meats." These were flavored sausages made by mixing pork or beef with eggs and spices, stuffed into an edible casing. Today they would be called hot dogs, but that term was not common in the 1930s and they were called wieners instead. Oscar F. Mayer had founded the company with his brother, Gottfried, in the German section of Chicago in 1883.

I camped outside the offices of the plant manager and was eventually able to see him. Then I launched into my pitch. "As a salesman, I could do a wonderful job for you," I told the manager. "I have four years' experience in pitching products at the world's fairs and in speaking with the general public. I can sell in two different German dialects."

That last selling point seemed to click in his mind, because 80 percent of his Midwestern customers were German butchers. I thought I had the skills necessary to land those accounts and just needed a chance to prove myself. "Well, I'm interested," he replied, "but I'm not the company advertising manager. If I can arrange for him to come up here from Chicago, would you be willing to come back for another interview?"

I thought I could fit it into my schedule.

Early the next week I returned to the Madison plant. The company's advertising manager began the interview by grilling me. "So, young man, I understand you speak fluent German, eh?"

"Yes, sir," I responded.

"Well, then, let's hear some."

I'd spoken just a few lines when he interrupted. "Hey, now, take it easy, take it easy. That's faster than I can go!"

I was hired. The employers at Oscar Mayer may have had their prejudices against hiring a midget as a salesman, but my combination of skills and experience had allowed me to sell them on my winning product: me.

I started at Oscar Mayer in late June 1937, beginning as a summer replacement in the accounting department. One week I worked at the accounts payable desk, and the following week I was employed at the accounts receivable desk. Within four months, I had rotated through everything but the secretarial department, learning the ropes.

It was very satisfying having a job that was not seasonal and enough income to live on my own. I rented an efficient

This 1950s version of the Wienermobile shows its classic lines.

little apartment within walking distance of the plant, but eventually got a company car—well, actually, two (and one of those was pretty special).

As it turned out, I was a good fit for *two* of the company's marketing innovations. Carl Mayer, a nephew of Oscar F., had created and drawn out schematics in 1936 for what was dubbed the Oscar Mayer Wienermobile: a thirteen-foot metal hot dog on wheels that would transport the company spokesperson. Carl had joined the company and become the head of marketing after graduating from the University of Wisconsin in 1927. (So Oscar's little nephew and this Little Oscar were fellow alums!)

Even in 1936, themed vehicles were not unheard of, although they were quite rare. The Moxie cola wagon had pioneered the vehicle-advertising concept back in the 1890s.

It was followed by the Pep-o-Mint Life Savers truck (shaped like a roll of candy) in 1918, the Zippo Car (shaped like a lighter on the body of a Chrysler Saratoga) in 1947, and today we have the popular Kissmobile (which holds up to 230,000 Hershey's Kisses) and Monster.com Land Rover (which, of course, looks like a mean, green monster).

Carl Mayer's other marketing coup was the cartoon character Little Oscar, conceived around the same time as the Wienermobile. As the Wienermobile developed, Carl thought about marrying the two concepts by employing a little person as an embodiment of the popular trademark character to ride around in the vehicle and peddle Oscar Mayer wieners. Little did I know that Carl's ideas would indirectly lead me to job security—by providing an opportunity for which I was uniquely qualified.

In my earliest days as Little Oscar, I dropped by a Chicago market in 1937.

The following fall, I moved from the Madison Oscar Mayer Company plant to the corporate headquarters in Chicago. There I worked three days a week in the accounting department and spent the remaining two days on the street as the first walking, talking Little Oscar.

The first and only Wienermobile had been built the year before, but it took a little time to train both the driver and me for our new, and highly visible, roles in the Oscar Mayer Company.

As Little Oscar, I had to talk about, and demonstrate the preparation of, the latest Oscar Mayer products.

The company paired me up with a professional chef, a German man who worked in the Madison division, helping to refine the recipes for many Oscar Mayer sausages. He showed me ways to incorporate Oscar Mayer products into everyday dishes. I learned how to prepare many of the company's products properly and was soon ready to try out my culinary skills as "Little Oscar: The World's Smallest Chef."

When I had transferred to the Chicago branch the previous summer, Oscar Mayer had given me a company car. At that point I had only driven a car a few times; my earliest lessons had come from my father in our family Ford. Now, as I tried to get my license, I got more of a runaround than a drive-around.

At the license bureau I took a test drive. When we finished, the inspector directed me to "go over to that guy," with whom I took another test drive. He sent me to another inspector, and *he* sent me to still another. Finally, my fourth instructor signed off on my license. The others had just not wanted to be responsible. Since the extra instruction probably helped me overall, I was not bothered.

Being four feet in height at the time, naturally I could not reach the pedals or see out of the windows without modifications. I had pedal extensions installed in the company car, which provided the extra five to six inches of reach that I needed to drive, and I sat on a stack of thick cushions to see over the dashboard. I quickly got used to these adjustments and did not even think about them after a while—it was just nice to be independent of the public transportation system and to finally be heading to work in style.

In my excitement as a new driver I did not realize that a turnoff on the road I was traveling was paved in yellow bricks and that deciding whether to take it—or not—would affect the rest of my life.

In full Little Oscar costume, I was ready to sell!

CHAPTER FIVE

My First Trip Down the Yellow Brick Road

FTER WORKING IN THE FAIRS AND expositions, I could safely guess that I knew about 80 percent of the show-business little people in the country during the late 1930s. I kept in touch with many of them and tried to keep my address book up to date as best I could, considering everyone's hectic lifestyle.

Right after moving to Chicago, I heard through our midget grapevine that Metro-Goldwyn-Mayer (MGM) Studios was going to make a picture starring Judy Garland and wanted all the little people it could possibly get. I knew the title was *The Wizard of Oz,* but I did not have the slightest inkling of what the film was about, who L. Frank Baum was, or what constituted a "Munchkin." This would soon change.

Oz's casting requirement was unheard of, and fulfilling it was a giant task even for the studio that boasted it had "more stars than there are in heaven." The call went out through all the major newspapers and via magazine ads, radio stations, and scouting agents. MGM, however, needed additional help with the project and sought the services of midget troupe impresario Leo Singer, who was internationally known for the great success of his Singer Midgets.

Asked if he could provide a minimum of 124 midgets for the film, Singer answered in the affirmative and signed a contract—the master Munchkin contract—on October 1, 1938, with Eddie Mannix, the vice president for Loew's Incorporated, which owned MGM Studios.

The contract was the easy part. Now Singer had the daunting task of finding and delivering as many little people as possible, *in six weeks.* They had to arrive at MGM Studios, in Culver City, California, by November 11, 1938. Since Singer's own troupe had dwindled down to perhaps thirty midgets at most, he had to round up more than eighty other little actors whom he had never met or seen.

Singer used the screening process employed by many film agents and carnival owners: requiring the submission of a full-length photograph. This was to make sure that an applicant was really a midget, versus a dwarf. (About five achondroplastic dwarfs were used in the picture, making them distinctly a Munchkin minority.) Bold friends or family members responded for some little people; others heard about the call second- or third-hand. In any event, MGM's mass inquiries had an effect, and it was not long before the studio's need for little people was known by most midgets working in show (or other) business across the country.

I received the word late in 1938, directly from Victor Bump, my friend from the Chicago World's Fair. He and his wife, Gladys—also a little person—owned a jewelry store in

Children love the stories of L. Frank Baum, shown here in 1908. But I had never read The Wizard of Oz—*and I still haven't.*

"These people were all made of china"

I knew and loved the work of W. W. Denslow from my childhood. This is one of his drawings from
The Wonderful Wizard of Oz, *an original pen-and-ink that became one of the color plates in the book.
The pencil lines show where the Cowardly Lion was going to be in the picture with Dorothy and Toto.*

Twenty-seven little people rode the bus to Munchkinland.

The driver is Frank Martz, who took the All-American Bus Line charter full of little people from New York City to Culver City.

Ohio. Although they did not want to leave their business unattended for such an uncertain venture, I was young enough at the time to think that going to California might be an enlightening and fun adventure.

The Oscar Mayer Company, however, didn't quite seem to share my youthful enthusiasm. I remember that fateful day when I boldly marched in to ask my boss for a leave of absence. Obviously surprised, he replied, "What's the matter, Mr. Raabe? Don't you like your job?"

"I like it swell," I quickly countered, "but if I am not good enough for you, or worth enough to you, to get a two-month leave of absence, then maybe this isn't the place for me to hang around." That was putting it rather bluntly (and, looking back, rather illogically). But passion persuades, and he agreed. Ultimately, this would be a decision that both the Oscar Mayer Company and I were glad we made.

Having obtained my employer's permission, I simply packed a few things and headed to California on my own. I was on the train west in the first week of November 1938. I had turned twenty-three two months before.

I left Chicago purely on a will-o'-the-wisp, not even considering how, when—or if—I would return home. What I *did* think about was the excitement and glamour of being in a real movie, and that thought was the driving force for my bold trip to the wonderful, but unknown to me, world of Hollywood!

About one-quarter of the total soon-to-be Munchkins took a more publicized means of transport: on November 5, twenty-eight little people boarded a chartered bus in New York City. I had previously worked with most of them, including Mitzi, Emma, and Billy Koestner; Jimmy Rosen; Margaret and Helen Hoy; Jack Glicken; and, of course, Mike and Ike Rogers.

The bus driver, John Crabtree, stopped in Pittsburgh to pick up two more little people, also friends of mine from the world's fairs: Charles Ludwig and Elmer Spangler. Future City Father Munchkin Matthew Raia and Lollipop Guild member Jerry Maren were also aboard.

Mrs. Sybilla D. Rogers, sixty-seven years old, brought the tally to thirty-one. She would not become a Munchkin, but had boarded in New York to accompany her adopted sons, Mike and Ike, who later reimbursed Singer for her round-trip fare.

I would have enjoyed riding the bus, too, since I knew most of its passengers; but my travel arrangements had already been made, and I did not even know about the bus until after it had arrived in California. Still, all roads seemed to lead to Oz for those of us little people who had heard about the film, and we were together soon enough.

I reached Culver City, about ten miles southwest of Hollywood, just a few days before the All-American Bus Line charter bus dropped off its Munchkins-in-waiting at the Adams and Culver Hotels on November 10. I was one of the few nonindependent little people who came to the studio without already having been contacted, or put under contract, by Singer.

"Nonindependent" means, oddly enough, that I was not already working in pictures and did not have an agent to

The master contract between Loew's—which owned MGM Studios—and Leo Singer gave Singer responsibility for hiring and managing the little people who would become Munchkins. Eddie Mannix signed in green, and Leo Singer signed boldly in black.

represent me. Since Singer had the master contract with MGM, my only choice was to sign up under him. I was not alone; most of the Munchkins had to sign this Faustian contract with Loew's Incorporated that gave Singer control of overseeing and handling our affairs as he saw fit.

This document was a simple stock contract, and though each of us signed his or her copy in November, all were dated October 1, 1938—the date on Singer's contract with MGM. If I had arrived a little bit later (after November 11), it would have been possible to sign up directly with MGM as an independent actor—due to Singer's failure to provide on schedule the number of little people he had contracted for. This would have meant more freedom and money for me—and cutting out Singer as the Munchkin middleman would have been nice. But I had no such luck.

MGM actually had wanted at least two hundred little people—far more than the minimum 124 that its contract required Singer to deliver. Instead, Singer fell short of the contracted goal. He was able to procure seventy-three midgets (perhaps more) in addition to his own troupe of thirty. The rest were independents, including the Doll family and Major Doyle. The Major brought in quite a few midgets himself, all of whom successfully sidestepped signing under Singer.

Those who didn't arrive on the highly publicized charter bus came by way of cars or other buses, or, like me, trains. Whatever our mode of transportation, collectively we were touted as one of the more interesting casting conundrums that the Hollywood studios had ever tried to solve, and such a large assembly of little people for a single film has yet to be matched today. When the studio marketing executives embarked on their very aggressive advertising campaign for *The Wizard of Oz*, they overlooked no detail or opportunity for exploitation—including us.

Some little people were independent actors who were able to sidestep Singer's contract. This group included Billy Curtis, Tommy Cottonaro, Major Doyle, Mickey Carroll, Colonel Casper, and Pat Walshe. Most of these guys had already worked in previous films and had agents to negotiate their deals. Because Singer was under the gun for only having delivered just over one hundred midgets to MGM, he eventually relented. By allowing these independents to sign up without being under his control, he fulfilled his end of the bargain: providing our final Munchkin magic number of 124.

One of the most *independent* independents to join the cast was the very vocal and boisterous Major Doyle, whom I had met back at the Chicago World's Fair. Quite a distinguished-looking gentleman, he expected to be taken seriously by everyone—and he dressed for the part, always wearing a suit and tie and carrying a cane.

Culver City, California
October 1, 1938.

Loew's Incorporated,
Culver City, California.

Gentlemen:

I hereby warrant to you that I have entered into a contract of employment with Leo Singer, whereby I have agreed to render my exclusive services for you in connection with the production of your photoplay "WIZARD OF OZ". I agree that in rendering such services I will carry out such instructions as you may give me, and will perform all services which may be required by you conscientiously and to the full limit of my ability and as, when and wherever you may request. I further agree to observe all of your studio rules and regulations.

I agree that I will look solely to Leo Singer for all compensation for the services which I am to render for you, and will not look to you or seek to hold you liable or responsible for the payment of any such compensation.

I hereby confirm the grant to you contained in the agreement between you and Leo Singer dated October 1, 1938, of all rights of every kind and character in and to all of my acts, poses, plays and appearances and in and to all recordations of my voice and all instrumental, musical and other sound effects produced by me, and in and to all of the results and proceeds of my services for you, and the right to use my name and likeness and reproductions of my voice and sound effects produced by me in connection with the advertising and exploitation thereof. I agree that you may use such photographs and recordings in said photoplay "WIZARD OF OZ" or in any other photoplay or photoplays and otherwise as you may desire.

All notices served upon Leo Singer in connection with the aforesaid agreement shall for all purposes be deemed to be notice to me of the matters contained in such notice.

Very truly yours,

_____

EXHIBIT "A"

The stock Munchkin contract was an addendum to Singer's master Munchkin contract. We all had to sign a copy of this page, in which we agree: "I hereby warrant to you that I have entered into a contract with Leo Singer, whereby I have agreed to render my exclusive services for you in connection with the production of your photoplay 'WIZARD OF OZ.'" This contract was dated October 1, 1938, but many people signed on different dates—I signed mine in November.

Now I'd like to dispel the rumors about Major Doyle and how he supposedly obtained the master contract over Leo Singer. In a nutshell, it was said that Major Doyle obtained the contract from the MGM casting director, William Grady, due to Singer's inability to provide enough little people. The rumor says that the original agreement with Singer was subsequently dissolved.

A further embellishment was added later—an incident dubbed "Major Doyle's Revenge." I have heard about this incident many times. It goes like this: The Major purportedly rubbed in his contractual coup by rerouting the buses filled with his midgets to stop by Singer's apartment building in New York City. Once the bus halted, word was sent up to Singer, and he was greeted with what can best be described as . . . shall I say . . . many mooning Munchkins!

The story is nothing more than an amusing anecdote, as well as one of the more outlandish (and factually incorrect) stories that have surrounded *The Wizard of Oz*. At the time the incident supposedly took place, Singer was actually residing in a private home in Culver City with his wife and troupe. This, and most other apocryphal stories regarding the Munchkins and other aspects of the making of the film, can easily be disproved by looking at the piles of MGM documents that have resurfaced over the years—Singer's contract, for instance.

Almost seventy during filming, Major Doyle was the movie's oldest Munchkin, and from what I knew of him from

our days at the world's fair, he would never have pulled a stunt like the "revenge" escapade. As for usurping the master contract, initially the Major did try to vie with Singer to handle the deal, but he settled for signing up as an independent with MGM and bringing a few fellow independents with him. I'd guess this was the full extent of "Major Doyle's Revenge"—although for Singer it might have been revenge enough. He was quite disturbed by anyone other than himself receiving commissions from MGM for the little people.

Pat Walshe was a special case in *The Wizard of Oz*. He played Nikko, the Wicked Witch of the West's Winged Mon-

Nikko, played by Pat Walshe, watches as the Wicked Witch directs the captain of her monkey army to bring back Dorothy and Toto.

key confidant, and was the only midget in the film who got an actual screen credit. All of the other Munchkins had uncredited roles as extras and were simply grouped collectively as "The Singer Midgets." Pat, a very nice, though very taciturn, gentleman, was quite an accomplished animal impersonator. Only a few midgets had the acrobatic and physical skills necessary to play both a Munchkin and a Winged Monkey. Pat was the only midget who did not play a Munchkin at all, but the part he did have kept him more than occupied long after the Munchkins had gone home.

Another common Munchkin misconception is that all of the little people who worked on *The Wizard of Oz* stayed in the Culver Hotel, but the truth is that the Culver had only forty-six rooms. Though many Munchkins certainly resided there, others stayed in additional rooms at the nearby Adams Hotel, and the rest of us—including me—were bivouacked in private homes.

The studio provided Singer and his wife, Wally, with a large private residence. The little people in his troupe also resided there, from founding member Charles Becker to relative newcomers Jakob Hofbauer, Nita Krebs, and Karl Slover. Though not as active or large as it once had been, the Singer Midgets remained among the most well-known and respected performing troupes in the country.

I resided with Arthur and May Housman. They had been bit players for years and were very nice to me. My living experience was comfortable; their home, a simple, single-story bungalow-style house, was within walking distance of the studio. They had no children of their own and seemed to enjoy having a young person around the house—especially May, who fed me better than my own mother did!

The Housmans gave me my first lessons on the inner workings of Hollywood and the various studios. As recurring bit players, they were always "on call" and made sure that at any given time one of them was in the house to monitor the telephone. With no answering machine or voice mail in those days, if an agent called and no one was home, the job was lost. Since bit players were not under contract, they worked for various studios, but most of the Housmans' films happened to be done at MGM.

Arthur had been in quite a number of films, starting as early as 1912. Later in his career, he gained a kind of notoriety as an actor adept at playing comical drunks. Character actors were commonly under studio contract, but even without a contract, Arthur was called upon frequently to play the same inebriated type.

I enjoyed listening to their stories of life in the movies, but their efforts seemed so great for so little gain. They were in the twilight of their careers, yet even after playing many film roles, they lived quite modestly and were obliged to continue working. Eventually I decided that if this was a Hollywood life, I didn't want to be part of it—at least not for a lifetime.

This rare still shows the Haunted Forest set, where the Winged Monkeys swoop down on Dorothy and Toto.

A photographer caught us on our way to MGM Studios for the first day of work on The Wizard of Oz.

The first day we reported to the studio was a holiday, Friday, November 11, and the streets of Culver City were packed with people and parades commemorating Armistice Day. Many of the little people woke up to the sounds of the parade music and thought it was a welcoming committee especially for them! That might not have been the case, but we were definitely welcomed by everyone at MGM Studios.

For the most part the studio treated us like real people—not as sideshow attractions or inferiors. Granted, we were labeled by the now-pejorative term "midgets" on every studio memo and letter that referred to us, but this was before our medical conditions—either being growth hormone deficient or having a genetic mutation—were understood by the general public. So for little people as a collective group, acceptance by the studio was a big step in the right direction.

Famed actor, fellow little person, and friend Billy Barty noted the significance of this in his foreword to the book *The Munchkins of Oz*: "For the first time, an opportunity was afforded little people, or midgets as they were called, to act independently as people, not freaks."

Though he was not a Munchkin in *Oz*, Billy Barty had played a small part (as the White Pawn) in the 1933 movie of *Alice in Wonderland*, with Gary Cooper, W. C. Fields, and Cary Grant; and he had played Mustard-Seed, a fairy, in 1935's *A Midsummer Night's Dream*, with James Cagney, Joe E. Brown, and Mickey Rooney. (Mickey had also played Billy's "big brother" in some of the early 1930s Mickey McGuire comedy shorts.)

It was these two box office failures that MGM producers closely examined when deciding how to depict the principal cast in *The Wizard of Oz* movie. The producers viewed *Alice in Wonderland* and *A Midsummer Night's Dream* as examples of what *not* to do when making a fantasy film. Most notably, they decided that the stars' faces should remain recognizable. In *Alice in Wonderland*, makeup had obscured them.

Billy's positive and prophetic sentiments about *The Wizard of Oz*'s importance to all little people cannot be understated. In 1957, he went on to further the independence of little people himself by creating an organization that provides support and information to little people and their families: the Little People of America (LPA). A British version of LPA followed, named the Restricted Growth Association (RGA); like the LPA, it is a thriving organization today.

Billy was a funny man who helped make some huge advances for all of us. He believed that little people should always stand up for themselves and that they could have a healthy sense of humor when doing so. "The name of my condition is cartilage-hair hypoplasia," he used to quip, "but you can just call me Billy."

Billy told me that he was too young to work in *The Wizard of Oz* film, but I think he might have been hired if he had not been so honest. Fern Formica, who played a Sleepy Head Munchkin and a Villager, was born a few months after Billy, in 1925 (Billy was born in 1924), but she kept her true age a secret in order to work in the film.

I am not sure what the exact minimum age limit was for us as Munchkins, but I do know that Marjorie Raia, the ten-year-old sister of Matthew Raia (one of my fellow City Father Munchkins), was certainly deemed too young. Margaret Pellegrini's age of fifteen was well known. (An adult little person, Jessie Kelley, was assigned to watch over her.) Margaret remembers Marjorie having some type of seizure on the set, and perhaps that is why she was sent back home to New York City by train in late November. Sadly, Marjorie recently passed away in her Port Richey, Florida, residence, at the age of seventy-five.

Our first casting call was scheduled for 8:00 A.M. Most of the little people dodged paradegoers while walking from the Culver Hotel at 9400 Culver Boulevard to one of the studio's main gates on Madison Avenue, just a few blocks southwest. I walked from the Housmans' home, just three blocks west of MGM's Overland Drive gate. The soundstages were to the left as you entered the studio grounds through this gate.

Many of us were grouped together for a mass publicity photograph to commemorate the little people's arrival and first day as employees of MGM Studios. We started at the corner of Overland Avenue and West Washington Boulevard, and helped by two police officers directing traffic, we continued our staged walk toward the studio. We had to repeat this two or three times before the cameraman got what he wanted. It was cold that day, but the press really loved the story, and each of the little people received a free eight-by-ten-inch photograph from the event.

Walking through the gates of MGM Studios was an amazing experience. "Huge" does not accurately describe the scene, and getting to where I wanted to go was hard, because I was constantly gawking at the surroundings. The studio was like a city within Culver City and occupied several full-sized city blocks, lined entirely by ten-foot walls. It was busy twenty-four hours a day—not surprising for a production company whose goal was to shoot one picture per week (though the actual number was around one every nine days).

The Munchkinland set was still being constructed and would be housed on Soundstage 27 by mid-December. Soundstages are large rectangular buildings inside which films are shot. When the mammoth sliding doors to a soundstage are closed, all of the ambient sound disappears. A small door was available for letting personnel in or out, but we quickly learned *never* to enter one of these doors if the light above it was red—that meant a movie was being filmed at that moment.

Instead of assembling at our future Munchkinland soundstage, we reported to a large dance rehearsal hall nearby. Throughout the years many Munchkins have vividly and vigorously reminisced about the splendor of the Munchkinland set. If working in the marvelously designed fantasyland was the most memorable and enjoyable part of doing the film—as it was for me—then a close second would be the wonderment of that first morning when we reported to the dance rehearsal hall to meet the full throng of Munchkins!

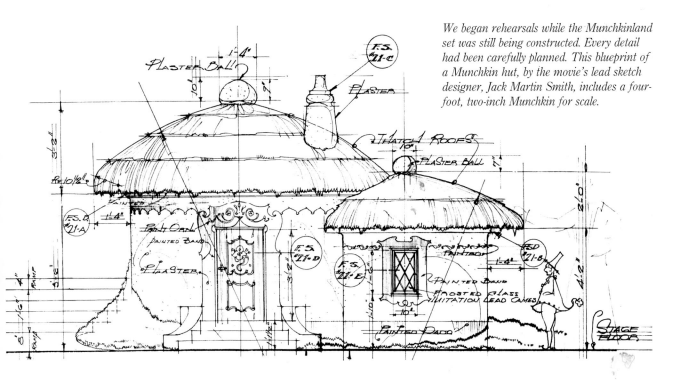

We began rehearsals while the Munchkinland set was still being constructed. Every detail had been carefully planned. This blueprint of a Munchkin hut, by the movie's lead sketch designer, Jack Martin Smith, includes a four-foot, two-inch Munchkin for scale.

▲ *Jack Martin Smith and Bill Horning created this concept watercolor of Munchkinland. Two Munchkins in the foreground shush each other so Dorothy will not be disturbed.*

▶ *Director Victor Fleming (seated, wearing the dark hat) looks at the Munchkinland blueprints with the set designers. A model of Munchkinland, complete with Dorothy's fallen farmhouse and the guard tower at the border, is visible to the right of the director.*

The idea of all of us being in one spot seemed to fascinate everyone, from the studio assistant journeymen to the biggest MGM stars; but we little people were the most curious and excited. Many of the midgets had never seen even one other little person before—much less more than a hundred in a single place! The feeling we all had is difficult to describe, but try to imagine our emotions. Imagine that you had remained the size of a child your entire life. You would be quite astonished to wake up one day to find yourself suddenly staring at eye level (or even looking down) at your father and mother! This is how many of us felt. It was simply thrilling.

One of the first little people who welcomed me was Jack Glicken, my roommate from the 1935 San Diego Exposition. Jack had been living in New York City when he first heard about MGM's casting call. He was still married to his wife, Mildred, and said they were enjoying the New York lifestyle.

It had been more than two years since I had heard from any of my little people friends and acquaintances who were here for the film, so this reunion was wonderful. Unfortunately, the picture's busy schedule didn't give us too much time for carousing. It had been stalled at various times due to casting difficulties and logistical requirements for all of the special effects, and because shooting a film in Technicolor was still a relatively new process.

The large rehearsal building consisted of a main area with a wide staircase on one side and a piano and folding chairs on the other. There were some small ancillary rooms, but the majority of the cast and crew congregated in the main open space.

The first order of business was to break us up into smaller groups so that we could be considered more closely for our prospective parts. The casting director was William Grady. His two assistants, W. L. Gordon and Leonard Murphy, assisted him in deciding which part (or parts) each of us would be assigned.

Thirty-five of the Munchkin roles had "special business." These were high-visibility parts that might also include a line or two of dialogue: the Mayor, the Barrister, the Coroner, the Town Crier, the Commander of the Munchkin Navy, the Sergeant-at-Arms, three Trumpeters, several City Fathers, Lullaby League dancers, Lollipop Guild tough boys, five Fiddlers, a Coach Driver, and a Coach Footman. The rest of the midgets filled in as assorted Munchkin Villagers.

It has been said that Singer gave his troupe the first crack at the most visible roles, but I cannot confirm or deny that. I do know that I had never met Mr. Singer before doing this film, yet I came away with the coveted Coroner part. The truth is that many factors came into play for each role, among them height, dancing or singing ability, and in the case of the Mayor, some specific characteristics that the director wanted to see.

In fact, the first Munchkin cast was the Mayor. Charles Becker won the role, due to his large beer belly and distinguishing facial features. His rounded face, real mustache, and naturally jolly appearance made him look the part before he even put on any makeup. (He was also one of Singer's favorites from his troupe, so I guess that was one position secured for the home team.)

Charles Becker, with his round belly and jolly face, makes a perfect Munchkin Mayor. Dorothy's other friend is Nita Krebs.

Nita Krebs, Olga Nardone, and Yvonne Moray danced through their scene as the Lullaby League representatives.

Next chosen were the three Lullaby League dancers, who had to be able to dance on their toes. Few little people had this ability, so it was the main consideration. Selected were Nita Krebs, Olga Nardone, and Yvonne Moray. I learned later that the casting director made a valiant attempt to cast Betty Tanner, but she vehemently declined. "I told them I could not do it [toe-dance] without bending my knees," she explained. As it turned out, "The other girls did bend their knees, but I just did not want to have that part!" Betty became a Villager instead and can be seen next to the very young Margaret Pellegrini, who was cast as the Villager wearing the blue flowerpot hat.

The Lollipop Guild members were up next, and here Grady's main concern seemed to be finding three midget men who stood the same height, shoulder to shoulder. Chosen were Jackie Gerlich, Jerry Maren, and Harry Doll, whose ages varied considerably.

Then I was lined up with about eight other fellas—rounded up like the usual (or unusual) suspects. W. L. Gor-don went down the row and peered keenly at each of us as we individually recited the lines for the part of the Coroner. I think I edged out my peers because I had previously done a bit of public speaking and had learned to enunciate a bit more distinctly. After listening to everyone, he paused for a minute, slowly sauntered back to me, and simply announced, in a deep, gravelly voice, "Okay, you're the Coroner."

When everyone was finally cast, we were measured for our costumes. MGM knew that the first location the audience would see in Technicolor would be Munchkinland, so no expense was spared in the creation and design of the Munchkin costumes. MGM's renowned Adrian was more than equal to this task—you could say he was almost born for it! His favorite book as a child had been *The Wonderful Wizard of Oz*. He had drawn many detailed sketches of the fantasy characters in his youth, and he actually sent home for his old notebooks for consultation. Ultimately, he produced a fabulous array of watercolor sketches to be approved by producer Mervyn LeRoy.

In the wardrobe room we were measured from head to toe—for everything from our outlandish hats to our felt shoes, and everything in between. The seamstresses and tailors used those measurements, along with the approved sketches, to make our costumes. These were so intricate and detailed that the costume department needed nearly five solid weeks to complete them all.

During those five weeks we continued to report to the dance rehearsal hall, where we were broken up into groups for the rehearsals. The regiment of twenty-five Munchkin Soldiers and the Sergeant-at-Arms practiced their marching steps regimen repeatedly, as if they were actually in the army. Some Munchkins were cast in multiple roles, so part of their day might be spent with the Soldiers, for instance, and the rest of their time with a group of Munchkin Villagers.

About two-thirds of the Munchkins had dancing or singing routines, so they were sent to work with the dance director, Bobby Connolly, and his assistants, the lovely Dona Massin and Arthur "Cowboy" Appell. Mainly, Connolly was in charge of the choreography, and the assistants personally trained the Munchkins how to perform the routines.

Dona, who was just twenty-one years old, took on the monumental task of teaching all the little people their dance steps. She spent most of her time with the Munchkins who had the biggest dancing parts but taught certain steps to every one of us at one time or another. I merely had to walk up seven steps to recite my lines, so I didn't work much with the dancing group. Still, I did get to see Dona quite often during rehearsals and was very much impressed with the kindness and understanding she demonstrated toward the little people.

She also worked extremely well with the gaggle of about half a dozen average-sized children who filled in as Munchkins in the background. Those of us who danced very little still had to practice the scene for the final song—when the entire Munchkinland village came alive and we sang "We're Off to See the Wizard" and danced in unison. It really wasn't much of a dance; basically, we just moved our hands and upper bodies while our feet remained securely planted.

Dona also had a cameo in the film, when Dorothy and the gang go to the Wash & Brush Up Co. She is one of the manicurists (the farthest woman on the left) who wave their scissors and give the Lion a once-over as they all gaily sing, "Clip-clip here, clip-clip there!" Mr. LeRoy cajoled her into taking the part because he thought she brought him luck. (She had had cameos in his previously successful films.)

Unfortunately, the employees of the Wash & Brush Up Co. were not the only ones adept at clipping. Later, because the film was running too long, the studio executives cut an elaborate "Jitter Bug" number that Dona had worked on tirelessly with Ray Bolger and Bert Lahr.

My friend Jerry Maren hands Dorothy the huge lollipop, a token of appreciation from the Lollipop Guild. He is flanked by Jackie Gerlich and Harry Doll.

More Munchkins than cards in a deck! There are at least fifty-five Munchkins in this wonderful photograph. I am sitting on the yellow brick road at the lower left. Victor Fleming is standing next to Leo Singer in the center of the picture. Daisy Doll is looking over the director's right shoulder.

While our costumes were being made, the masterful Jack Dawn, head of MGM's makeup department at that time, created our makeup appliances. He had previously worked on such films as Tod Browning's *Mark of the Vampire* in 1935, with Bela Lugosi; *The Good Earth* in 1937, with Luise Rainer and Paul Muni; and *Marie Antoinette* in 1938, with Norma Shearer.

Jack was a gaunt-looking man, in his mid-forties, with dark hair and glasses. Typically only four to six men worked under his direction in the makeup department; but this film needed at least a score more, so the call went out for additional makeup artists and apprentices.

Each character's unique makeup was created by Jack; then the regular crew of seasoned men from the department, and their underlings, applied it. He took us aside, one by one, and asked what parts we played and what lines we had, if any.

Plaster casts were made for each male Munchkin face—the lady Munchkins did not wear any prosthetics. A lubricant was applied to our faces and then a thin coat of plaster covered that. This shell made a created image of our faces and was used to make a positive mold in the form of a thick plaster bust. Once these busts were ready, the department could experiment with various facial appliances and application techniques.

Referring to our character biographies, individual facial molds, and the costumes in Adrian's sketches, Jack created our master makeups. A still photograph was taken the first time our makeup was applied. Later, when filming began, the crew simply pulled these images each day for reference and reapplied our makeup exactly as Jack had designed it.

For a final costume fitting reference photograph, Murray Wood, Charles Becker, Billy Curtis, and I line up to show off our suits by Adrian. The Mayor and the Braggart (Billy) seem to have the same penchant for bowties and chains.

Adrian's costume sketches captured the whimsy of the Munchkins.

In this rare shot, the dance director, Bobby Connolly (in the foreground, wearing a hat), and Victor Fleming (hunched over) watch Munchkinland come to life.

While all of the costume fittings and makeup tests proceeded, we continued to rehearse our parts in the film. We were each given a mimeographed script of the "Munchkinland Musical Sequence," which consisted of all the Munchkin lines and the songs "Ding-Dong! The Witch Is Dead" and "We're Off to See the Wizard." The script denoted individual parts for the Good Witch, Dorothy, the Mayor, the Barrister, and the Coroner. It also had the parts for Munchkins #1 and #2, Fathers #1 and #2, the Three Tots (the Lullaby League dancers), and the Three Tough Kids (the Lollipop Guild). This was all we knew of *The Wizard of Oz*, and it served as our only guide to the overall plot.

We practiced the singing portion of our script next to the piano in the rehearsal hall, led and accompanied by our pianist, Eddie Becker (no relation to the Mayor). Some of the vocal and orchestral arrangers who worked on the picture have claimed that none of the little people could carry a tune. But the truth is that many of these Munchkin musicians had had plenty of experience working as singers or dancers on Broadway or the vaudeville circuits.

▲ *Victor Fleming directs Jack Glicken while makeup man Charles Schram checks the Munchkin makeup from behind Dorothy.*

▶ *Bobby Connolly, the dance director, studies the model of Munchkinland.*

This overhead shot shows just how large Munchkinland was. The ponies, Wizard and Oz, are making their way toward Dorothy and Glinda.

As time went by, we were all able to piece together the individual routines into the single Munchkinland sequence. We continually rehearsed the whole scenario, from the lines, "Come out, come out, wherever you are," to "We're Off to See the Wizard," sung as Dorothy leaves Munchkinland for the Emerald City.

Behind the piano, a large set of bleachers mimicked the many staircases on the Munchkinland set. About twenty-five Munchkins practiced going up and down them while singing, "Ding-Dong! The Witch Is Dead." Everyone in the *Oz* production seemed to be a perfectionist. All were adamant about detail: We had to be on the same exact yellow brick, on the same note, and in the same specific physical position every time we practiced.

One thing I have always been asked over the years is what I thought about working on the Munchkinland set: What were the smells, sights, and sounds that I remember? Writing this book gives me a chance to recount as many of those memories as I can in a single spot. I hope this will answer most of the questions asked of me during the sixty-six years since I first set foot in Munchkinland.

Audiences have always been impressed and enchanted by the amazing transformation from black-and-white (originally sepia) to color that Dorothy experiences when she opens the door on Munchkinland. Even though viewing this scene on film is spectacular, walking into that enchanting land for real was one hundred times—one hundred and twenty-four times, to be precise—better.

At the old watering hole, Judy Garland chats with a group of Munchkins. Olga Nardone, of the Lullaby League, is on her left and Jerry Maren, from the Lollipop Guild, is to her right.

Munchkin Villagers sing "Ding-Dong! The Witch Is Dead" as they dance up the steps. I'm standing next to Dorothy, watching the marching Munchkin Soldiers below us.

Tarps protect the yellow brick road before filming begins. Notice that the water in the pond is still crystal clear.

It was during the last two weeks of December, the final two weeks of 1938, that we first stepped into the land of Lilliput. Numerous workers had labored around the clock to get this enormous set ready, and its completion timed out perfectly with our being ready with our parts. On the first morning we filmed the Munchkinland sequence, we discovered our village almost simultaneously, each filing onto the set after our makeup had been applied.

I recall an amazing contrast—not unlike that of Dorothy's arrival. From outside of the plainly painted, windowless soundstage, we walked into the wide expanse of an amazing fantasyland that one could only have dreamed of before it was actually built by the MGM prop masters. Flowers and trees were everywhere. Twenty-foot hollyhocks reached upward like skyscrapers. Real trees were rooted into the ground—which even smelled like fresh dirt—and towered over us to touch the ninety-foot-high soundstage ceiling.

We entered the heart of the set via the wide expanse of the yellow brick road. It led invitingly into Munchkinland through a break in the four-foot-high wall that bordered the village. In front of the entrance a prop sunflower "grew," its head as large as a truck tire; and to our right, a turreted guard tower rose atop the wall. These were decorated in

bright blues and reds, and had obviously not been painted too long before our arrival.

The first day I saw the yellow brick road, it was still partially covered by protective drop cloths. It began in the center of Munchkinland, curling outward from a lollipop-looking shape, then leaving the village and, ultimately, reaching the Emerald City. The road was made of Masonite—compressed wood and plastic—so it had a little more give underfoot than real bricks; but it was still quite solid.

A stream as wide as the yellow brick road wound through the center of the Munchkinland set. Huge patches of blue, yellow, white, red, and orange flowers lined the riverbanks. A Japanese-style bridge spanned the width of the stream just before it flowed into a large pond, which was bordered by a two-foot-high wall. In the pond floated water lilies up to four feet in diameter, and at one edge of it, a stack of four circular platforms—steps, really—descended into the water.

Above the topmost platform an enormous, inverted yellow flower served as a canopy, creating a pavilion; on this spot Dorothy first stands with Glinda, the Good Witch of the North, and they sing about the "miracle" that had occurred. That was the biggest flower in Munchkinland by far—although many of the buds were larger than most of

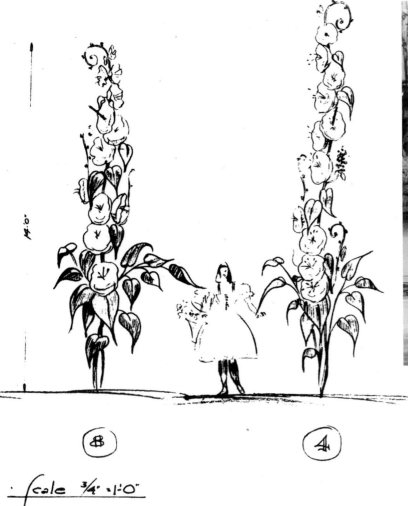

The hollyhocks in Munchkinland grow up to sixteen feet tall. At left, this never-before-seen concept sketch drawn by Jack Martin Smith includes a tiny Dorothy to show the scale. Above, you can see how Dorothy and Toto are dwarfed by the giant flowers.

our heads and the diameters of several were wider than most of us were tall.

The river was only about two feet in depth but looked much deeper due to its dark blue coloring (later I would find out why it was so blue). The pond was equally deep, and equally blue. The set's rich detailing heightened the realism for many of us discovering this panorama; it took some Munchkins a few days to finally believe that everything had been built and was not *really* real.

The Munchkins' directive to "Follow the yellow brick road" sounds like a no-brainer right up the Scarecrow's alley. In truth, there really was an alternate path: the *red* brick road. Like its better-remembered twin, it originated in the center of Munchkinland, but whereas the yellow path led past Dorothy's fallen farmhouse, toward the Emerald City, the red one passed by the Munchkin town hall and toward the soundstage wall—to Quadling Country, I suppose! The next time you watch the film, look under the boots

of the twenty-five Munchkin Soldiers when they come marching in, and beneath the white, flower-shaped carriage that transports Dorothy to town hall—you'll see the red brick road.

All of the houses of Munchkinland were shaped like mushrooms, with painted plaster exteriors and layered, straw-thatched roofs; and each was crowned with a rounded white cupola. Yet they varied considerably. There were fat, square windows; thin, rectangular windows; and oval or triangular windows. There were short, stubby houses and tall, thin houses built like towers.

What I always thought added to the allure of these miniature homes were their beautiful trimmings and colors. Every single window and door had ornate decorative painted borders in swirling pastel hues of purple, green, and blue. The tops of the walls, under the eaves, were intricately painted with a wonderful array of colors and patterns. So were the many double and Dutch doors.

An assistant cameraman performs a color setup for the next scene as Judy Garland waits.

The cameramen on the boom come in for a closeup on Dorothy.

The splendor and fantasy of these sets reminded me of the animated dwarfs' domicile in Walt Disney's earlier *Snow White and the Seven Dwarfs*. Since MGM's publicity department dubbed *The Wizard of Oz* the "biggest sensation since *Snow White*," maybe there was an even deeper (or more commercial) connection.

Munchkin town hall, or civic center, was on the farthest right side of Munchkinland, directly opposite the fallen farmhouse. The seven steps leading up to it border the red brick road, just before it turns to end at the soundstage wall. Eventually I would stand on these steps with Judy Garland. A decorative tassel with numerous blue-painted balls hanging from its fringes encircled the thatched roof, distinguishing the town hall from other buildings. There was also a single lantern in front of the hall; from the audience's perspective, it hung directly to the left of where my character stood at the top of the steps. Only two more lanterns appeared on the set, flanking the Munchkin Bridge. (Since they were not operable, it was for the best that Dorothy and Toto landed in our little "ditch" during the daylight hours.)

In the film the Mayor and the City Fathers are seen stepping out of the doors of the town hall, heralded first by the three Munchkin Trumpeters. If you reversed this path and headed *into* the hall, you would see a white wall to your left—the last edge visible to the camera. I am not fond of bursting any bubbles—not even Glinda's—by ruining the magic of our little land, but the area past this white wall inside the hall was nothing but supportive planking and was open in the back. Between the back of this set and the painted background was at least a ten-foot gap. We were not supposed to walk there—and would not have wanted to, anyway, given all of the obstructions, such as lighting equipment. The back of the town hall provided a nice off-camera area for the City Fathers' departure, but the building was just a facade, like Dorothy's farmhouse.

To the viewers' left of the town hall stood a series of stairways, still part of the on-camera decor. The largest one led up, around, and over many of the Munchkin houses, which were clumped together in a tight and cozy little semicircle. All of the stairways were gray-painted Masonite that gave the appearance of stone and was very sturdy. The yellow brick road, the red brick road, and the light- and dark-gray tiling that made up the rest of the Munchkinland floor were also made of this material.

Anyone beginning the ascent of the stairway to the left of the town hall would first encounter the Sleepy Head nest perched on top of one of the Munchkin hut roofs. Made of interwoven branches, it held five mini-Munchkin beds: green, cracked-open little eggs lined with pink satin sheets

Munchkin Villager Frank Cucksey peers into the camera on the relatively barren Munchkinland set.

and pillows. These matched the pink bonnets and night-gowns worn by the Sleepy Head Munchkins.

The stairway continued beyond the nest, rising no fewer than thirty steps, to meet a bridge that spanned a few Munchkin hut roofs before connecting to a set of stairs on the other side. These led back down to the ground level of the Munchkinland set. On film, nearly sixty Munchkins run all the way up the stairs—first passing me at the town hall entrance, where I stand with the other City Fathers, then crossing the bridge to head back *down* the stairs on the other side of Munchkinland—all the while merrily singing, "Ding-Dong! The Witch Is Dead."

The red brick road bordered the Munchkin town hall. Directly opposite, and obstructing the yellow brick road, lay Dorothy's fallen farmhouse, which had sailed into Munchkinland on a gargantuan gale (carrying a Gale). Amazingly, that house never lost a single shingle or left a shard of glass on the grounds of Munchkinland ... although several hinges did seem to be unhitched!

Past the house was the border of Munchkinland—and the wall through which we all had entered the set. Stationed in the opening on top of the Munchkin guard tower, on the audience's right, was the Sergeant-at-Arms (played by Prince Denis). He waves his little sword at Dorothy as she

Jack Glicken, next to Dorothy and Toto, wears a costume other than his regular City Father regalia.

passes the village wall, heading toward the Emerald City. Of course, the fabulous rolling hills behind her did not exist, except as a matte painting that was inserted later, and her journey would not last long, since the road came to an abrupt stop at the bottom of the soundstage wall.

Not all of the Munchkin houses were accessible, unless you were extremely thin! Several were just cutouts painted on muslin, and each of these was attached to a sturdy contoured frame. They were used to blend into the areas between the painted backdrops and the three-dimensional set pieces to make the set look larger. The cutouts gradually decreased in size and were quite effective in creating the illusion of a city.

Also painted on muslin was the background: Munchkinland's rolling hills, meadows, farmland, and a large cliff. These huge, heavy, white canvas backdrops—as large as four hundred feet long and forty feet wide—had been painted on Soundstage 26, directly across from the Munchkinland set, back in early September. Similar drops

were used for all of the backgrounds in the film. Behind the backdrops, of course, were the plain white—well, whitish—walls of the soundstage. The backs of the framed set pieces were not squared, but rounded, and the backdrops followed these curves. This rounded quality gave Munchkinland a more realistic and panoramic look, deceptively masking its true rectangular shape and limited acreage.

I was especially interested in the various plants throughout the Munchkinland set. Although I never had a chance to see the faux poppy field, I did see every flower (high and low) in Munchkinland. I was so impressed with how big and ornate everything was—not to mention how expensive. Each of the largest flowers had cost more than one hundred dollars to make and install. (And in 1938, one hundred dollars went a very long way.) Nowadays, they could simply be added digitally, in any quantity, by computers, but I do not think the exact look of richness and realism can be duplicated by such a technique.

▲ This Munchkinland set still, taken before filming began, reveals the secret of Dorothy's farmhouse: It's just a facade. The inside area by the door was used for the transformation scene from sepia to Technicolor, executed seamlessly by Judy Garland and her double, Bobbie Koshay.

◄ City Father Jack Glicken, wearing his brown polka-dot costume, reflects deeply as the assistant color cameraman strolls past the Munchkin town hall.

We could roam around the set quite freely when no shooting was going on, but the areas with grass and flowers were off-limits, lest they be damaged. That is not to say that no one ever walked in these areas. One of these spots, for instance, was just above the riverbank near the bridge, on the side toward Dorothy's farmhouse. This is where the first Munchkins pop their heads up to catch a glimpse of the newly arrived Dorothy—and where the audience catches its first glimpse of us.

The insides of the Munchkin houses were unfinished and rough, which is quite common in Hollywood. You could enter most of them without too much trouble, but some structures—such as the bell tower behind the town hall—were inaccessible, built just for what the camera could see. Little pedestals were installed inside a few of the huts, underneath the windows. These supported the half-dozen or so little girls who filled in the background gaps as additional Munchkins. When you watch the film, you can see many of them peering through window and door openings, waving. They all wore Munchkin costumes, too, but some of their garments were rather dull in comparison to those worn by more prominent adult Munchkins.

I remember that a few of the child actors became so fond of the houses that quite often they stayed in them when the cameras weren't rolling! Who could blame them? Even the children of the biggest MGM stars quite adored those tiny abodes. Jack Haley brought his five-year-old son, Jack Haley Jr., to the set, and Norma Shearer came with her two kids: Irving Thalberg Jr., who was eight, and his sister, Katherine, who was four. They, and many other children, had the rare and wonderful opportunity of seeing Munchkinland for real—it was an experience none of them would soon forget.

Discovering and exploring the magnificence of the Munchkinland set for the first time made me suddenly remember "Jack and the Beanstalk," which I'd read as a child in my favorite *One Ring Circus and Other Short Stories* book—the one written and illustrated by William Wallace Denslow. Even though at twenty-three I was an adult whereas Jack was a child, his fantasy seemed to be coming to life before my very eyes.

Yet the only "giant" I would see in my fantasy world appeared to me later, in the slightly smaller and more feminine form of Judy Garland—a young girl with a huge personality who was to become one of Hollywood's biggest stars.

Setting up for the Dorothy's departure, where we escort her to the border of Munchkinland. I am standing way in the background, past the guard tower, behind the Munchkin Soldiers, but just in front of the pavilion steps. In the foreground, George Ministeri walks toward Nita Krebs. The Town Crier, Mickey Carroll, wearing a purple coat, sits on the edge of the Munchkin pond.

Judy Garland pauses before the cameras roll. Note the yellow brick road—and the red brick road. In the window is a "child Munchkin," wearing a comparatively drab gray and white costume. Below her is the Captain of the Munchkin Army, Victor Wetter, and to his left is Dolly Kramer, wearing the burgundy flowerpot hat.

Norma Shearer dropped by with her children, and was thronged by star-struck Munchkins.

Mervyn LeRoy, the producer, brought his four-year-old son, Warner LeRoy, to visit the set.

CHAPTER SIX

Ding-Dong! The Witch Is Dead!

Coroner: 1. An officer of a county, district, or municipality, originally charged with maintaining the rights of the private property of the crown; in modern times his chief function is to hold inquests on the bodies of those supposed to have died by violence or accident.

OXFORD ENGLISH DICTIONARY

EHEARSALS, MAKEUP TESTS, AND COStume fittings continued for five of the seven weeks that we were to spend on *The Wizard of Oz*. Finally we were ready to commence filming, and on the morning of December 13, 1938, I reported to makeup for my first day as the Munchkin Coroner.

The makeup Department had been assembled in Rehearsal Hall 8, and this is where we were to report for our makeup applications for the next two weeks.

The hall was arranged with a long row of chairs facing large lighted mirrors. We arrived at seven in the morning, headed to our designated section of the hall, and were out by eight. We were divided into groups according to our particular parts, and the same assistant makeup man was assigned to us each time for consistency. The Munchkin Soldiers reported to one area, the Lollipop Guild tough guys to another, and so on. I reported to the City Fathers group in the center of the hall.

Younger assistants acted as gofers for the assistant makeup men. They brought in trays of the appliances that had been made from our plaster facial sculptures the previous day. Under Jack Dawn's tutelage the department was very efficient—we were up to our ears in extra cheeks and noses, in case one was incorrectly applied.

My hair was slicked back with some type of grease or pomade that flattened the top of my head, readying it for application of the notoriously irritating bald skullcap. These latex caps were tightly adhered to our heads with a thick spirit gum. The stuff really did the trick—my makeup didn't come loose during the entire filming. But removal of the skullcaps was definitely not fun. I suppose the sticky stuff is called "spirit gum" because you would have to be inebriated in order not to feel the pain when they snipped the cap behind the ears and ripped it off your head!

Makeup was applied around the edges of the skullcap so that it blended with the skin tone.

Putting the dyed, coarse yak hair on our heads was the next step. Bright orange hair was applied to my head, upper lip, and chin. Spraying it with a hardening substance allowed the hair to be molded into various points and swirls. My beard came to a long point that curled under toward my chin, and my mustache went up in a handlebar style. A little circular piece of latex added to my nose gave it a more bulbous effect.

I had a feeling I didn't look like twenty-three anymore.

In the opening scene as Dorothy steps out of her fallen farmhouse, she takes in a panoramic view of the apparently empty Munchkinland. One of the prime features of our village was its large pond in the center of the city square. In the film, lovely blue water ripples in the stream and big lily pads bob around.

Can you believe how young the Coroner looks? I'm standing next to Judy Garland and Charles Becker as the Mayor.

Initially, about a dozen little white ducklings were also in the pond. They spent their days swimming in circles around the lily pads and waddling amid the flowers on the riverbanks. In nature, a pond only appears blue if it reflects the blue sky, but catwalks and arc lamps formed the sky of Munchkinland. The prop men tried to solve this problem by adding bottles of bluing solution to the pond. Unfortunately, this also turned the ducklings blue!

So the pond was drained and dried and the bottom was painted blue in order to create the desired effect. The prop men's off-screen services were still required whenever the pond or stream was on camera, though. With a large wooden paddle, a pair of them created the nice undulating ripples seen on the water's surface. The blue ducks did not return.

As Dorothy exits her now-dilapidated farmhouse, she looks around for a while before observing, "Toto, I've a feeling we're not in Kansas anymore. . . ." Then she concludes, "We must be over the rainbow!" Judging by all of the colors surrounding her, she might well have believed herself to be *in* the rainbow.

As it turned out, the farmhouse was the last part of the Munchkinland set to be built. Its blueprint was finally approved in early November, though the layout of Munchkinland itself had been finalized in August. The house actually looked very much like the facade seen in the 1902 stage version of *The Wizard of Oz*—that setting might even have been used for reference by the MGM art department, but I can't say for certain.

Since the farmhouse's rendezvous with the Wicked Witch of the East prompted my character's pronouncement, I am glad that it fell into our little hamlet. To be precise, four farmhouses were used in the film. The first was the full-sized version used in the opening Kansas farm sequence; it was completely built and decorated, both inside and out. The second was the distressed-looking farmhouse that fell onto Munchkinland. Just enough of it was built for the camera to see—including part of the interior, just inside the door behind the porch. It was this door that Dorothy opened onto the enchanting Munchkinland in the film's famous transition from sepia to color.

Dorothy looks out over the Munchkinland panorama. This Kodachrome was taken as a publicity photograph; Dorothy never stood in this particular spot in the film.

(This house, of course, figures prominently in a later classic scene—the one of most interest to me—since it was the official "cause of death" for the Wicked Witch of the East.)

To the audience's right of the front door are the legs of said Witch. Her striped-stockinged feet, still wearing the magical ruby slippers, protrude from the house's foundation, directly under the window of what would be Uncle Henry and Aunt Em's room. Through the torn curtains, a strangely shaped wooden object juts out the window. People sometimes ask me if I know what this object is, and the answer is yes, I do. It is simply one of the legs from Aunt Em's overturned rocking chair and looks odd because of its curved shape and because it is upside down.

The other two versions of the Gale home were made for special effects. One was the miniature used for the scene in which the house falls through the air, dropped by the "twister," to land in Oz. This house was filmed from above as it was dropped onto the floor of a soundstage. Because the floor had been painted to look like the sky, when the film was played in reverse, the house appeared to fall toward the camera instead of away from it.

The fourth farmhouse was used in the cyclone sequence as the twister approaches the Gale farm. It was just a facade and was slightly smaller in proportion to the full-sized house used in the opening sequence. Wind machines on the soundstage bombarded the facade with flying debris and bent the model trees.

The fourth farmhouse was used in the cyclone sequence as the twister approaches the Gale farm. The entire farm was built at one-third scale, so that the thirty-five-foot-high muslin tornado would look more menacing. The top of the muslin funnel was attached to a framework that ran the full length of the soundstage, and the bottom was guided into an S-shaped slot in the floor. Fuller's earth (an absorbent clay) and wind machines on the soundstage bombarded the facade with flying debris that bent the model trees.

There was also a separate set built for the shot when Dorothy is in her room, inside the tornado's funnel. She stares out of her window incredulously at the objects and creatures flying by.

Dorothy explains how she came to Munchkinland.

Once she's landed in Oz, a bewildered Dorothy asks Glinda, "Oh, but if you please, what are Munchkins?"

When Glinda gently responds, "The little people who live in this land. It's Munchkinland—and you are their national heroine, my dear," it becomes clear that L. Frank Baum was truly ahead of his time. She refers to us with the term that most of us now prefer.

As the Munchkins begin to tiptoe from their hiding spots, Glinda sings about Dorothy falling from the sky. (Billie Burke's singing voice was dubbed by Lorraine Bridges, who also filled in vocally for one of the Lullaby League ladies.) The first Munchkin seen on camera is little Olga Nardone, in her Munchkin Villager outfit. She is better known for being the centermost, and tiniest, of the Lullaby League dancers, and she also played one of the five Sleepy Head Munchkins.

◀ *Choreographer Bobby Connolly and director Victor Fleming guide Judy Garland as a prop man brings Billie Burke a new star-studded wand.*

▼ *Dorothy looks over at Olga Nardone, Margaret Pellegrini, and Fern Formica in this shot, done on December 29 or 30, 1938.*

I am standing on the top step by
Munchkin town hall. Toto is just
below me. Jack Glicken is to my left
and Charles Becker, the Mayor, is
holding his hat out as Judy Garland,
Little Billy Rhodes, and Matthew Raia
look on. Jerry Maren is visible in the
lower right-hand area. The Soldiers
closest to him are Parnell Elmer St.
Aubin and, to his left, one step lower,
the mustachioed Charles Royale.

More than half the Munchkins prepare to film. This behind-the-scenes photograph has never been published before.

Olga is the most reclusive of the nine surviving Munchkins—so much so that I have not seen her since 1938. None of us other eight knows why she does not participate in the various *Oz*-related events occurring today, but we certainly respect her privacy. It's too bad, though, because she was as cute as a button, and I think *Oz* fans would have loved seeing her throughout the years.

The overall filming process intrigued me, and when I did not have a part to play in the action I could be found off camera, watching intently. Most of the other Munchkins would hang out around the bridge in Munchkinland, or sit along the sides of the houses, while waiting for the long tracking shots or their particular close-ups. Another favorite spot to sit—and I enjoyed this one, too—was along the ledge of the Munchkinland pond. Even director Victor Fleming sat there occasionally, especially when directing us on how to perform a specific scene.

Victor Fleming was an amazing director and will forever be a screen legend for having directed both *Gone with the Wind* and *The Wizard of Oz* in the same year. I found out

later that he had the reputation of being a stern, tough guy, but he was very understanding and congenial when dealing with the little people. He never barked orders at us, but proposed instead, "Well, let's do it this way," or "Let's try it that way." He was quite kind with the little people, and I think we all respected him more as a director and a man because of his patience and politeness.

Victor seemed to know innately exactly where to group the little people. The effect he desired—and achieved—was making us too-few Munchkins appear to be a multitude. We were shifted around to several locations during the same scene, which helped foster the illusion of a large population. Today's technology can catch where these shifts occur, but it is still difficult. To me they are similar to the "beaming" of people that occurs on the *Star Trek* series. One second you might see Harry Doll standing to the left of Judy Garland in the background; in the next he's behind her shoulder.

The City Fathers and I were beamed at the end of our sequence, when we escort Dorothy to the border of Munchkinland. Following Glinda's instructions, Dorothy follows the yellow brick road—starting at its lollipop-shaped epicenter—past the wall and guard tower, turning once to wave good-bye before starting her journey to the Emerald City. Somehow the City Fathers and I leap from the heart of our village to line Dorothy's path as she departs Munchkinland. This sequence looks fairly seamless in the finished film. As Dorothy finally takes her leave, I can be seen not only tipping, but actually doffing, my Coroner's hat—the only time that my bald head was viewed on camera.

The apparently magical shifting of Munchkins around the set was augmented by the movement of a few average-sized children. They were used in the background to fill in the blank spaces. Also, multiple parts were given to some Munchkin actors. A few of them are seen so briefly that I've always wondered whether it was worth all of Adrian's trouble to design a separate costume for each role.

Before Glinda completes her Kansas song about Dorothy, a few of the little people playing extra roles can be seen fleetingly. While Dorothy and Glinda stroll past the farmhouse, watch for Lollipop Guild member Harry Doll to make a unique entrance through a manhole—or was it a Munchkinhole? Here his only costume change was the addition of a red bandanna around his neck and a corncob pipe. A continuity error occurs in the next shot when the manhole disappears completely, replaced by the smooth yellow brick road surface. My guess is that having a second hole in the set—the Witch's elevator shaft being the first—created an unnecessary safety hazard. Mickey Carroll can be seen here in one of his many roles, too: a Munchkin Crier. Watch for his purple coat and silver bell.

With Dorothy and Glinda positioned up on the canopied platform by the pond, kind of a daisy dais, the second of the E. Y. "Yip" Harburg and Harold Arlen songs commences.

Their songs were very catchy and clever, due in no small part to the wit and talent of Mr. Harburg's lyrics. Not only did he pen all of these songs for the film, he was also one of the uncredited screenwriters. Nearly all of the rhythmical Gilbert-and-Sullivan-inspired dialogue in the film was written by him, too—such as the City Fathers' "You'll be a bust in the hall of fame" exchange and even *my* lines as the Coroner!

After Dorothy sings about the wind beginning to pitch, and the Witch "flying on her broomstick, thumbing for a hitch," Billy Curtis appears in what has to be the largest hat in Munchkinland: tall and gray, adorned with a single long-stemmed plumelike flower. His interjection as the Braggart Munchkin—"And, oh, what happened then was rich!"—is the first line in the film spoken by a little person.

"What happened then" is revealed by the full chorus of Munchkin Villagers: "It landed on the Wicked Witch in the middle of a ditch. Which was not a healthy sit-u-a-tion for the Wicked Witch." It was, however, very healthy for the business of the Munchkin Coroner!

Just before this song ends, the plumed platoon of twenty-five Munchkin Soldiers marches in on the red brick road, led by George Ministeri (driving the coach with the two miniature horses) with Victor Wetter, the Captain of the Soldiers, at his side. The only distinguishable difference between Victor's costume and the other Soldiers' was the top of his hat: He had three feather plumes, while the others had only two—yet another intricate detail of Adrian's.

The coach halts at the foot of the pavilion by the pond, where five steps lead up to where Dorothy and Glinda are standing. Very few scenes occur in which the pair is not perched on some type of raised platform; elevating Dorothy and Glinda accentuated the diminutive size of the Munchkins.

Frank Cucksey and Prince Leon present Dorothy with their thank-you bouquets. They had the only unaltered Munchkin speaking roles in the film.

Victor Fleming directs a group of Munchkins, including, from left, an unidentified Munchkin Soldier, Frank Cucksey as a Villager, Jerry Maren as a member of the Lollipop Guild, one of three Munchkin Heralds, a barely visible Lullaby League dancer, and one of the five Fiddlers.

The Captain escorts Dorothy to the flower-shaped coach, and two stately Munchkins, played by Leon Polinsky and Frank Cucksey, present her with a bouquet of rainbow-colored flowers. (The omnipresence of rainbow colors in Munchkinland, seen in such gifts as the bouquet and the lollipop, was carefully devised—from the vivid hues of the huge set to the full spectrum of colorful opulence displayed in the costumes.) "We thank you very sweetly, for doing it so neatly" and "You've killed her so completely, that we thank you very sweetly," Dorothy is informed. Leon and Frank delivered these lines so sweetly that they were the only two Munchkins whose voices were not later dubbed over by professional vocalists.

The coach reaches town hall just as the chorus of "Ding-Dong! The Witch Is Dead" fades, and the first Munchkins to exit from the building's multicolored double doors are the three Trumpeters. Lead Trumpeter Karl "Karchy" Slover is followed by Kayo Erickson and Major Mite, whose real name was Clarence Howerton. At slightly more than three feet tall, these half-pint heralds were among the smallest Munchkins on the set.

Karl, who was in Leo Singer's troupe for many years, is the last surviving Singer midget. He lives in Tampa, Florida, near me, and travels frequently to the Oz conventions, which are more like reunions for all of the remaining Munchkins. He often relays a story about the Trumpeter's entrance. Originally, Kayo had been directed to be the first Trumpeter exiting town hall—but he kept missing his cue. Karl would tell him to get going, but he still wouldn't budge. Then, when Karl gave him a little push, Kayo blurted, "Hey, don't shove!"

Victor Fleming was not happy. He told them that when he said, "Come out," they had better do so right away, without any delays—the film had been delayed enough. Did they have any suggestions, he asked. Karl replied that if *he* were in front, he would "make dern sure" that the Trumpeters came out on cue. Fleming directed them to switch their order; now Karl was in front and Kayo was in the center.

In the shot used in the movie, Karl did come out immediately, but again, Kayo wouldn't budge. This time Major Mite gave him a shove, and they all moved out together. Since the jockeying happened off camera, inside the Munchkin town hall, it's not noticeable on film. Some have suggested Kayo might have been narcoleptic, but I can't say for sure. The few times I spoke with him he seemed like a very nice fellow, and he had enjoyed his travels with the Harvey Williams midget troupe before the *Oz* filming.

In true clown car fashion, next to exit town hall are the City Fathers, led by the Mayor. Only my old friend Jack Glicken had been seen before—in the background, on the bridge when Glinda first arrived in Munchkinland. He is best known as the City Father in the brown polka-dot uniform who interjects his verification that the Witch is "spiritually, physically" dead.

The Mayor's tall stovepipe hat barely clears the doorway of town hall. He doffs it immediately to Dorothy, meets her at the coach, and escorts her to the top of the stairs. It was

probably a good idea that he took her hand to assist her, because the miniature ponies didn't want to stand still and the carriage wobbled a bit as she left it.

The ponies were aptly named Wizard and Oz. Although we weren't allowed to pet Toto, I was able to pet the ponies, thanks to their trainer, Mr. Gilman. I told him about the time I had been bucked off the former circus pony at the San Diego Exposition because I hadn't known the commands for its tricks. He said that the only thing tricky about this obstinate little duo was getting them to stop or start. They were great once you got them going, but that took a little coaxing. The same went for stopping—which is why the best take of Dorothy stepping off the carriage shows Wizard and Oz still in motion.

Dorothy looks back at her footman, William O'Docharty, while a stoic George Ministeri steers the ponies, Wizard and Oz.

The Mayor's oversized gold pocket watch, complete with fob and chain, was his most distinguishing prop. To give you an idea of how exacting MGM was at this time, I'll just note that the watch was made after an approved blueprint had been sent to the prop department!

Charles Becker, the very affable gentleman who played the Mayor, had a thick German accent and had been with Singer longer than any other midget. Some of the Munchkins moved the hands on his nonrunning watch as a kind of "running" joke. It wasn't funny, though, and he'd an-grily curse the culprits in German; he knew that continuity was important in any film.

Despite Charles's vigilance, the hands on his watch are not static during the Mayor's time in front of the camera. The timepiece reads five thirty when he first meets Judy at the coach, then goes backward (or forward, to the early morning) to five o'clock as they reach the top of the stairs.

An example of the Munchkins' voices being dubbed occurs in this scene. Lively banter begins when the City Fathers first talk to Dorothy. If you listen closely, you can hear that the

The Mayor lauds Dorothy. Keep an eye on his big watch!

voices of the Mayor and the Second City Father (played by Matthew Raia in an orange polka-dot costume) are one and the same. Billy Bletcher, a midget actor known for providing numerous voices for films and cartoons, dubbed the voices for these two Munchkins.

But in the final City Father lines, the voices mysteriously change. "From now on, you'll be history," declares the Mayor in Bletcher's voice. Then another voice is dubbed for the Barrister's line, "You'll be hist—" Most likely this was Pinto Colvig, who was the voice of Grumpy and Sleepy in Walt Disney's *Snow White and the Seven Dwarfs*. When the Mayor adds, "You'll be a bust," he speaks in the voice of the Barrister!

Over the years, much controversy has arisen about the use of our actual voices in the finished film. MGM seemed to me quite ahead of its time technologically, and for a very long time I thought they had just manipulated the recordings of our own voices. While we were filming, a boom mike had recorded all of the sound.

But a few years ago, I heard some selections from the movie's newly released deluxe soundtrack—the kind of recording that's made when a trove of material is found tucked away in a vault, or in someone's attic, and becomes the impetus for a rerelease. One of the tracks was of the Munchkin voices before and after they were altered. Having heard those recordings and listened to the voices jumping around from character to character, I now believe, as I stated above, that all of the Munchkin voices were dubbed, including mine. The only exceptions were the two beaus who present Dorothy with flowers.

The last time I met Buddy Ebsen at a celebrity function was in the late 1990s, in Long Beach, California. Buddy was originally cast as the Tin Woodman, then was sidelined by a reaction to the aluminum dust used in his makeup and replaced by Jack Haley. I kidded him during that last visit that he was just as much a part of *The Wizard of Oz* as the Munchkins. I reasoned that we were there in body, but not voice, while he was there in voice, but not in body! As many *Oz* fans know, Buddy's voice can still be heard on both reprisals of "We're Off to See the Wizard."

I was deeply saddened by Buddy's death, at ninety-five, on July 6, 2003. He and his charming wife (whose name just happens to be Dorothy) helped me out on this project by providing photos of Buddy and me. I acquired an original still photograph of Buddy in his Tin Woodman makeup, taken in October 1938, from an esteemed Oz collector. Reproductions of this photo had been featured in numerous books about the filming of Oz. It was even published in Buddy's own autobiography, *The Other Side of Oz*.

I didn't learn until after his death that Buddy had signed the original photograph I had sent to him for my book. He had been hospitalized due to a recent stroke and was not doing too well. Because he could not write or paint at this point (and Buddy had been an excellent painter), Dorothy put his signature on the photograph with a rubber stamp, then Buddy wrote over the outline in a silver-paint pen. This took place in late June 2003; it was one of the final autographs he completed from the hospital bed that he never left.

This photo is more special to me than words can describe, and is further proof that this erstwhile Tin Man always possessed a huge and caring heart.

Buddy Ebsen kindly autographed this October 1938 photograph for me in late June 2003. It was one of his last autographs.

Not until the end of the first week of shooting was I finally able to voice my solo proclamation. The Coroner was a rather macabre Munchkin, but a fun role to play. I remember being a little nervous about delivering my lines, but I tried to put my best foot forward without tripping as I traipsed up the stairs to Dorothy and the other City Fathers. With seven steps and thirteen seconds of dialogue, all I needed to jinx me further was to walk under a ladder, step on a crack, or see a black cat cross my path.

As if this weren't enough, my costume's number was also thirteen. Wardrobe assigned each of us a number to facilitate our dressing every morning. As Jack Dawn's department did with makeup, the wardrobe department kept still photographs of each of our costumes in a notebook. Corresponding numbers were written in the lower right-hand corners of all of the stills required to depict a single costume.

I wish the technology were available to enable the readers of this book to simply push a button and hear audio of me reciting my lines during the filming, at age twenty-three or

Photographs were taken of every Munchkin costume and placed in costume key books for reference. Each costume had an assigned number—mine was number thirteen!

even at my current age of eighty-nine! Until that's possible, and for those of you who don't have them memorized, the lines went like this.

> As Coroner, I must aver
> I thoroughly examined her.
> And she's not only merely dead,
> She's really, most sincerely dead.

When first attempting this incantation, I tried not to look down at the steps too much, but worried about tripping on my long, dark purple robe. While averring, I also was averting—my eyes, that is—from Judy Garland. I was, after all, supposed to deliver my lines directly to the Mayor, but I also thought that looking directly at Judy might throw me off a little. I idolized this youngster and didn't want to look foolish in front of her.

One thing that Judy Garland and I might have in common is that throughout the years I have probably recited my proclamation about the Witch as many times as she sang her signature "Over the Rainbow" song. Like her, I never grow tired of repeating it because it seems to make the Oz fans so happy.

A question frequently asked of me is, "What does 'aver' mean?" It is not a commonly used word and simply means to swear, affirm, or verify an action. I have always been a fan of Mr. Harburg's catchy lyrics and would never have doctored the script had I been given the chance—even though I was technically an M.D. (a "Munchkin Doctor," of course).

Recently, with so many of the former Munchkin actors being sincerely deceased themselves, I sometimes wonder if the casting director somehow knew I would stick around so long. I cannot know when I will depart this Munchkin coil—but I *do* know that I am nearly out of blank scrolls!

My heavy felt costume was made from three different layers of material: a baby-blue inner lining, the dark purple outer layer, and a trim of light green around my hands to match the band of green on my hat. I was one of the few Munchkins who didn't have to wear shoes made entirely of felt. My black shoes are visible in the film, and the only felt used in their construction lined the soles, to lessen the sound of walking on the soundstage floor.

Filmmakers generally ensure that nothing seen on screen is "out of period" for the time in which the action takes place. Actors may not wear personal jewelry, for instance (to prevent such flubs as Roman soldiers sporting wristwatches in some of the old gladiator movies). For some reason no one mentioned this to me, so the Coroner wears a gold University of Wisconsin ring on his left hand. (Go, Badgers!) It's quite visible in all of my scenes and in the still shots taken of my character.

The most distinctive part of my costume was the large, dark purple hat, with its curlicued, or scrolled, ends. It did not fit snugly onto my head, but rested on the very top, held in place by a purple ribbon that was tied with a bow at the back of my skull. I couldn't tie it myself, so someone from the costume department had to secure it for me. The brim of the hat was fifteen inches across, and the crown was four inches high—which made me seem much taller than I actually was, along with looking more distinguished and formidable.

That hat was sold at an auction in Beverly Hills, California, on December 13, 1998—sixty years to the day that we started filming in Munchkinland! I attended the event and was asked to try on the hat, to see if it still fit. It did, and the new owner was very happy with his *Oz* memento. It only cost him $19,000! The Wicked Witch's hat—worn, of course, by Margaret Hamilton in the film—was auctioned off at the same event, for twice as much!

My original Munchkin Coroner hat was auctioned off in 1998 for $19,000, and again in 2005, on eBay, for $34,000.

Fans sometimes ask me, "Was something legible written on your certificate of death, and if so, what was it?" The answer is, yes, but only to make the prop look more authentic on camera. According to a conversation that I had with former prop master Jackie Ackerman while writing this book, one of his fellow prop men, Earl Hayes, made the scroll.

Jackie worked as a prop man at MGM for more than sixty years, and *The Wizard of Oz* was one of his favorite projects. Many people might wonder how Bert Lahr moved his tail as the Cowardly Lion throughout the film—well, Jackie is the best person in the world to ask, since he was the one who controlled the movement.

Up in the catwalks (the rafters of the soundstages where lighting and other equipment was installed), he worked a pole, which was attached to a wire, which was attached to the tail, and thereby wagged said tail as the Lion lumbered around. (Lions, and tigers, and catwalks . . . oh, my!) Jackie's favorite scene while working the tail occurred when Dorothy, the Tin Woodman, Scarecrow, and Toto first meet up with the Cowardly Lion in his forest. After Dorothy slaps him for chasing Toto, the Lion wipes his eyes with his tail. The scene ends with the comrades interlocking arms and setting off together while reprising "We're Off to See the Wizard." (Although the ebbing voice of the Tin Woodman is that of Buddy Ebsen, not Jack Haley.)

Jackie told me how he managed this, and how he came to acquire the job of chief tail-wagger for the Cowardly Lion. "Harry Edwards was a first prop man on the film and was a lot older than myself. I was a third prop man and had such wonderful jobs as polishing the yellow brick road over and

High above the Munchkinland set, Jackie Ackerman worked the Cowardly Lion's energetic tail.

I had a good time playing the Munchkin Coroner and have always been grateful for my "lucky thirteen" seconds of total screen time that it took to walk up the seven steps and read my lines.

over with a cedar mop," said Jackie. "He had to climb up the ladder to the catwalks to work the Lion's tail. It was really hot up there, and he got tired of constantly going up and down the ladder. One day he finally told me, 'Jackie, when you see the Lion come on the set, up you go!'

"I climbed up that thing like a monkey. There was a fishing pole stashed up there with the line for the Lion's tail, in between the lights. I let the fishing line down so Harry could tie the line to the Lion's tail. Whenever Bert Lahr walked along, I stayed with him and wagged his tail at the same time. I tried to stay away from the lights in the catwalks [because], boy, they were really hot!

"In one scene the Lion sat down on that log and picked up his tail to dry his tears off. When he let go of it, [his tail] would have went *plop*, like that, but I had the tension on the line all the time he was wiping the tears. I kept the tension until he let go, and then I let his tail down slowly and commenced wagging it again. It was really a fun thing for me to do and I was glad that no one else wanted to do it. . . . Harry had the job at first, but I ended up doing it, so I consider myself the one who worked the Lion's tail in *The Wizard of Oz*, and I am proud of that."

One question I had to ask Jackie during this conversation was about the date of the Witch's demise on the scroll:

Earl Hayes, the property manager for The Wizard of Oz, *made the death certificate. This is what it said.*

May 6, 1938—nineteen years to the day after the death of L. Frank Baum.

"Really? That is interesting," Jackie responded, "but it is just a coincidence. We tried to make the props look very authentic, but we were always under the gun to get these things out fast and did not have too much time to think about every detail."

Careful scrutiny of the actual writing on the scroll prop reveals that it is very detailed, but also not meant to be taken literally.

Whether or not Earl Hayes actually tried to make an intentional connection seems unlikely, in my opinion, but it still is an eerie and ominous coincidence. Ironically, the film not only keeps Baum's story alive, but adds to his immortality. Also, note the nonsensical name of "W. W. Barrister, M.D." It's an unintentional combination of the characters of the Wicked Witch and the Barrister, plus the Coroner's credentials as a Doctor of Medicine. This writing filled the space on the section of the scroll, but was not legible on even the biggest of theater screens.

Due to our intense rehearsal period while our costumes were being made, our performances required very few retakes. I don't recall the exact number of takes needed for my scene, but there were no more than three or four. Many factors can cause a retake. For example, an actor might deliver his lines perfectly, but to a camera he is ill positioned or out of focus; conversely, the actor might flub his lines, though the camera captures his image perfectly.

I thought I was "dead-on" in reciting my lines, although, of course, I'm a little biased. Two separate shots were needed for the delivery of my pronouncement of death. The first was a continuous shot of me walking up the steps, unfurling the scroll, and reading the findings to the Mayor. The second was of me standing next to the other City Fathers and Dorothy as the Mayor decreed, "Yes, let the joyous news be spread. The Wicked Old Witch at last is dead!"

All of my lines were spoken in the first shot, so I was able to comfortably look around a bit in the second. Judy had been watching me the whole time in the first shot, so I didn't peer at the little dear until the latter. To the audience, I look quite stoic, but I remember feeling very excited and proud to be in this scene, standing next to Judy Garland. At sixteen, she was still a kid (compared to my mature twenty-three), but I was very impressed with her career thus far, and the genuine kindness and radiant personality that she displayed on the *Oz* set only reinforced my admiration. I even managed to give her an impromptu bow when she looked at me on camera.

Technicolor looked great on the big screen, but was certainly not easy to film. The studio brought in 150 arc

The most famous Munchkin publicity photograph was widely used for Oz promotional posters and lobby cards. The actors are, from left to right, Jack Glicken, a City Father; Johnny Winters, Commander of the Munchkin Navy; me, with the Certificate of Death; Judy Garland; Little Billy Rhodes, the Barrister; Charles Becker, the Mayor; Matthew Raia, a City Father; and Jakob Hofbauer, a Munchkin Soldier. This is my favorite picture with Judy Garland. She was only four foot eleven, but she dwarfs all of us!

The picture was used again for a special set of playing cards made in England. The entire deck had different hand-painted scenes from the film. My Certificate of Death looks even more ominous in this red color.

This British puzzle, manufactured in 1940, uses a painting very similar to the lobby card, but here my scroll is rolled up.

Judy Garland gets some coaching from the director, Victor Fleming, while Munchkin Coach Driver George Ministeri rests. A young property assistant holds Toto—dispelling the myth that only Toto's trainer, Carl Spitz, handled the dog.

The assistant cameraman holds a large "lilly," a color adjustment tool for the Technicolor team. Judy Garland looks through her script; Bert Lahr is visible in the lower left-hand corner of the picture.

lamps—each three feet in diameter, and very expensive, to say the least. Hanging from the ceiling, these lamps generated an immense amount of heat, raising the temperature to extreme levels. Most of the actors were burdened with heavy makeup, cumbersome costumes, or both. As the Scarecrow, Ray Bolger had a rough time with the latex that covered his head, simulating burlap. Most of the Munchkins wore thick felt costumes, and the men's skullcaps trapped their body heat, causing perspiration to pour down the backs of their necks. Worst of all was Bert Lahr's heavy Lion's costume.

The chief electrician on the film was A. W. Brown. Each time the director yelled, "Cut!" Mr. Brown immediately ordered, "Save your arcs!" This was the cue for the lamps to be temporarily turned off, saving electricity and letting the temperature cool slightly. The Munchkins' instinctive response to this statement was, "Save your arches"—which meant squatting down on whatever yellow brick or step we were standing on at the time, until filming resumed.

When the lamps were turned on, an electrician carried a light meter around the set, checking each flower and thatched roof for hot spots (areas where light was reflected back into the camera, which would require an adjustment). The twenty-foot-tall cellophane hollyhocks were notorious for causing such reflections. When a hot spot was discovered, the electrician directed an assistant to fan out the light (widen the beam) in order to diffuse its intensity.

As if the arc lamps, backlights, top lights, and klieg lights weren't enough, key lights were added to the electrical mix. These smallest of instruments were used to light up the actors' eyes. I found out from Mr. Brown that using these lights was made more difficult by the performers themselves. Many actors and actresses feel they are photogenic on only one side of their face and will try to favor that side as much as possible during shoots. So the key lights have to be moved and readjusted frequently to stay with the favored side. I didn't have enough face time on film as the Coroner to worry about such countenance conundrums.

Not surprisingly, this production was notable for using the most electricity of any film up till its time. To support the extra electrical load, Southern California Edison provided two enormous emergency generators, which sat just outside the lot. These prodigious machines hinted to passersby of the wondrous, and also very secretive, goings-on inside the soundstages.

More Clark Kent-style quick costume changes appear when the lights and cameras focus on the Munchkins during our singing and dancing reprisal of the "Ding-Dong! The Witch Is Dead" scene. Munchkin Heralds (the Trumpeters) Kayo Erickson and Karl Slover stand behind me while Margaret Pellegrini dances her dainty self up the stairs, dressed in her classic baby-blue flowerpot Villager outfit. The crowd pauses at the Sleepy Head nest before continuing up the stairs. In the blink of an eye, Margaret and Kayo (now playing Sleepy Head Munchkins) are seen within two of the five green Sleepy Head egg beds, in pink nightgowns and bonnets.

Two of the other Sleepy Heads were Olga Nardone and Fern Formica—respectively, the smallest and youngest female Munchkins. Fern was a whopping thirteen (a fact that was kept quiet by Leo Singer); the next youngest was Margaret Pellegrini, who was just fifteen years old at the time.

"I helped them in and out of the giant bird's nest," recalled prop master Jackie Ackerman. "They were the little Munchkins that raised their heads from the beds. I used to handle them like little babies, almost." When we spoke in the summer of 2004, Jackie seemed pleased to learn that Olga and Margaret were still alive and well. It is quite amazing that two of the nine of us still living were in the bird's nest (although they *were* the youngest, to begin with).

Yet age in years does not always matter. At ninety-one, Jackie is even older than I am—but he remembers six and a half decades ago as if it were yesterday, from the comfort of

Jerry Maren and Harry Doll joke as other Munchkins look on. Billy Curtis is the first Munchkin in the back row, wearing a very tall hat with a long-stemmed flower. To Billy's left is Dolly Kramer, wearing her burgundy flowerpot hat. The Munchkin lady next to her has an identical hat—what are the odds they shop at the same store?

The Lullaby League scene pauses, as Judy Garland looks down at Charles Becker, the Mayor. The right side of my scrolled hat is visible just to the right of the Barrister, Little Billy Rhodes.

The Lollipop Guild consisted of Jackie Gerlich, Jerry Maren (here in a rare moment without his signature cheroot), and Harry Doll (the oldest of these "boys" at age thirty-six).

his apartment in the Actors' Home in Los Angeles (where Billie Burke spent her last years).

It may not be like yesterday to me, but I certainly remember my two weeks on the Munchkinland set clearly. Climbing past the awakened Sleepy Heads, the marching Munchkins celebrate in song the Witch's having gone below, "where the goblins go . . . " When they finally march back down the other side of the stairs, they rally near the yellow brick road's lollipop swirl, to the left of town hall. They're just in time to witness Dorothy's welcoming by the committees of Lullaby League ladies and Lollipop Guild boys (also known as the three Little Tough Guys).

Ladies first—especially if they are "little ladies": The Lullaby League dancers all wear pink dresses and hats. This, the third costume for center dancer Olga, was very reminiscent of her Sleepy Head Munchkin attire. According to Jackie, Earl Hayes made the miniature scrolls from which the actresses pretend to read when welcoming Dorothy to Munchkinland.

One of the most memorable scenes from the Munchkinland sequence is the Lollipop Guild trio's salute to Dorothy immediately following the Lullaby League's. The tough boys' colorful costumes simultaneously match and clash with one another. Each boy's shorts are a different color, but all are torn in the same pattern at the bottom. Their striped stockings match their shorts and their shirts of red-brown, green, and blue. They do, however, all have the same gray-colored shoes.

My friend Jerry Maren, the center Little Tough Guy, holds the Guild's namesake lollipop in his left hand. "I wanted to keep that lollipop," he has told me in the past, "but they wouldn't let me have it. That's how it goes!" I guess most of us have gotten the fuzzy end of the lollipop at one time or another—which reminds me: Where is my original Certificate of Death scroll? I wouldn't mind owning that prop—and I would be sure to hold on to it, too.

On Jerry's left is Harry Doll, wearing the blue top and gray shorts. That he was able to play such a youth even in his mid thirties is impressive. He was an accomplished actor who had top billing with Lon Chaney in *The Unholy 3* in 1930, and played Hans in *Freaks* in 1932.

On Jerry's right is Jackie Gerlich. Both he and Harry were with the Ringling Bros. and Barnum & Bailey circus prior to *The Wizard of Oz*, although they performed in different parts of the country. At fourteen, Jackie was the youngest of the Lollipop Guild. This scene shows particularly well how Dorothy's height was accentuated by having her standing on the steps instead of at ground level.

After the Lollipop Guild's presentation, the entire gaggle of Munchkins flocks to Dorothy to continue the official welcoming song. Closest to the guest of honor is little Fern, in a green-and-yellow dress, with a tiny brown hat atop her curly blonde hair. She was always a little timid, being so young, and oftentimes would look around to see what the other Munchkin ladies were doing. She can be seen doing so here, at the end of the Munchkins' welcoming song.

When *The Wizard of Oz* conventions became popular, Fern was the first of us to have a replica of her costume made especially for those affairs. This started a trend, and now most of the surviving Munchkins, including myself, wear replica costumes to such appearances. She has been gone for some time, though I was her senior by a decade.

The City Fathers belt the final salute to Dorothy—and quite poorly, I might add. This is another glaring example of the blatant use of bad dubbing of our voices. In this scene the Mayor begins by telling Dorothy, "From now on, you'll be history," in the voice of Billy Bletcher. The Barrister echoes, "You'll be hist—" in the voice of Pinto Colvig. Then Matthew Raia, the City Father in the orange polka-dot costume, repeats the same line in a third voice—probably also provided by Billy Bletcher. When the Mayor concludes, *this* time he sings in the same voice as the Barrister! (Well, at least his pocket watch was still set at five o'clock!)

As much as I would like to rush past this City Fathers scene without mentioning my peccadillo-laden performance, it is best that I point out my mistake, rather than wait for someone else to do it for me in the future. The group of City Fathers had just two lines to recite as an ensemble. These are delivered in the scene where national heroine Dorothy is feted for having just dispatched the Witch. The first line

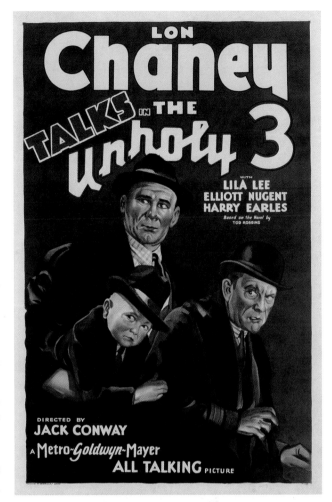

Harry Doll (also known as Harry Earles) is featured in this one-sheet poster for the 1930 remake of The Unholy 3. *The movie also starred Lon Chaney and Elliott Nugent.*

was, "And we will glorify your name!" That went off without a hitch (or a stitch), but I completely blew my line when everyone—except for me—sang the next and final line: "In the hall of fame!" I just simply missed the cue, but no one has ever brought it to my attention…out of kindness or simply because it wasn't noticed.

The scene quickly transitions to everyone marching toward Dorothy and the Good Witch, Glinda, who both viewed this procession unfold from the raised pavilion platform. My scroll magically appears in my right hand for this final shot of the Fathers. While we walk, the Barrister and Mayor lead Dorothy by the hand. I am next to Johnny Winters, who was the Commander of the Munchkin Navy. (If my coauthor, Naval Lieutenant Daniel Kinske, had been with me at that moment, he would have had to follow the orders of that atom-sized admiral!)

As the entire group reaches the Good Witch, we all throw our hats up in the air. Here, with accidental prescience, some of the lady Munchkins scream, foreshadowing the unexpected appearance of the Wicked Witch of the West.

Technically speaking, this is the single scene in which I am on screen at the same time as the Wicked Witch—but, in fact, her entrance was actually made by Margaret Hamilton's stunt double, Betty Danko.

I did meet Margaret on the set, though, and contrary to her rather menacing screen character, she was the nicest adult actress there. A hardworking single mother, she did whatever it took to care for her son, Hamilton. She was very professional and cordial, and always wore a smile. She seemed to empathize with the little people more than most others and really treated us as equals. Judy Garland was

great, too, but she was still a girl and spent most of her time in school with her tutor. So it was the Wicked Witch of the West—enemy of the Munchkins and perpetual pest—who spoke to us the most and treated us the best.

In the Munchkinland scene, the smoke does not even clear before I run across the right side of the screen and out of view of the camera. The Mayor and the Barrister don't make a beeline, so those actors got their exercise for the day. First the Barrister runs to the left, past the fountain, after almost crashing into our confused Town Crier (played by Mickey Carroll); the Crier hugs the ledge of the fountain as the Mayor swerves around him.

None other than Jerry Maren, still in Lollipop Guild garb, executes the most acrobatic running maneuver: In the background, behind Margaret Hamilton's left shoulder, an

Betty Danko, Margaret Hamilton's double, arrives in Munchkinland amid a cloud of smoke. Very soon, Margaret will step into Betty's place.

Margaret Hamilton, Judy Garland, and Billie Burke chat between takes.

extremely nimble Munchkin actually jumps into the front window of a Munchkin house. Jerry's legs can still be seen kicking as the Witch makes her way toward the feet of her dead sister. *His* feet stay in the window so long that the Witch of the East's feet actually shrivel into nothingness before he finally disappears into the house—just as Margaret Hamilton (not her stunt double) exits!

One lone Munchkin Soldier can be seen skulking in the background as the Wicked Witch of the West marches back to Dorothy, demanding to know what became of the slippers. Jerry's character never gets close to the Witch, but at least he performs his duties honorably by trying to protect the village!

All of us knew where the trapdoor was, and we were told many times to stay away from the opening. During our last dance rehearsal, on Saturday, December 11, head dance director Bobby Connolly again warned us not to go near the trap-door. Ironically, in the midst of this speech, *he* fell in. Falling down the pit was bad enough, but he landed on Betty Danko, who was preparing to test the mechanical catapult that would soon be used to launch the Wicked Witch of the West into Munchkinland. She was not seriously hurt, but did suffer some minor injuries to her back, while Mr. Connolly took quite a beating to his pride.

In hindsight, these early problems could have been viewed as a bad omen for the Witch's future fiery entrance—Munchkinland was not a safe place for evildoing witches, it seems—but Christmas was approaching, and the goal was for our sequence to be in the can before 1938 was itself extinguished.

Red smoke without fire announces the entrance of the Wicked Witch of the West (still Betty Danko at this point, on the catapult). I have heard many Oz fans and historians say that Betty's back was toward the camera when she came up, but that is incorrect, at least from what I saw. She arrived in Munchkinland facing the camera, her feet firmly planted on the platform to brace against the blast from the six-foot-wide wind machines (positioned off camera, left of the farmhouse). Witchlike, Betty gyrated her gaunt body toward the Munchkins but remained on the catapult surface until the wind and smoke cleared. Her head dipped down so that the brim of her hat and the broom in her hand obscured her face. She took one step off the catapult, toward the right, and—

At that moment, director Fleming yelled, "Cut," and Margaret Hamilton stepped in to take Betty's place. Facing the camera and brandishing the broom, she looked very menacing and maniacal.

The director adjusts the brim of the Wicked Witch's hat while Dorothy holds a handkerchief and Nikko clutches Dorothy's basket. Note the soft slippers that Judy Garland is wearing.

The thin metal covering of the eight-foot-deep pit was painted light gray to resemble the simulated stone slate surrounding it. As I mentioned earlier, this "slate" consisted of two-toned, irregular shapes of gray-painted Masonite, so the opening of the trapdoor was perfectly camouflaged. If, watching the movie, you look on the ground just in front of Glinda and just to the right of the farmhouse, you can see a large rectangular outline among the much smaller surrounding faux slate outlines. This rectangle is the largest piece of gray flooring on the set, and the only one that an average-sized person could fit through. It's not hard to find—once you know where to look.

Just a few feet in front of the trapdoor opening, a straight line seems to cut through the floor. This "line" is really formed by a series of tiny holes in the floor—openings for the two sets of tubes that made the Wicked Witch's departure so ominous. One set carried the smoke; the other, the flames. The tubes themselves were not visible, but it is easy to spot their openings because the line they form is so long that it bisects an adjoining lighter gray square. The tubes

were positioned beneath this straight line—they did *not* encircle the elevator opening, as some books have erroneously noted. They were, however, close enough to generate extremely intense heat near that area—especially for Margaret Hamilton. Had the tubes actually encircled the opening, I would have had to "aver" her, too!

Not everything had been peachy during the filming of *The Wizard of Oz* to date. Before I got there, Buddy Ebsen had nearly died from inhaling Jack Dawn's concoction of aluminum dust makeup; more recently, Bobby Connolly had performed his accidental duet with Betty Danko in the pit, and poor fellow Munchkin Elsie Schultz had been hit by a car while Christmas shopping on December 21. (She was forced to return home to recover from her injuries.)

But the worst accident that occurred during *The Wizard of Oz* filming happened right on the Munchkinland set. It was the day before Christmas Eve and the holiday weekend. Most of the cast and crew had heard about Elsie's accident just two days previously, and we, especially the little people, were still thinking about her health.

The scene that was shot on that Friday morning, December 23, was the one where the Witch threatens Dorothy and Toto, then climactically departs from Munchkinland. When the Wicked Witch first arrived in our little village, most of the Munchkins scattered or fell to the ground cowering—and most of them held their positions for the entire Witch sequence. Since my character had run off camera, I was not in the departure sequence at all—but I was on the town hall side of the set, watching intently.

There was always a lot of sitting around and waiting for various things to be set up before a scene could be filmed. This setup was especially complex, with good reason due to the inherent danger of the real flames that would emanate from the tube. The technicians tested the apparatus and then conferred with the director to make sure that the flames were of the right height and intensity. Most importantly, they had to be timed perfectly.

The Witch arrived in Munchkinland accompanied by just the red smoke, but she departed in smoke and flames. The difficulty was in coordinating the flames and the smoke exactly so that Margaret would have enough time to get on the elevator masked by the smoke and be safely underneath the set before the flames spewed forth. Margaret's double would not be able to perform in this dangerous scene since it had to be a seamless take—a fact that must have haunted Victor Fleming and producer Mervyn LeRoy long afterward.

The Wicked Witch delivers a blistering harangue to Glinda and Dorothy, demanding the ruby slippers and warning Dorothy, "I'll get you, my pretty, and your little dog, too!" She backs away from Dorothy and Glinda, turning half to the left, then 360 degrees left, to end with her back toward the camera. If you look closely, you can see Margaret clutch her broom close to her body and tuck in her arms as she slowly descends in the elevator. She had barely completed this action and ceased her cackling when the flames went a-crackling—with perfect spacing and timing. Everything looked pretty good, but Victor Fleming wanted one more take to be on the safe side. Unfortunately, it was lunchtime; and regardless of how much the director or producer may have wanted to push onward, they were obliged to let the crew have a break.

After all of the cast and crew had returned from lunch, Victor still wanted to shoot the Witch's departure scene again, even though the previous take had been nearly perfect. The technicians returned to test the timing of the

Victor Fleming explains a scene to Margaret Hamilton, Judy Garland, and Billie Burke as the Munchkins rest in the background.

This Kodachrome of Billie Burke, Judy Garland, and Toto was featured in the July 17, 1939, issue of Life *magazine.*

smoke and flames. This time, however, there was a problem with getting them to synch up properly. In hindsight, this should have registered as another bad omen.

As the afternoon wore on, the director became increasingly displeased with the lack of progress, since so much valuable shooting time was lost each time the flames and smoke had to be reset after a misfire. Technical problems, a lethargic cast and crew, and executing a dangerous precision stunt the Friday before Christmas did not make a good recipe for success.

Because of the elevator's prominent location between the farmhouse and the pond, almost everyone saw Margaret's descent. The smoke plumed, then the flames—and for a moment, everything seemed to have gone as planned. Then a shock wave of shouting voices began to ripple across the set. In the tumult a darting figure caught my eye, running toward the elevator. It was a prop man who had been stationed off camera, holding a soaking-wet blanket

as a safety precaution. Seeing this, I knew something had gone horribly wrong.

A large crowd surrounded the elevator opening, so it was impossible—especially at my height—to see exactly what was going on. Eventually the throng dispersed: At the end of the day everyone went home for Christmas break, unsure of exactly what had happened on that final take.

We found out later that the flames had come too quickly in succession after the smoke and the elevator had not fully lowered Margaret beneath the set. The flames immediately set her broom on fire, and that fire jumped to her green makeup—which was copper based and very flammable. Luckily, her intrepid makeup man, Jack Young, saw what had happened and jumped down into the elevator—which must have been crowded by then, what with the prop man and his wet blanket. Margaret's face and right hand were badly burned, and she did not return to the set until February.

Many Munchkins remained unclear about the details of Margaret's accident, because most of us only had three more working days left on the film after Christmas break. Only years later was I able to learn exactly what had happened to Margaret and to piece together the correct sequence of events. Still, I had always felt that it must have been a sad Christmastime for her and her young son, Hamilton. At least she seemed much happier recalling the events when I next saw her again, some forty years later!

There have been numerous versions of this story, varying as to how severely Margaret was burned and who helped her. Many of these are so outlandish that it's hard to imagine anyone ever believed them. My favorite is that a fellow Munchkin used his hat to scoop up some pond water to douse the flames. My only certainties are that Margaret did not return to the set while any of the Munchkins were there and that the first near-perfect take is the one you see in the film.

Everyone was very concerned about Margaret's condition, but most of us (the Munchkins at least) did not realize the extent of her injuries, so we kept to our rigorous schedule and continued shooting that afternoon. It is important to note that *The Wizard of Oz* was not filmed sequentially, but I can best remember the details by describing the scenes as if they *had* been.

After the Wicked Witch disappears, the Good Witch notes the smell of sulfur. As we stand around Dorothy and Glinda, you can see me on the right side of the screen. The height of my Coroner's hat is always a "dead" giveaway when trying to locate my character. After Glinda kisses Dorothy's forehead (an allusion to the magical protective kiss in L. Frank Baum's book), she traces graceful swirls in the air with her star-laden scepter. (The next time you watch the film, listen for the clinking sound of Billie's wand hitting her crown. The prop men made sure that duplicate scepters were available, since time could not be wasted in waiting for any prop replacements.)

Just before Glinda leaves Munchkinland in her bubble, she eases Dorothy's trepidation by directing her to follow the yellow brick road. Floating away in her special-effects pink sphere, Glinda first hovers over the red brick road, then zooms off to disappear in the background.

Billie Burke did not have to suffer for *her* special-effects exit. Once the bubble starts to float, the Good Witch is no longer visible within. The double exposure for this scene was done later, in post-production, in 1939, but the Munchkins' double takes were filmed on December 29 and 30. Most of the Munchkins—including me—had completed our last day's filming on the set on the 28th, but about twenty little people were retained for such touch-up and background shots.

Of course, Dorothy finally does begin to follow her designated path, and several Munchkins keep her on track. The Mayor is the first to direct her to "Follow the yellow brick road," while adjusting the stuffing around his waist. The City Father played by Matthew Raia is the second to echo the phrase—in a very deep Billy Bletcher baritone voice. Nita Krebs delivers her final line when she repeats Glinda's directions in a high-octave "chipmunk-dubbed" voice. The Barrister is the last to bellow out "Follow the yellow brick road," before the entire gaggle of Munchkins breaks into "We're Off to See the Wizard." We modify the lyrics slightly—"*You're* off to see the Wizard"—since we, regrettably, will not be following Dorothy on her journey.

Just before Dorothy passes through the Munchkinland gate, the five Fiddlers join her near the farmhouse whence she came. Looking to the right of the movie screen, near Toto, you can see the Wicked Witch's trapdoor in the ground. City Father Billy Curtis and a Soldier stand on the edge of the cover. This is the best point in the film to view the line of perforations that cuts through the simulated slate to release the flames and smoke, just in front of the trapdoor. (Look for the small, light gray square in front of Billy that is suspiciously segmented.)

I dutifully doff my Coroner's cap as Dorothy passes the line of City Fathers, and we all resume our little Munchkin jingle and jig. Lollipop Guild member Harry Doll gives Dorothy a final salute, Munchkin Villager Margaret Pellegrini dances her way past the Munchkin wall—still wearing her blue flowerpot hat—and our Munchkin Sergeant-at-Arms, Prince Dennis, salutes by swinging his sword from his watch station in the guard tower.

When the shot switches to Dorothy heading down the yellow brick road, we all wave a final farewell. This background is really just a matte painting (called a Newcombe shot after its inventor) that was inserted in post-production. All we saw was a prop man, up in the catwalk at the end of the soundstage, waving a white handkerchief. That was our cue to wave a gleeful goodbye to our homesick, but hearty, heroine.

The lavish backgrounds needed for *The Wizard of Oz* proved too expensive to be built as normal sets or miniatures. Fortunately, a recent innovation in filmmaking was the Newcombe shot, pioneered by special-effects newcomer Warren Newcombe.

Newcombe shots involved creating matte paintings (a very wide painting of the desired background scenery), filming them, and later superimposing live-action footage. The results looked very convincing, as if, for example, Dorothy and Toto really were dancing down an endless yellow brick road stretching far into the distance. "The beauty of a matte shot is that you can become God," Alfred Hitchcock once said.

The matte paintings used for Newcombe shots had a dark, unfinished area in the lower part of the painting. That was where the characters would appear. If the matte painting was intended to be used simply to establish the look of the background—for example, if it just needed to be there while Dorothy talked to Glinda, so the moviegoer could see the road stretching away in the background—it would be labeled an "all over painting." For all over paintings, the artists filled in the whole scene, without leaving any unfinished parts, since there was no need to insert footage of the actors.

MGM's matte paintings were done in a twenty-two-by-twenty-eight-inch size (coincidentally, the standard size of a theatrical half-sheet movie poster) on quarter-inch-thick particleboard with a black veneer very similar to the finish on a blackboard. The "paintings" themselves were actually drawings created with pastel chalks and pencils—all of which made for breathtaking backgrounds, colorful, and convincingly three-dimensional.

This matte painting of the yellow brick road leading into the distance was prepared for a Newcombe shot—that is, the footage showing the actors and the foreground scenery would be married with this painting to create a convincing whole.

The finished shot combines the matte painting with live action. The little Munchkin guard tower at the left was an actual piece of scenery, and its unusual roof helped the special-effects department match up the two shots seamlessly.

▲ *Standing in the field of poppies, Dorothy and her three friends see the Emerald City for the first time in this all over painting. The columns of the Emerald City were pierced with small holes, and light shining through them produced the sparkle that makes the city look jewel-like and "emerald" rather than merely green.*

◄ *Matte paintings were remarkably small, considering the vistas they represented. Daniel Kinske holds the twenty-two-by-twenty-eight-inch matte painting of the Emerald City at the Cinema and Television Library at the University of Southern California.*

Nearly all of the matte paintings from *The Wizard of Oz* were thrown in the trash by workers clearing out an old MGM storage building in the 1970s. But fate took a hand. The drawings caught the eye of a scrupulous scavenger, who ended up donating them to the Cinema and Television Library at the nearby University of Southern California. Now the unwanted drawings are among the treasures of the library's collection.

Carefully housed in a darkened room, the drawings look fresh and bright, almost as if they were painted very recently. Though they seem quaint, they were the latest in cutting-edge special-effects technology in the 1930s. Their rich, illustrated quality adds to the story-book feel of *The Wizard of Oz*.

◀ *The Gatekeeper, played by Frank Morgan in one of his multiple roles, guarded the Emerald City of this matte painting.*

The castle of the Wicked Witch of the West, shrouded in mist, is truly menacing in this matte painting. Note the river at bottom left.

◀ *The black area at the top of this Newcombe-shot painting shows where the live-action footage would be blended in to create the finished scene at the Witch's castle.*

CHAPTER SEVEN

More Stars Than
There Are in Heaven

DREAMS DID NOT JUST COME TRUE IN Hollywood—they were *made* there. Being away from my home and family was of little importance at that time compared with the idea of being part of a motion picture—especially one in which "the dreams that you dare to dream really do come true." Although seeing so many of my fellow little people again was great, the real treat for me was working with the film's leading stars—and finding that, in fact, "more stars than there are in heaven" *were* walking around on Earth at the MGM lots.

I was able to see Ray Bolger, Jack Haley, Bert Lahr, and Frank Morgan during my time at the studio . . . but not as much as I wanted to. I did obtain their autographs and thought they were very polite and respectful to all of the little people who worked on the film. In real life, these great actors did have brains, hearts, and courage. Throughout the years they had only kind words to say about Judy Garland and the little people—even when rumors and innuendos might have tempted otherwise.

Ray Bolger was the most affable of the four, and though he played a brainless scarecrow, he was very witty and intelligent. His gift of a rare, deluxe-bound edition of Edgar Allen Poe's *The Raven* to Judy Garland was very clever . . . especially since the trained crow in our film actually was a raven (not a crow, as one might assume) named Jimmy. The raven was used in the first scene after Munchkinland, when Dorothy stumbles across the Scarecrow, and also in numerous promotional shots—such as one in which he "feeds" straw to Ray while perched on his shoulder! Jimmy the raven also appeared in Frank Capra's *It's a Wonderful Life*, in 1946, but was nevermore so perfectly paired with an actor as he was when "cawed upon" to work with the Scarecrow.

Bert Lahr was somewhat more reserved and quiet, but was still kind and polite to everyone. He frequently visited the Munchkinland set and talked to Victor Fleming while watching a few scenes being shot. Some actors want more direction than others, and being the nervous type, Bert might have been getting additional clarification on his upcoming scenes. The job of director seemed almost godlike back then, which I respected. (Although as the Coroner, the closest thing I could have been to a director was a funeral director.)

Jack Haley, on loan from Twentieth Century Fox Studios to replace Buddy Ebsen as the Tin Woodman, was also very kind to all of the little people while working on the film. Jack performed with Shirley Temple in a few of her films while they were both at Fox. As I've mentioned, Jack brought his young son, Jack Haley Jr., to the set to show him around,

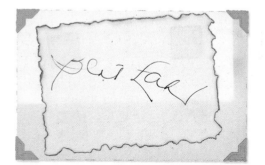

Bert Lahr and Jack Haley kindly gave me their autographs.

▶ *The big MGM star Norma Shearer signs an autograph to Harry Doll as his two sisters, Tiny and Daisy Doll, look on. Victor Fleming is on the right side, and Munchkin Villager Olga Nardone, with her hand wrapped around the director's finger, is nearby.*

▼ *Leo Singer's Midget Troupe visits Charlie Chaplin on the set of* Shoulder Arms *in 1918. Future Munchkin Mayor Charles Becker is near Chaplin's right arm; both Charlies have mustaches.*

and a few publicity photos were taken of them together. Many of *The Wizard of Oz* cast and crew brought in their children to view the Munchkinland set, as did many other MGM stars.

Jack Haley Jr. later became a successful television director and producer, and wrote the introduction to my favorite book about *The Wizard of Oz* film, *The Wizard of Oz: The Official Anniversary Pictorial History*, by John Fricke, William Stillman, and Jay Scarfone. Jack Jr. also directed *The Wonderful Wizard of Oz: The Making of a Movie Classic* television special, in 1989, narrated by the lovely and angelic Angela Lansbury.

This son of the Tin Woodman was actually married to a daughter of Dorothy Gale for a few years—Liza Minnelli. Although the elder Jack was present at the ceremony, Judy had died five years previously. Tragically, Jack Haley Jr. passed away too soon, on April 21, 2001. I fondly remember seeing him at many *Wizard of Oz* conventions during the 1980s, and find it rather bleak that he, too, is now somewhere over the rainbow.

Even given the grandeur that was typical of MGM, the Munchkinland set and the little people were a magnificent sight to see. We indirectly owe our participation in the film to former child star Jackie Coogan, and somewhat more indirectly to Charlie Chaplin. In 1921 Chaplin had personally picked Jackie to star in an eight-reeler aptly titled *The Kid* after seeing him in another film, *A Day's Pleasure*, in 1919. Jackie had become Hollywood's first child star and self-made millionaire. Unfortunately, his parents took advantage of him, and the Child Actors' Bill, quickly nicknamed the "Coogan Law," was passed to protect the children of California. It limited the amount of work they could do each day, and protected their earnings from being squandered by their parents. This bill was not officially passed until 1939, but the public uproar over Jackie's taking his parents to court in 1935 began a ripple effect that caused many changes in the film industry almost immediately.

Before finding Jackie, Charlie had been visited by another group of little people—a group that the Coogan Law would never have applied to. That was Leo Singer's Midget Troupe, which, in 1918, tramped through the World War I set of the Little Tramp's *Shoulder Arms* between takes. One of those midgets was Charlie Becker, who was not shy about talking to the other Charlie. He would later recall, "Chaplin was great fun to meet and surprised me by being so well spoken and refined—he also seemed to like the fact that I was the only midget that had a mustache like him."

Charlie Becker could not have foreseen that soon midgets would be doing much more than merely touring movie

A rare autographed picture of Charles Becker—forever immortalized as the Mayor of Munchkinland.

sets—they would become actors themselves (like Harry Doll in *The Unholy 3*). Using child actors had become expensive due to the schooling, breaks, and recess now required thanks to the Coogan-inspired legislation. The MGM executives used an innovative solution to this problem by hiring small-stature adults to play the Munchkins.

The irony is that even after children's pay and benefits began to be protected, the little peoples' salaries were left exposed—a weakness that was soon exploited by midget troupe impresario Singer. The master contract for the acquisition and employment of the 124 midgets deemed Singer not only the sole supplier, but the *employer*, of all the little people who would work on the film. He was paid two hundred dollars a week for the month of October for the acquisition stage of hiring the midget actors, and one hundred dollars a week to oversee them once filming commenced.

Maybe it was this cut in *his* pay that caused Singer to take a substantial chunk of ours. We were each supposed to get one hundred dollars a week for our roles as Munchkins—but

The October 1, 1938, stock contract between Leo Singer and the little people was revised and signed on November 21, 1938, by twenty-four of the film's 124 total Munchkins.

most of us received just half of that. Some got more than fifty dollars, some less, but the average was fifty bucks a week. I found out long after that even the master contract stipulated our pay would be sixty-six dollars minimum—but none of the little people was privy to that contract. What we did see was the contract's appendix, labeled "Exhibit A" and created for Singer by the parent company of MGM, Loews Inc., when we signed our allegiance on copies.

But at the end of the Depression, the money we made was still very good, and we little people are forever grateful to that cute little Coogan "kid" and his lovable, laudable tramp.

There were plenty of children in Munchkinland—but they were mainly visitors, brought by their famous parents. Our unique presence drew many of the MGM stars and starlets. From Clark Gable to Greta Garbo, they came to peek at Munchkinland and its inhabitants. Those with families usually brought their children, who toured (and sometimes played in) Munchkinland. We gave the kiddies our autographs, and in return, we asked the famous parents for theirs. Often we were told, "Gee, I'm sorry, I don't have any pictures with me, but my dressing room is over on [such-

and-such] lot. Come on over and I will give you an autographed picture."

I had missed opportunities to collect autographs in the past—such as Edward G. Robinson's when he visited the Chicago World's Fair—but at MGM I took many stars up on their offer. Visiting their dressing rooms, I obtained celebrity signatures from Spencer Tracy, Fanny Brice, Jeanette MacDonald, Nelson Eddy, Edward Arnold, Norma Shearer, William Powell, Victor McLaglen, Walter Pidgeon, Florence Rice, James Stewart, Joan Crawford, Johnny Weissmuller, Wallace Beery, Hedy Lamarr, and the "Roberts," Montgomery, Young, Taylor, and Benchley.

Some stars, such as Mickey Rooney and Myrna Loy, visited the set quite frequently. Mickey might have been only eighteen, but he edged out Fox's Shirley Temple in 1938 as the number-one box-office draw in the entire country! He was very amiable and stopped by every day at lunch to see Judy Garland, whom he was sweet on at the time. Mickey is just as rowdy, raucous, eccentric, talented, funny, and wonderful today as he was then—the only difference is that he has a little less hair now.

Spencer Tracy was a big, and very nice,
guy who liked the little people immensely.
He wrote, "To Meinhardt with very best
wishes. Spencer Tracy Dec. 1938." Robert
Montgomery, Edward Arnold, Nelson
Eddy, and Jeanette MacDonald all gave me
signed photographs.

▲ *Judy Garland and Mickey Rooney came up through the MGM ranks together and were America's Sweethearts in the 1930s.*

▶ *Mickey Rooney visited Ray Bolger on the set of* The Wizard of Oz—*in between shooting one of three Andy Hardy pictures he made in 1939.*

I was most impressed with Hedy Lamarr, originally from Austria, who in the late '30s had literally escaped from her former husband (a munitions dealer and Nazi sympathizer) and the increasingly horrible conditions in Europe. She was extremely intelligent, and for a few minutes on one of her visits I enjoyed talking to her in German—a language that was not exactly looked upon favorably in those pre-WWII days.

The stars I saw most often were, of course, those in the Munchkinland sequences: Billie Burke, Margaret Hamilton, and Judy Garland. I remember Miss Burke coming to the set in full makeup and looking very dignified. She didn't mingle with the little people like the rest of the cast, but she would occasionally pull a chair outside her dressing room and chat with whomever stopped by to see her. I was able to say hello on a few occasions, but our rare leisure time never permitted a longer conversation. Unlike Judy Garland, who was sixteen, and Margaret Hamilton, who was thirty-six, Billie was in her early fifties, so it is understandable that she was slightly more aloof with her much younger—and, in our case, smaller—costars.

My friend Karl Slover, the first Munchkin Trumpeter, often relays a story about the first day he saw Billie walk on the set. (Karl's charm and omnipresent grin were endearing; most people who met him instantly adored him, and this is still true today.) "She had on a black dress, a black hat, and black gloves—all black," Karl recalls. "She looked like she must've been a hundred years old or something. She also had a black cane and—with her body hunched over—walked over to Victor Fleming, who responded, seemingly vehement, 'What's the matter, coming in here like that, all hunched over? Stand up straight.'

"At which Billie Burke stood fully upright and proceeded to take off her hat, throw down her gloves and cane, and answer, 'If I am going to work with these wonderful little people, then they should know what I really look like in real life—so what do you think about that!'

"'Well, that is something,' muttered an incredulous Fleming."

Karl was amazed at the transition from the lady in black to the Good Witch in pink: "When I saw her [Miss Burke] during the shooting, I thought to myself she looked about thirty years old—she was *beautiful*. What they can do with makeup and such."

Billie's father was an internationally renowned circus clown named Billy Burke, and that was the name she adopted when first starting out in show business as a young adult—her birth name was Mary William Ethelbert Appleton Burke. As a child she toured with him throughout Europe and America. It is fitting that someone exposed to show business so early in life would end up marrying *the* great showman, Florenz Ziegfeld. After his dazzling career, though, he lost their fortune in the stock market crash of 1929, and Miss Burke supported him until his death in 1932.

She had stopped acting after her marriage, but the financial difficulties caused her to return to films in 1936, after a twenty-year hiatus from stage and screen roles. Her first project was, of all things, *The Great Ziegfeld*. Miss Burke worked behind the scenes, having the surreal experience of coaching Myrna Loy, who played . . . Billie Burke. William Powell portrayed Ziegfeld, Ray Bolger and Frank Morgan were in the cast, and the film won the Oscar for Best Picture that year.

Margaret Hamilton was, ironically, the sweetest of all the adult players. She talked to all of us quite frequently and was very friendly. Though the filming of *The Wizard of Oz* was very difficult for everyone, it was, of course, especially traumatic for Margaret—but she was a real trouper.

▲ *Billie Burke inscribed this photo to my fellow Munchkin and friend Harry Doll. It says, "To Harry, with all fond wishes. Billie Burke 1938."*

◄ *Margaret Hamilton gave me a signed photograph of herself for Christmas 1938. It says, "Best wishes to Meinhardt—from Margaret Hamilton (W.W.W.)." I bet you can guess what the W.W.W. stands for!*

Around Christmas in 1938 she gave each of the little people an inscribed and autographed picture of herself. I still have mine today. She would write "W.W.W." next to her name to denote her Wicked Witch of the West character. (Now it would probably be misconstrued as the World Wide Web.)

To misquote the great Cary Grant: "Judy, Judy, Judy!" Of all the stars I met and worked with on *The Wizard of Oz*, Judy Garland was the nicest and most charismatic. Though only sixteen, she had already been a performer for more than a decade. Yet she treated all of the little people as though they were professionals in the same category as herself.

It would be a mistake to say that Judy Garland merely starred in *The Wizard of Oz*—she **made** *The Wizard of Oz*! Every member of the cast and crew knew that she was perfect for the part, and she gave the performance of a lifetime.

Some memories fade or become clouded as time passes, but I will never forget my time spent working with Judy, nor how sincerely wonderful she was to all of us. Whenever there was a break in the action during the filming, she sat down on the steps and chatted amiably. Judy was full of spunk and pep, and just being around her cheered me up— even if I was feeling fine already. She had one of those rare personalities that could brighten up a room—or a 31,888-square-foot soundstage—simply by being in it.

It was fitting that MGM chose to make one of Judy's dreams comes true on the childlike and magical Munchkin-land set. Here they announced that she had moved up from "featured" to "star" player. In late November 1938, all of the Munchkins and other cast members gathered on our set, where a brand-new star trailer on wheels was topped off with a large red ribbon and bow. We waited for her to come in,

Munchkins love Dorothy! Here, Townsman Frank Cucksey, smoking Fiddler, and Soldier Charles Royale watch Judy Garland reading the latest issue of Life *magazine, from December 26, 1938..*

then yelled, "Merry Christmas, Judy!" It was a little early for such Yuletide yodeling, but she was teary-eyed just the same.

She knew what a big deal her new stardom was, and it made her so happy that I personally think it made the *Oz* film all the more special for her. This put her in the same category as such MGM stars as Clark Gable, Joan Crawford, Myrna Loy, Greta Garbo, Spencer Tracy, William Powell, and the Marx Brothers. I felt fortunate just being able to witness this transformation firsthand—especially since it affected someone who is still so beloved today.

I don't remember all of the times I spoke with Judy, but I do remember her giving me an autographed photograph of herself, for Christmas. That's when she told me about having been at the Chicago World's Fair, too, after I mentioned what had led me to MGM. It was not exactly the headiest banter of the century, but I was really thrilled and ecstatic to be conversing with such a movie star—and I quite literally looked up to her. Judy took the time to thoughtfully autograph and personalize a photograph for each of the 124 Munchkins. Her photo is still very dear to me, and I have never forgotten her lovely inscription: "For Meinhardt, a perfect Coroner, *and* person, too, love from Judy."

I always remember the Judy Garland in that picture: the caring brown eyes; dark, curly, cascading hair; soft dimpled and rosy cheeks; a never-ending smile; and enough love for the whole world. Tragically, life ended too soon, on the saddest day of June—June 22, 1969. I don't know what caused her life to burn out so quickly, or why she seemed to become such a tragic figure throughout the years, but I choose to remember her as only the cast and crew of *The Wizard of Oz* did: a cute, funny, giggly, and amazingly talented little girl from Minnesota—with a heart big enough for the whole world, and *Oz*.

CHAPTER EIGHT

Wake Up, You Sleepy Head

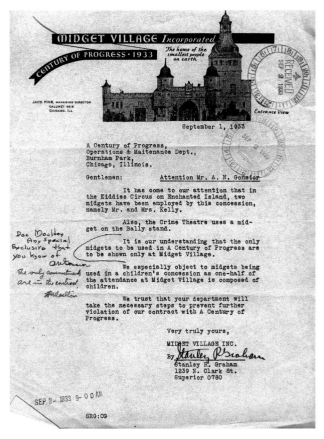

F COURSE, DOROTHY WAS NOT THE only one who was homesick in the Land of Oz. Multiple delays occurred during the inception and filming of *The Wizard of Oz*, and what with the five directors, fourteen writers, multiple cast changes, technical and logistical delays, and our under-age star's limited working hours, there was little time to waste on the set. The filming of the Munchkinland sequence spanned the Thanksgiving and Christmas holidays. We were only given a three-day respite for both holidays combined, but it was enough of a break to tide us over.

For Thanksgiving, I asked fellow Munchkin Margaret Pellegrini (née Margaret Williams) if she would like to see a movie with me that evening. Luckily, she said yes. Margaret was (and still is) a beautiful small-town girl who has always been fast to laugh and smile. She originally hailed from Alabama, and this was her first foray into any type of show business. I was quite a bit older than she, but was very happy to enjoy the pleasure of her company. (Little people do not get the chance to see other little people very often, so I would have been remiss to not call on at least *one* little miss during my time in California.)

I met Margaret at the Culver Hotel, where she was rooming with another female Munchkin, Jessie Kelley, who was in her thirties at the time. Jessie had been placed there to help take care of Margaret, who was only fifteen. Unfortunately for both of them, Jessie was going through a terrible divorce from her estranged little-person husband, Charley Kelley. He was quite abusive to her throughout the film—so much so that Margaret and Jessie were later moved to another hotel and their exact whereabouts were kept secret to protect them from him.

That Charley was causing problems was no surprise to me, but that Jessie and Charley had not divorced long ago was. I had seen them several times when they were working as the main grocers in the Midget Village grocery at the

Chicago World's Fair, in 1933 and 1934. Even then, the Village managers floated around interoffice memos singling out the Kelleys' bad behavior. "These two midgets have always been more or less troublemakers. . . ." notes one, dated September 19, 1933. It was written by Midget Village manager Stanley Graham, who, like all of the managers, was average sized. He referred to the couple, but Charley, of course, was the true culprit. Jessie was merely guilty by association.

As this letter reveals, the manager of Midget Village was already concerned about the Kelleys' behavior in 1933.

Little people did not get the chance to socialize with other little people often in those days, so I enjoyed my time in Oz! Here I am outside Soundstage 27 with Prince Denis (Sergeant-at-Arms), Matthew Raia (a City Father), and Robert Kanter (Soldier) on Seventh Avenue, inside MGM's Lot 1.

Jessie was such a gentle and kind little lady; in fact, the couple remained in charge of the Midget Village grocery only due to her extra-hard work and charismatic personality. All of the fairground concessions were inspected, and once the Kelleys received the highest grade on their monthly inspection of any establishment on the entire fairground.

Charley Kelley caused innumerable problems during his employment at MGM. These ranged from dragging his wife by the hair through the lobby of the Culver Hotel, to bringing a pair of guns (complete with matching holsters) inside the studio on the second day of . . . well, shooting. He looked like a cross between a cowboy and a bellboy. I never heard what became of him after *Oz* ended. The good news is that Jessie found a better "Charlie" while working on the film: She and Munchkin Mayor Charles Becker got engaged, and were married in 1940. They remained husband and wife until his death, just after Christmas in 1968.

Previous to our date, Margaret Pellegrini had spent the earlier part of Thanksgiving sightseeing around the Los Angeles area with Henry and Dolly Kramer. Henry was a man of average stature who managed a midget troupe bearing his surname. His leading lady, Dolly, headlined this Kramer Midget Troupe. Dolly was a gorgeous, gregarious, and garrulous little person. She was quite the singer in her day and was well known for her resemblance to Kate Smith, in both looks and the enormous range of her rafter-rattling voice.

The Kramer traveling troupe had found Margaret in 1937, while she was visiting the Tennessee State Fair. At the tender age of thirteen, she had not been ready for show business; still, she scribbled down her address for them, wistfully figuring that would be "all she wrote." She had no way then of knowing that our future boss, Leo Singer,

would fall "short" in his quest for little people and would desperately seek to subcontract other companies—such as Henry Kramer's. Margaret's soon-to-be roommate, Jessie, had been in show business as part of this same Kramer troupe before the *Oz* film. Margaret began traveling with the Kramers after the filming, then stopped in the early 1940s to settle down and raise a family.

I entered the Culver Hotel on Thanksgiving evening for my date with Margaret, but I was a little nervous. I loitered in the expansive first-floor lobby—which was two floors high—before finally heading up to the third floor. Bearing a box of Whitman's chocolates, I met this sweet little southern belle at her door. I took her to a restaurant that I had previously scoped out because it served southern food and was within walking distance of the hotel.

We enjoyed dining on a large buffet-style spread and had fun getting to know each other better. She chatted about growing up in a small town in Alabama—where her nickname was Lil'bama—and about how exciting it was to be working in the movies. After we finished our apple pie *à la mode* (my absolutely favorite dessert—with chocolate ice cream) at the restaurant, we walked to a nearby movie theater and saw *Man-Proof*, starring Myrna Loy and Walter Pidgeon. Geographically the theater was very close to MGM, and I'm sure it was part of the Loew's distributor chain that owned MGM, due to the preponderance of MGM films that were shown there.

I didn't care too much for the film, since my companion was so wonderful—but I would meet both of the leads on the studio lot in the following month. Margaret and I had a good time that evening, and it made me less distraught about being away from my family during the Thanksgiving holidays.

Charley Kelley continued to cause the lion's share of trouble for MGM, and his melees greatly contributed to the Munchkin stories of misbehavior that were embellished over time. The last big problem he caused for Jessie—and for Margaret, who was in the right place at the wrong time—was knocking on their door at the Culver Hotel, swaggering in, waving a dagger, and nearly scaring Lil'bama to death.

Jessie quickly diffused the situation that evening, and the following Monday Singer severely reprimanded Charley for his actions. Though Charley was not fired from the film, Singer was at the end of his rope in dealing with this troublemaker, and sternly let him know that he *would* be fired if any further problems occurred. It was at this point that Margaret and Jessie were secretly moved to the Vine Manor Hotel, on Hollywood and Vine (now also known as Bob Hope Square), as a precaution against further similar incidents.

Over the years many tall tales regarding Munchkin mischief have grown to epic proportions in the realm of Hollywood folklore. The escapades of Charley Kelley were real—but he was one of only three or four true troublemakers. Out of 124, that does not constitute a majority.

The Matina twins, Mike and Ike, were more rambunctious and rowdy than average, but they were still professional on the set. They, like Charley, had worked at the Chicago World's Fair. Having known them in the past, I was not surprised to hear that on occasion they became intoxicated and quarreled at the Culver Hotel. In Chicago they had been paid to fight each other in the boxing ring. They were still going at it round after round in Culver City—but these "rounds" were liquid in nature. Getting plastered exaggerated their punk-drunk personalities.

This is not to say I did not like Mike and Ike, because I did. It was just that I did not hang out with them all that much; with those sorts of fellows you had to be a drinker or you would soon find yourself left behind.

However, I did know their older brother, Leo, who played a Munchkin Villager, pretty well. A full decade older than his younger brothers, he was very mild mannered and easygoing—the polar opposite of the turbo-charged twins. Leo said those two had been quarreling nearly from the cradle and would continue to do so until the grave. "They always make up," he added, "and usually in the same fashion that the fighting begins: by drinking together."

Considering how hard we worked on the film, you could not blame these two for wanting to blow off a little steam during their free time. I know for a fact that many average-sized studio employees and actors did the very same thing—except they were not being watched under a microscope like the Munchkins.

Most of the people who worked on *The Wizard of Oz* have generally agreed that they had no clue how popular the movie would become over time. The same is true for the Munchkins, regarding the rumors surrounding our employment at MGM. We had no idea that the antics of a few individuals would start rumors that over the years would grow to overshadow our hard work. The simple fact is that if any of these outlandish occurrences had actually happened, the papers of the time would have had a field day with all of the publicity.

Nevertheless, I have been asked, interviewed, and quoted (and sometimes misquoted) innumerable times about the rumors regarding the Munchkins. Now, sixty-five years after the filming, I can *finally* give you the official Coroner's report.

Any rumor can only grow if it is told over and over again. In 1938 there were no real issues to speak of, and it would be years later before I even heard of any disparaging stories about the little people. Studio publicity was known to exaggerate back then—but more in the line of claiming that the hollyhocks in Munchkinland were thirty feet high instead of twenty, or that sixty-five shades of paint were used to decorate the set instead of twenty.

Personally, I never saw any difficulties arise on the set between Victor Fleming and any of the Munchkins. I can't imagine one of us having time to get in trouble, given our hectic schedule: working six days a week, from six in the morning to six at night.

Because of the sheer number of people on the Munchkinland set, I certainly can't speak for everyone—but if someone

Mervyn LeRoy, center, watches the dual-screened "dailies."

Hard at work! Producer Mervyn LeRoy, Judy Garland, and director Victor Fleming (holding Toto) watch Olga Nardone, Tiny Doll, Jerry Maren, and Mickey Carroll (Fiddler) while Prince Denis oversees everything from atop the guard tower.

was drunk or tipsy on the job, I sure do not remember it. What anyone—little or big—did off the set was his or her business.

You have to remember that *The Wizard of Oz* was filmed fewer than twenty years after women gained the right to vote in this country. At that time the civil rights movement was not even a blip on the radar—so you can imagine how midgets ranked in precedence in the late 1930s. The general opinion regarding the capabilities of little people was "small bodies, small minds." We never had a "Munchkin Movement" per se, but little people as a whole kept taking small steps toward independence. So though the rumors back then painted pictures of us running rampant and sliding down banisters, I have lived long enough to see little people become teachers, doctors, and lawyers.

It was a well-known fact that each morning MGM screen veteran—and wonderful Wizard—Frank Morgan carried to the set a black bag containing little bottles of champagne and similar libations. But since he always delivered the goods in his performance, his eccentricity was never questioned. I certainly do not blame Frank for occasionally adding a little flavor to his tank, in part because he never judged anyone else.

None of the actors on the film had anything bad to say about the Munchkins at the time, although they had plenty of opportunity to relay such information. Years later Judy Garland regaled Jack Paar with some obviously fictitious stories about the Munchkins. Her humorous tales did not surprise me—but the fact that the public actually believed the blather did.

It was a little disappointing to hear Judy's comments about working with the little people on *The Wizard of Oz*, when she appeared on Paar's show in the early '60s. But she was not the same giddy young girl that we as Munchkins had known, and by the time I was made aware of her remarks she had already died. Her death affected me far worse than any of her apocryphal anecdotes.

Judy told Paar that the Munchkins were "little drunks" and that after we got smashed each night in Culver City, we were picked up in butterfly nets. But Judy also said the Munchkins were two inches high and there were thousands of us. These gross exaggerations might have hinted to Paar's audience that her reminiscing was in jest, yet many people focused on the partly plausible idea that we were all really just diminutive drunkards.

Judy's joking comments never really bothered me, but stories with no foundation in truth, published in books on the movie—they bothered me. One of the first books mentioning details about *The Wizard of Oz* was written by John Lahr, Bert's son. Called *Notes on a Cowardly Lion: The Biography of Bert Lahr*, it was released in 1969, just two years after Bert's death. The book is the first to mention the fictitious Major Doyle's Revenge story, in a quote by William Grady, who is erroneously labeled the film's casting director. Grady also maintains that he—not Leo Singer—brought all of the midgets to Culver City. That claim is easily disproved by the plethora of MGM paperwork charging Singer with overall responsibility—not to mention the little people being billed as "The Singer Midgets" in the film and its promotional materials.

According to John Lahr, "Major Doyle's Revenge, as it became known in movie circles, was not the last the movie executives heard from the midgets. Once they got to Culver City, there was a problem controlling them. The polyglot group of little people came from a wide range of professions. Many of the Munchkins were midgets who, in fact, made their living by panhandling, pimping, and whoring. Assistants were ordered to watch the crew of midgets, who brandished knives and often conceived passions for other, larger, Metro personnel."

This statement by the author is sandwiched between two *true* (and rather humorous) anecdotes regarding the Munchkins, which might make Major Doyle's Revenge seem more credible to an unsuspecting reader.

Just six years later a book called *The World of Entertainment: Hollywood's Greatest Musicals*, written by Hugh Fordin, was released. One of the musicals covered was, of course, *The Wizard of Oz*. The fantastically false figure of 350 Munchkins, which had appeared in the Lahr book, was quoted again—and with worse narrative: "These 350 midgets—where did they come from? Partly from Leo Singer, partly from Major Doyle. Wherever, they were the most deformed unpleasant bunch of 'adults' imaginable. Culver City and the Metro lot were crawling with them. They propositioned everybody; in the commissary, filled to capacity during lunchtime, they were constantly underfoot. This unholy assemblage of pimps, hookers and gamblers infested the Metro lot and all of the community."

I guess the panhandling midgets had changed vocations—or taken vacations—by the time this book came out, in 1975. Maybe if I had written this book thirty years ago, I would have had to change the title to *Pimping, Whoring, and Gambling: The Munchkins' Guide to the Making of* The Wizard of Oz—since back then gossip about Munchkins was taken as gospel.

It took three decades after the movie's initial release for the first books about it to be published, and less than a decade after that for most of the Munchkin rumors to trickle out. Judy's fabricated stories and the books that misrepresented the Munchkins really laid the foundation for the myths. So deeply rooted are these tales that a film came out in 1981 called *Under the Rainbow*, based on the purported shenanigans of the Munchkins.

Though the movie is bad, at best (noted film critic Leonard Maltin called it the "Wicked Witch's revenge"), I thought it was so outrageous that it actually seems kind of funny—but I benefit from the joy of seeing such friends in it as Billy Barty and original Munchkins Jerry Maren and Ruth Duccini.

The film starred Chevy Chase as Bruce Thorpe, a government Secret Service agent assigned to protect the Duke and Duchess of Luchow (played by Joseph Maher and Eve Arden) from a Sicilian assassin. The would-be assassin's father had failed to kill the duke's father, and the son is trying to rectify the mistake.

Carrie Fisher plays Annie Clark, an attractive special-talent coordinator assigned to take care of the little people prior to filming *The Wizard of Oz*. In the subplot a tiny Nazi spy (played by Billy Barty) is to turn over a map of America's coastal defenses to a Japanese spy (played by Mako). After this map accidentally ends up in Carrie Fisher's *The Wizard of Oz* script, the two spies spend the rest of the movie in its pursuit. Meanwhile the assassin is after the duke, and the drunken, elfin extras wreak havoc on the hotel.

Under the Rainbow was based largely on negative stories about the Munchkins, but it was farcical in nature, and I enjoyed it, knowing not to take it too seriously. The actor playing the Coroner is at right.

More than a hundred little people were gathered for *Under the Rainbow*; fewer than fifteen were actually midgets, and the rest were dwarfs. Billy Barty greatly assisted the filmmakers in finding many small actors through his Little People of America organization.

Surprisingly, the involvement of Jerry Maren and Ruth Duccini was not played up or publicized, except for a brief notation in the movie's press kit. Jerry can be seen throughout the film cracking jokes and smoking a cigar. He and Eve Arden had been paired together more than forty years previously in the Marx Brothers film *At the Circus*, produced by Mervyn LeRoy and written by Irving Brecher—the first writer assigned to *The Wizard of Oz* script.

It is nice to see my friends—most of them long gone—even in such a silly movie. In fact, it was flattering in *Under the Rainbow* to see an actor playing the Munchkin Coroner, running around throughout the movie in his costume. *Under the Rainbow* was too steeped in slapstick to be taken literally, but for some reason many people chose to believe it was an accurate portrayal. Not for another eight years would there be any substantial effort to disprove the Munchkin myths.

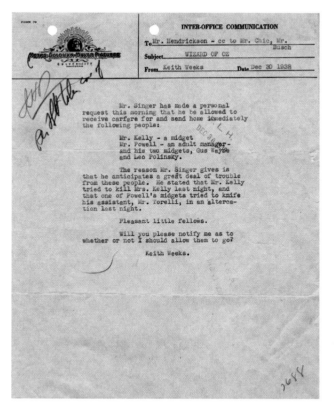

In this interoffice memo, Oz production manager Keith Weeks mentions Munchkin problems. Sadly, Weeks sided blindly with Singer's story—which was erroneous, at least as far as Gus Wayne and Prince Leon were concerned.

Those efforts were made in 1989, which heralded the fiftieth anniversary of *The Wizard of Oz* film and an amazing resurgence of interest—not that it had ever waned too much—in all things *Oz*. Ray Bolger had been the last of the film's principals to pass on, in 1987. Since none of these actors had survived to enjoy the jubilee festivities, the Munchkins found themselves in high demand for interviews and appearances. The sheer luck of our longevity—and our newfound popularity—helped us to begin slowly dispelling the distasteful Munchkin myths. Documentaries and books looked more deeply into the making of the film and quickly proved that the exaggerations regarding our days on the set were just that. The most accurate book to come out at that time—and my favorite to date—was *The Wizard of Oz: The Official 50th Anniversary Pictorial History*, written by my longtime friend John Fricke. He did a wonderful job of telling the facts in a delightfully entertaining way while deftly disproving the Munchkin rumors and myths.

Whether exaggerated in *Under the Rainbow* or in *Oz*-themed books, most authentic Munchkin problems could usually be traced back to a few isolated events involving Charley Kelley or Mike and Ike Matina. An interoffice memo at MGM does list Charley and two other midgets as causing problems, but only the reference to Charley has any merit. The other two little people listed—along with their manager, Mr. Powell—were Gus Wayne and Prince Leon Polinsky. (Leon played the Munchkin who told Dorothy, "We thank you very sweetly for doing it so neatly," in an undubbed voice.) Having known both Gus and Leon well, I think it is obvious that their inclusion was based upon false pretenses. Singer originated this complaint due to a financial problem he was having with Gus's manager.

I have never spent much time pondering the Munchkin myths, though they have amused me at times with their sheer outrageousness. My memories of *Oz* are not clouded by eccentric escapades, but are brightened by small day-to-day occurrences on the set: seeing the amazing special effects in the Wicked Witch of the West's fiery appearance; chatting with an excited young Judy Garland as we all sat by the Munchkin pond, comparing our funny costumes; or hearing Judy talk about how "out of this world" Bert Lahr, Jack Haley, and Ray Bolger looked in their wonderful makeup and costumes—just passing the time in a fun way while awaiting the next set-up. It was simply an exciting episode of my youth, and I still cherish the memories today.

In early November of 1938, I met Edgar Allen Woolf, one of many writers who had worked on *The Wizard of Oz*. (He had officially signed off the film the previous July, along

with his longtime writing partner Florence Ryerson.) Edgar was visiting one of the restaurants that I sampled on a Sunday afternoon, and our mutual interest in exotic cuisines and the finer points of cooking kindled our unlikely friendship. On quite a few of my Sundays off from filming, I rode around with Edgar to lesser-known and unusual restaurants in the Los Angeles area. We tried everything from Hawaiian to Indian cuisine. I took notes of any recipes I could find, along with historical tidbits about the restaurants themselves, and acquired more than two hundred before leaving Hollywood and Mr. Woolf.

I'm quite certain that Edgar never ate an Oscar Mayer product in his life, but he did enjoy hearing about my exploits on the novel Wienermobile. This was long before a West Coast Little Oscar came into the picture; in fact, technically, there were *no* Little Oscars at the time, since I was on furlough for the film. I told Edgar about the German chef who had shown me some good tips and new recipes using the Oscar Mayer products, and I gave him some of my grandmother's old-world German recipes.

Edgar was a world-class cook, famous in Hollywood for the parties that showcased his culinary creations. He even cooked for the famous brunches that were held by Louis B. Mayer at his beach house for the big producers and executives. Many an actor's career could be made or broken at these brunches: one minute he might be looking at an illustrious future; in another he could be chewed up like one of

Edgar's tasty hors d'oeuvres. Being late—or, worse, not showing up—was a cardinal sin to the stout host with clout.

Though Edgar thoroughly enjoyed cooking brunches for Mayer (or "L. B.," as everyone called him)—it was, in fact, L. B. who had become Edgar's meal ticket. Edgar had been writing sketches and plays in New York when he hosted a dinner party attended by Mr. Mayer. Very impressed with Edgar's cooking skills—and hoping to be impressed with his writing ability—L. B. invited him to MGM.

Edgar had been assigned to work on *The Wizard of Oz* script with Florence in June 1938—around the same time that English writer Noël Langley, who had written the film's first script, had been taken off the job. Rotating scriptwriters was a common practice in those days, and Noël's removal did not reflect adversely upon his talent in any way. In fact, he would return to the script again, from August until Halloween.

All told, the movie had contributions from thirteen writers. These included Irving Brecher, who was under the personal contract of producer Mervyn LeRoy and pumped up some of the gags for the principal characters before being reassigned as the sole screenwriter on LeRoy's *At the Circus*; and Herman Mankiewicz, who went on to write *Citizen Kane*. Only Noël Langley, Florence Ryerson, and Edgar Allen Woolf would receive screen credit, however. Many of Noël's contributions remain in the film, such as the talking apple trees, the ruby-colored slippers (which were silver in

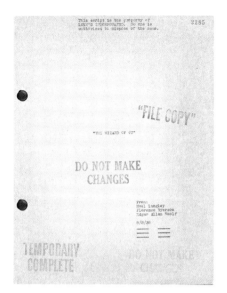

On August 8, 1938, this copy of the script for The Wizard of Oz *went into the MGM files. Edgar Allen Woolf and Florence Ryerson were two of the credited writers.*

Memories of a SCREENWRITER

It happened an eon ago, yet in my mind's eye certain scenes are still seeable in glorious Technicolor. I was at my MGM typewriter writing some hopefully comic material for the Oz clowns—the Cowardly Lion, the Tin and Straw Men—when my friend, the brilliant lyricist Yip Harburg, phoned to invite me to his office down the hall. "I think you might want to hear a new song Arlen and I are going to run through with the kid who's going to play Dorothy, what's her name, Judy Something."

Minutes later I experienced the unforgettable magic of hearing the lovely, nervous, and incredibly talented star-to-be, Judy Garland, singing "Over the Rainbow." It was years later that I had another moment of magic when I first heard Judy sing "The Trolley Song" for the movie I was writing—Meet Me in St. Louis.

Matchless memories I never would have dared to dream that I would ever have when I was a young kid in the Bronx.

IRVING BRECHER
First screenwriter for
The Wizard of Oz

the book), and having the Wicked Witch of the West make her first appearance in Munchkinland.

One of Florence and Edgar's most important contributions was multiplying the incarnations, and hence, the visibility of *The Wizard of Oz*'s title character. Instead of simply being the humbug Wizard, he was also to play the roles of the Emerald City Gatekeeper ("Who rang that bell?"); the Cabby; a mushy mustachioed Soldier; and, in the Kansas sequence, Professor Marvel. This idea was very popular among the film's producers, who especially liked the Kansas casting. (It's likely that double-casting the farmhands and the Woodman, Scarecrow, and Lion was probably "borrowed" from Larry Semon's 1925 silent version of *The Wizard of Oz*.)

LeRoy first offered the part of the Wizard to his favorite candidate, popular radio comedian Ed Wynn. This was before Florence and Edgar expanded the role, so Wynn turned it down, thinking it too small. Next up was W. C. Fields, who haggled over money for so long that time for any additional negotiations ran out.

Frank Morgan was on MGM's list of contract players, but initially was not a serious contender for the role of the Wizard. However, as hopes of Fields's playing the part fiz-

zled, Morgan stepped in to provide a very funny screen test. He landed the Wizard role on September 22.

Florence and Edgar also brought back the Deadly Poppy Field scene, and gave the Wicked Witch of the West her famed clipped-winged companion, the Flying Monkey named Nikko.

The most lasting contribution of the writing team was adding Dorothy's "There's no place like home," which she recites as she taps—*not* clicks—her heels together three times before waking up in her soft Kansas bed during the final scene. This now-famous line became the movie's main motif, and it would be unimaginable to think of *The Wizard of Oz* without that wonderful theme. It came from the final paragraph of the original Baum book, in which Aunt Em asks Dorothy, "Where in the world did you come from?" To which she replies, "From the Land of Oz...and here is Toto, too. And oh, Aunt Em! I'm so glad to be at home again!" Florence and Edgar finished their final version of the screenplay by the end of July.

Edgar was interested to know that Harry and Daisy Doll, who played Hans and Frieda, the leads in *Freaks*, were portraying Munchkins in the *Oz* film. I told him that their other siblings, Tiny and Gracie Doll, also played Munchkin villagers. (Edgar had previously met Olga Baclanova, the average-sized Russian actress who was the cunning Cleopatra in *Freaks*. She had performed in *The Great Lover*, a film he had written in 1931, which also starred Adolphe Menjou and Irene Dunne.)

Another little person who had acted in *Freaks* was not allowed to work on *The Wizard of Oz*. Angelo Rossitto, who had played Angeleno in the earlier film, was turned down because he was a dwarf. Why, I don't know, since at least five of our 124 little people were dwarfs. Perhaps it was because independent actors such as Angelo frustrated Leo Singer since he could not pocket any of their salaries.

One of the restaurants I visited with Edgar was the famous Brown Derby on Wilshire Boulevard. Shaped like its namesake hat, it was frequented by the big Hollywood names—countless caricatures of famous stars adorned the walls of the restaurant as a testament to that fact. Most of these drawings were the work of Frank "Pancho" Willmarth, who drew them all in person. Edgar was very quick to point out his own portrait, which accentuated his wavy, flaming red hair. With its walls of drawings and show-biz clientele, the Derby was similar to Sardi's in New York City. Though I have eaten in both restaurants, my own portrait has never been drawn by their artists. However, I am very proud of the fact that another great caricaturist—*the* caricaturist, as far as I am concerned—drew me for the jacket of this book. Al Hirschfeld was one of the greats.

I corresponded a few times with Edgar when I moved back to Chicago to work for Oscar Mayer, but I eventually lost touch with him, just as I did the many other people I met while working on *Oz*. I found out years later that Edgar had died on December 8, 1943, in a freak accident. He had tripped on his dog's leash and fallen down the staircase in his own home.

My frequent trips to innumerable Los Angeles exotic eateries were adventures purely to satisfy my own distinct tastes, and were, of course, a luxury. But during the work week I still ate well, thanks to the studio. All of the Munchkins were issued meal cards, which were punched each time we ate, so no money ever changed hands. We had to arrive at the studio very early to eat breakfast and still make it to the makeup area by six o'clock. We had our breakfasts and dinners at the studio commissary—though the breakfast was continental, at best. A special arrangement had been made between the studio and a local restaurant named Marie's, so that the Munchkins could eat dinner there instead of in the commissary—but only if the shooting was done for the day.

Our lunches were served closer to the *Oz* sets, on an adjoining soundstage. Our lunchtime varied with each day's schedule; when there was a break in the action for our partic-

Brittingham provided the Munchkins with a daily buffet in an adjoining soundstage. Margaret Pellegrini, wearing her flowerpot hat, carries a tray of treats.

ular Munchkin role, that would be our cue to grab lunch. The tables and chairs were lowered to accommodate the little people, and a large van from Brittingham Commissary catered the meal, buffet-style, on location every day. We simply lined up to receive our trays and whatever the menu du jour was.

Since we were in costume during our lunch meals, it was customary to wear our street jackets over our Munchkin attire when eating. A smock type of bib was also available, and though these looked silly, they proved to be quite functional. Due to the exotic nature of Adrian's sometimes billowing and oversized costumes, bibs did not fit everyone, but getting any stains on these expensive, and one-of-a-kind, outfits was definitely frowned upon.

Judy Garland ate at our little impromptu commissary a few times, to be sociable and polite, but had most of her lunches in the regular studio commissary. That was for the entire studio lot, so seeing many of the leading MGM stars there was not uncommon. The advantage of being a Munchkin was that not only did we know who *they* were, but *they* had a pretty good idea which film we were working on. The one star I remember having a conversation with was Robert Montgomery. A very distinguished-looking gentleman, he was polite enough to ask if he could sit with me—which I thought was very noble. We did not exactly become pals, but we did have a nice conversation about current events and *The Wizard of Oz* film.

Just as we had little free time in the evening after the day's shooting, we had limited free time during the shooting. Some downtime was inevitable, however: when the big slider doors were opened to cool down the temperature from the oppressively hot overhead lights, or when we waited for Judy to get out of school for a scene that could not be done with her double.

It was during one of these periods that I was able to visit another *Oz* set while they were filming. I didn't make a habit of roaming around, but was I young and naturally curious about some technical aspects of filming, and in only a few days we would be finished shooting in Munchkinland. On this occasion I visited the Jitter Bug Forest set that was directly around the corner from Munchkinland, on Soundstage 26—both were on the old Seventh Avenue of Lot 1.

Right next to the Jitter Bug Forest was the Haunted Forest set; its soundstage had previously housed the Cornfield with the Scarecrow, and later the Apple Orchard.

Though I knew very well that this was only a set, it was dark and eerie, and I will never forget looking up at the deceivingly large Haunted Forest sign with awe . . . but if you had been me, would you have turned back?

The Jitter Bug Forest was designed to showcase the Jitter Bug dance of Dorothy and her companions; its trees moved around and swayed with the dancing. You won't remember this scene, because it had to be cut when the film ran too long.

The only scene in the film that does appear on the Jitter Bug set is the one in which the Wicked Witch sends her Winged Monkey army after Dorothy and Toto, attempting to retrieve the magical ruby slippers.

Also remaining is a line spoken by the Witch that refers to the missing dance. You can hear it in her orders to the Winged Monkey Captain: "Take your army to the Haunted Forest and bring me that girl and her dog. Do what you like with the others, but I want her alive and unharmed! They'll give you no trouble, I promise you that. I've sent a little insect on ahead to take the fight out of them!" In the screenplay, that "little insect" was the Jitter Bug—a pink-and-blue mosquitolike insect that caused anyone it bit to go into a dance.

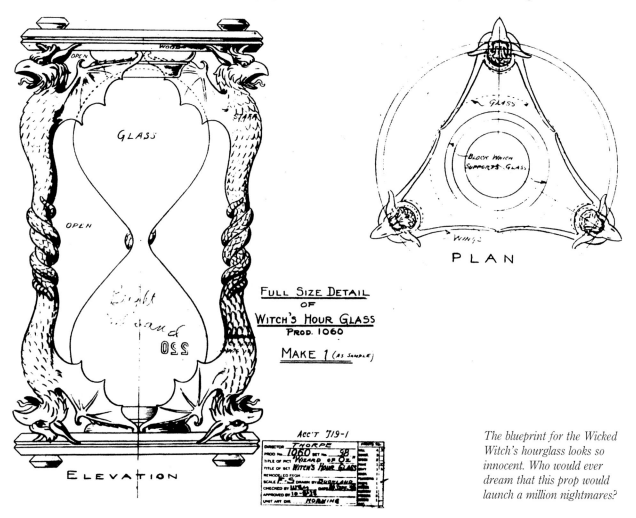

The blueprint for the Wicked Witch's hourglass looks so innocent. Who would ever dream that this prop would launch a million nightmares?

The Winged Monkey army flies through the sky . . . but this army is made up entirely of six-inch puppets on wires.

Although MGM's footage for the Jitter Bug dance has been lost, the film's songwriter, Harold Arlen, loved making home movies and captured the scene on film. His footage does exist and can be viewed among the bonus materials on Warner Bros.'s 1998 digitally remastered version of the movie.

In the completed film the Cowardly Lion, Scarecrow, Tin Woodman, and Dorothy are seen walking up to the Haunted Forest sign (which was actually on the Jitter Bug Forest set), carrying tools clearly intended for the Jitter Bug scene and no other purpose. The Scarecrow brandishes a silver cap gun and the Tin Woodman wields a monkey wrench—which the Winged Monkeys later wrench away from him. In one paw the Lion slings a butterfly net over his right shoulder and in the other holds a Flit gun (a pump for spraying insects) labeled WITCH REMOVER.

In the final screenplay, the Jitter Bug bites our heroes, and they launch into the lost song-and-dance number. Rehearsing and filming this segment required more than five weeks, and that was a great deal of work to lose in the final edit. However, leaving out this scene was better than cutting Judy Garland's *Over the Rainbow* rendition. That actually happened three times, before Arthur Freed thankfully intervened—altering the course of film history.

I enjoyed viewing the filming on the Jitter Bug Forest set. When I visited they were shooting Dorothy's capture by two Winged Monkeys who flew her to the Witch's Castle. The monkeys were actually lifting Judy's stunt-double, Bobbie Koshay, but since only her back is visible in the film, you can't tell the difference.

The Winged Monkeys were played by stuntmen—they were diminutive, but certainly not small enough to be considered midgets. Many fans assume that all of the monkeys were played by the Munchkin actors, but I only know of a few. Little people Harry Monty and Walter Miller did play both Munchkins and monkeys. Harry had been a circus acrobat before the film and was very capable physically; such prowess was needed for the dangerous stunts the monkeys had to perform. Walter can be seen grabbing Toto and flying off with him when Dorothy is abducted.

The stuntmen had harnesses under their costumes, connected to the thin wires that supported them, giving the illusion of flight. I guess that later on in the filming some of these stuntmen were hospitalized when their wires broke and they came crashing down to the ground. Today these wires can be digitally erased from the film, so thicker and safer supports can be used.

What I saw when I visited the set was a pair of Winged Monkeys, each grabbing one of Bobbie's arms. They were collectively yanked up in the air about ten to fifteen feet before the unit director yelled, "Cut." The wire operators then lowered the trio down and prepared to raise them again.

What impressed me most was looking up and seeing hundreds of Winged Monkeys flying through the sky. They were, in fact, eight-inch rubber puppets. Wires were attached to their bodies and the wings, then secured to a large rail on the soundstage ceiling. The prop men pulled this rail on a pulley and the monkeys' wings flapped up and down. Their tails were actually pipe cleaners bent into S shapes.

Many people don't know this, but a tiny Dorothy puppet was used for this scene also. If you look very closely, when the monkeys carrying Dorothy are very high in the sky, you can see the small puppet's legs kicking back and forth. This was not very high-tech, but was better than most special effects in those pre-Ray Harryhausen years.

Throughout the years, I have seen one or two of the rubber monkey props in the hands of some very avid Oz collectors, but I have yet to hear of the Dorothy puppet resurfacing. For all I know, to this day she may still be flying around somewhere over the rainbow, flailing her tiny legs and shrilling a muffled scream.

The whirlwind of Oz never stopped for any of us while we were rehearsing, filming, and carousing on the Munchkinland set. So it was rather shocking when the flurry of activity suddenly ceased as quickly as it had started—though our transition from Munchkin citizens back to civilians was not completely smooth. One slight problem cropped up when the studio wanted to retain all of the little people for two extra days, December 29 and 30, for touch-up shots—and Singer refused. His contract (paragraph four, section e) clearly stated that the studio could keep as many little people as it needed for retakes or additional work on previously filmed scenes, but for an unknown reason he fought MGM on this.

Financially, it would have been better for Singer (who would have been paid one hundred dollars per midget per week) to retain all of us. Though essentially the studio won on this point, Singer did get MGM to agree to keep only about twenty Munchkins for those two extra days. Personally, I think that even though Singer is widely remembered for his shrewd, and seemingly shady, business dealings with the Munchkins, he was still a rather sentimental man and wanted all of the little people to have a chance to get home before the holiday season ended. Perhaps the kindly spirit of the Oz story affected him in a positive way.

I was not one of the score of Munchkins retained for the final two days, but I still had a little time before my train was scheduled to depart Los Angeles, on January 2, 1939. I wanted to stick around long enough to see the fiftieth annual Tournament of Roses Parade in Pasadena. A day or two before the parade, I went there to case out the area, found the route, and located a good spot to view the floats. A billboard that sported a walkway just above the heads of the crowd offered a great vantage point. I simply grabbed some coffee and other goodies and camped out up there with my suitcase hours before the parade began.

Munchkin and Winged Monkey Walter Miller holds Toto (a rare privilege) in preparation for the kidnapping scene in the Haunted Forest. Harry Monty is the only other midget actor known to have played both a Munchkin and a Winged Monkey.

Even though *The Wizard of Oz* was still filming and would not be released for another eight months, MGM, wasting no marketing opportunities, entered a *Wizard of Oz*-themed float (with "Culver City" written on both sides), made of multicolored tissues and pastel pom-poms that looked like flowers. From a miniature Munchkinland, a yellow brick road led out to the front of the float.

Eleven cast members rode on board. The principal characters were actually represented by stand-ins for Judy Garland, Bert Lahr, Ray Bolger, and Jack Haley, but with their costumes on it was hard to tell the difference. The Scarecrow perpetually oiled the Tin Woodman, and Bobbie Koshay, posing as Dorothy, waved to the crowd. At the rear of the float, in front of the Munchkinland houses, were Charles Becker in his Mayor outfit, Karl Slover as a Trumpeter, Freddie Retter as a Fiddler, and Billy Curtis as a Soldier. Makeup man Jack Young accompanied the group to ensure that no one had problems with the prosthetics. On the tail end of the float rode three female Munchkins, including Nita Krebs and Olga Nardone—two-thirds of the Lullaby League. They waved to people, too, and the crowd—especially the children—showed great enthusiasm for the float, which was a good omen.

Sadly, that was the last time I would ever see many of the actors, Charles and Freddie among them. Luckily, I still see Karl Slover a few times a year at *Wizard of Oz* conventions—except now we both get to ride on *Oz*-themed floats!

I had already said good-bye to my hosts, the Housmans, and given them my address in Chicago. After the parade, I enjoyed one last taste of some exotic Californian cuisine, then boarded the train, the brand-new Union Pacific Challenger, back to my life in Chicago.

The train was unique in that an entire car was reserved exclusively for ladies traveling with small children, complete with a specially assigned stewardess who watched the children when the mothers needed to leave the car. I was riding in the third-class coach section, and on my first day aboard, the stewardess from the special car approached me to inquire if I was traveling alone. I told her yes, and she asked, could I sleep by myself? Well, she was very beautiful and I thought maybe she was flirting with me. As it turned out, she thought I was a child and wanted to take me back to the children's car.

To make matters worse, a group of gentlemen sitting next to me thought the whole scenario was too funny for words. The stewardess eventually realized I was a midget and apologized before leaving. But every time she passed us for the next two days, the guys sitting by me made snide comments such as, "Hey, Junior here wants his breakfast!" I knew I was not in *Oz* anymore.

To promote the movie, a Wizard of Oz *float was entered in the Tournament of Roses Parade on New Year's Day 1939, months before the film was finished, much less released. The principal actors' doubles played Dorothy, the Scarecrow, the Tin Man, and the Cowardly Lion; and they were joined by seven Munchkins, four men in front and three ladies riding at the rear of the float.*

These four brownies on Culver City's "Wizard of Oz" float intrigued the children.

Karl Slover, Charles Becker, and Billy Curtis ride the Munchkin float in the parade. Seeing the parade was the last thing I did in California before heading home, and I remember seeing this wonderful float very well. The yellow brick road leading up to the Munchkin hut was made of yellow flowers, of course, and the hut itself was multicolored. This clipping is from the morning edition of the January 3, 1939, Los Angeles Times.

ART
for Oz's Sake

Long before Judy Garland stepped into a Technicolor Munchkinland in 1939, the innovative use of color in L. Frank Baum's book *The Wonderful Wizard of Oz* made it an exciting adventure for innumerable children. Lavish tipped-in color illustrations and duotone drawings, all created by artist W. W. Denslow, made it the ultimate picture book of its day and riveted young readers with what would become their most beloved book.

This turn-of-the-century page turner has been America's national fairy tale for more than one hundred years. In the introduction to the centennial edition of *The Annotated Wizard of Oz*, its editor, Michael Patrick Hearn, commented on the book's successful use of color: "The extensive color work in *The Wonderful Wizard of Oz* revolutionized the design of American children's books. They would never be so wan and boring again. Baum and Denslow proved that novelty could sell."

L. Frank Baum and William Wallace Denslow first met in 1898. Though they were both already accomplished professionals, it was their collaboration that would secure their immortality. *Father Goose, His Book* was their first project together, and the nursery rhymes storybook was a smashing success-so much so that it was praised not only by critics, but from such luminaries of the day as Mark Twain (Denslow had previously provided an illustration for his book *A Tramp Abroad* in 1880) and Admiral George Dewey, the hero of the Spanish-American War.

Denslow's flying monkeys looked remarkably like their "real" counterparts in the MGM movie.

◀ Strangely enough, Denslow's lion did bear a resemblance to Bert Lahr.

▲ The scene where Dorothy and the Scarecrow meet the Tin Woodman is not unlike this striking drawing.

◀ Our Wicked Witch was much more frightening than the book's version— but she was pretty scary, too!

In the summer of 1899, Baum choose Denslow to work with him on his next book, tentatively titled *The City of Oz*. Denslow created more than a hundred original black-and-white line drawings, but from the beginning he and Baum planned for the book to be packed with color. Every picture was to be printed in color, either as a duotone appearing in the text or one of twenty-four more elaborate full-color tipped-in plates. (The colors vary depending on where the characters are in the story—for example, Kansas scenes are gray and the Emerald City is, of course, green.) When their publisher worried that the color printing would be too expensive, Baum and Denslow paid the costs of including the plates. The book was released on May 15, 1900—the author's forty-fourth birthday—and it immediately took its place in the pantheon of classic children's literature.

Judy Garland was older than the little girl of the original book, but her Dorothy had the same all-American spunk. Toto, played by a Cairn terrier named Terry, was probably the movie character who looked the most like her original drawing.

* "The Scarecrow sat in the big throne and the others stood respectfully before him."
natural.

The rare prints and manuscript division at the New York Public Library currently holds thirty-seven of Denslow's original pen-and-ink illustrations from the original *The Wonderful Wizard of Oz*. In the year 2000 a few of these national treasures were loaned to the Library of Congress for an exhibit showcasing the 100th anniversary of the book—but as incredible as it seems, these images of the original Denslow drawings have never been viewed by the general public or published in any book.

The bold black ink lines on these examples look just as vivid today as they did when they were first drawn, more than 105 years ago. Still-visible pencil lines show where the artist first placed, replaced, and even erased characters completely. The several tiers of barely legible guidelines used by Denslow to hand-paint all of the titles and lettering in the original book are a testament to his precise draftsmanship. The elegant images themselves are an iconic part of our collective memory.

—DANIEL KINSKE

CHAPTER NINE

From Louis B. Mayer
to Oscar Mayer

OLLOWING THE YELLOW BRICK ROAD DID
not end when I left MGM Studios and the
Munchkinland set. Upon my return to Chicago I
was welcomed back at my old job at Oscar Mayer.
My bosses, who had not wanted to give me a leave of absence
for the film before, were suddenly very interested in my role
as a Munchkin and in the fact that I had a speaking part.

Ironically for me, one of the very first "premieres" of *The
Wizard of Oz* occurred at the Strand Theatre, in
Oconomowoc, Wisconsin—just thirteen miles from my
hometown of Watertown! The date, August 12, 1939, is also
known as the official anniversary date of the film.

Harley and Ruth Huebner owned the Strand, where *Oz*
played for five days, through August 16. Those Wisconsin
moviegoers were the first among the general public to see the
great classic that would eventually be adored by billions
worldwide. (A few sneak previews had been shown earlier, for
the MGM executives who made last-minute changes in the
film.) My parents and sister saw the movie at the Strand on
the opening night, before I even had a chance. Since Chicago
is 120 miles south of Oconomowoc, I was not able to make it
there for what would have been my first trip back to Oz!

The Strand showed matinees on Saturday, Sunday, and
Wednesday, and included a Disney cartoon: *Mickey's Par-
rot.* This was an unintentional, but fitting, homage to Walt
Disney, since the enormous success of his *Snow White and
the Seven Dwarfs* fantasy had encouraged the bigwigs at
MGM to attempt the filming of *Oz.* My family was elated to
see me on the big screen in full color, even though I wasn't
there in person. I have always been happy that both of my
parents were still around to see the film.

In an article in the July 20, 1979, issue of *The Milwaukee
Journal,* Ruth Huebner was asked if she knew why the

Two technicians carry the separated sound and film for The
Wizard of Oz, *which was still in production, after a test screening.
Note the posters for* Boys Town, *starring Spencer Tracy and
Mickey Rooney—I had met them both in Hollywood.*

The East Coast premiere, on August 17, 1939, of The Wizard of Oz *at the Capitol Theatre in New York City featured live shows by Mickey Rooney and Judy Garland. They drew thousands upon thousands of fans to see the film.*

Strand had been selected for the *Oz* premiere. She replied that she and her husband had never been given a specific reason by the Milwaukee film distributor but thought the ultimate call had been made by the studio executives at MGM. Sadly, the Huebners' majestic theater has long since been torn down and turned into a parking lot.

The fervor of opening night in Oconomowoc did not match that of opening night in Los Angeles, held at Grauman's Chinese Theatre three days later, on August 15. Notable attendees included Maud Gage Baum (L. Frank Baum's widow), Fred Stone (the original Scarecrow from the 1902 stage musical), Chico Marx, Wallace Beery, Eddie Cantor, Edgar Bergen, Harold Lloyd, Allan Jones, and Douglas Fairbanks Jr. Nor did Wisconsonians experience the energy and mayhem generated at the New York opening, on August 17—when thousands upon thousands of fans lined up at Loew's Capitol Theatre to see Judy Garland and Mickey Rooney. Judy and Mickey would spend the next three weeks at the Capitol, performing five times a day between shows—an unbelievably successful marketing venture by MGM.

I was unable to attend the big-city premieres, but a caricature of my Coroner character did appear at Grauman's. I wish I had been there. All attendees received deluxe opening-night programs, which contained facts about the film, biographies of the principal actors, and many ornate decorative drawings. One of these depicted the Munchkin Coroner reading his scroll.

So rare are these programs today that they routinely fetch thousands of dollars each. Jerry Maren and some other little people wore Munchkin costumes and makeup to ballyhoo the picture. For some reason Jerry was dressed in the Mayor's costume and held my Certificate of Death scroll prop. "I grabbed one of the programs as a souvenir and years later sold it for over a thousand dollars," Jerry told me. "Later I thought, 'Oh, brother—if I would have known how much they would be worth, I would have grabbed a whole handful of them!'"

A rare and unexpected opportunity soon fell into my lap that allowed me to see *The Wizard of Oz* as often as I liked. Arrangements were made between Oscar Mayer and the Balaban and Katz theater chain for me to travel with the picture for its initial run throughout Illinois, Wisconsin, Indiana, and lower Michigan, to promote the film as Little Oscar. A special billboard was designed for my appearances at these theaters, featuring a picture of me in my Little Oscar outfit and noting that I had been in the movie. We parked the Wienermobile right in front of each theater for further publicity, and to keep the supplies we needed close at hand.

Before each showing I gave a five-minute introduction to the film. I told a little bit about the story and advised the audience on what to look for in the film. My Little Oscar persona held everyone's interest. They didn't yet know what a Munchkin was, so my real recognition came after the film.

After my monologue, I headed to the lobby to prepare weenie samples to be given to the audience after the movie. During the showings, I usually sat in the theater until the Munchkinland sequence was over. Of course, this was long before the age of laser discs, VHS tapes, DVDs, and even the now-ubiquitous television set, so I had to see it while I could. When a film's run ended . . . that was it! Who knew that *The Wizard of Oz* would break that rule, among many others, with its rereleases in 1949 and 1955. The year following the second rerelease brought the annual television presentation.

I saw the film during the first leg of the road show, which began in the second week of August 1939. The tour started out in Chicago—fitting because this is where Baum's book was written—then headed north to Wisconsin. Having gotten a handle on my job after the first few showings, I was able to view the film along with the audience in one of the Chicago theaters. The experience was unforgettable; the film was amazing.

Seeing *Oz* all together made me really feel proud of having played a part in its genesis. Munchkinland seemed even bigger on the screen, and watching the Munchkins dance around was fabulous. I enjoyed seeing my character march up the steps—up the entire movie screen—to Dorothy and the Mayor to deliver the death pronouncement. Talk about an out-of-body experience! A little irony is that back then I was amazed at how much older I looked with the beard and mustache. Now when I see the film, I marvel at how young that Munchkin looks!

In my mind the scene that stole the picture was in the first few minutes of the film. Judy Garland singing *Over the Rainbow* was simply heartwarming and beautiful. I had known Judy as a giddy, affable young girl on the set. Here was another side of her that showed why both she and her song remain in our hearts, even today.

After a few months of viewing the movie scores of times, and the Munchkinland sequence even more often, I changed

I'm wearing my very first mock-up of my Munchkin Coroner costume over my Little Oscar costume. This was for a promotional tour for Oscar Mayer in 1942; we were raffling off the little supercharged 38 pedal car to one lucky kid.

tactics. I immediately went to the theater's lobby, or outside with the Wienermobile, to begin setting up my meat samples and other Oscar Mayer advertising hoopla. Still, I could tell which scene was playing at any given time by listening to the audience's reaction. There was mesmerized silence when Judy sang "Over the Rainbow," and peals of laughter rang out during the Munchkinland sequence. Distraught mothers ran out of the theater, holding their screaming children, whenever the Wicked Witch or Winged Monkeys appeared. I helped the women calm their kiddies by giving them a tour of the Wienermobile or a balloon to play with.

Many elements of the *The Wizard of Oz* film have remained universal despite the passage of time. Whether this is solely due to the theme of home and family, or should be credited to the cinematic prowess of the film itself, no one can say. Yet the children's reaction of wonderment and awe never fades. Seeing this response in each new generation of children is why I continue to attend *Wizard of Oz* festivals across the country—more than sixty-six years after its original release. *Some* of the kids who saw the film in the 1930s don't look as young as they used to, but thanks to L. Frank Baum, they are still young at heart.

Though I hadn't been able to see the Oconomowoc premiere with my family, practically in our own backyard, I do remember my feeling of satisfaction and accomplishment when I toured my hometown to promote the film, in late August 1939. In Watertown all MGM productions were booked exclusively at the Classic Theatre. I spent the entire four-day run of the film there, August 20 through 23, making an appearance at each show.

I became something of a local celebrity instead of just being known as a little squirt. I was celebrated for my role as a Munchkin—and for my then-current and equally unique Little Oscar job. That felt good, and I felt then, as I still feel now, extremely fortunate to have had a part in what would become a great classic. *Oz* was kind of a sleeper during its initial release in 1939; it had to compete with such titles as *Gone with the Wind*, *The Hunchback of Notre Dame*, *Stagecoach*, and *Mr. Smith Goes to Washington*. Needless to say, the box-office competition was a little stiff that year!

Even though I had had to fight for the two months' leave necessary to film my role, Oscar Mayer couldn't wait to get me on the road to promote its products with the film for six months. All told, I ended up spending eight months with *The Wizard of Oz* in one form or another. Being constantly on the road and promoting Oscar Mayer products across the Midwest was a lonely existence at times. I didn't dream that it could be a blessing in disguise.

The Witch frightened Dorothy—and countless innocent children!

▲ At the twelfth annual Academy Awards, in 1940, Mickey Rooney presented Judy Garland with her special Oscar. Judy sang a very poignant "Over the Rainbow" as the star-packed audience and Bob Hope, the emcee, listened. The Oscar was a miniature one, and Judy called it her "Munchkin award."

◀ I stand on the top step, watching Judy Garland read over her lines while the next shot is being set up. Seeing the movie in my hometown, I felt so proud for having been a part of this great film.

149

CHAPTER TEN

If I Only
Had a Heart

BSERVERS OF *THE WIZARD OF OZ* eventually realize that the characters are searching for qualities and traits that they already possessed. Unlike the Tin Woodman, I knew I had a heart, but for the longest time I thought its only purpose was to pump blood—until I saw the most beautiful little creature in the world in a small town in Ohio. I realized at that moment just how powerful the heart is; and even though mine might have skipped a beat, thankfully, I did not: I immediately sought to meet that little princess.

I had been back at Oscar Mayer for a few weeks and was in full swing in my work as Little Oscar. By the time 1940 rolled around I had transferred back to the Madison, Wisconsin, plant and was making regular rounds in the Wienermobile. Our route swung through many of the major cities of Illinois, Ohio, Michigan, and, of course, Wisconsin. Occasionally we would also make runs to the East Coast, to Maryland and Virginia.

One weekend in the fall of 1941, I was making my normal stop in Akron, Ohio. To quote the Munchkin Braggart, "Oh, what happened then was rich!" As I pitched the meats and other canned eats to various customers, I found one butcher who had a pitch for *me*. He confided that the daughter of one of his best customers worked at the Mayflower Hotel as a cigarette girl, and she was also a little person. Even the brainless Scarecrow could guess where I was headed that night!

I made my living by talking and pitching products as a salesperson, and I was quite confident most of the time, yet I was at a complete loss for words from the moment I saw that young girl in the hotel lobby. I must aver that she was the most drop-dead gorgeous girl I had ever seen (luckily, I didn't have far to drop), and I instantly fell in love with her.

Her name was Marie Hartline, and she had grown up in Akron. Her long, brown hair cascaded down to her shoulders and she had the sweetest smile I had ever seen—a smile that many of her friends and family continue to remember fondly.

I had never used tobacco or drunk coffee—stunts your growth, you know—but that evening Miss Hartline must have thought I was a lifelong chain-smoker. My purchases were really just fueled by my burning desire to do anything I could to keep talking with this divine little lady. Nearly a carton of cigarettes and many packs of gum later, I had learned quite a lot about her.

In the late 1920s, when she was twelve or thirteen, Marie had coaxed her mother into letting her see the vaudeville show of Rose's Royal Midget Troupe when it visited Akron. Mrs. Hartline didn't want her going alone, so Marie had to take her sister along. Though the sister was younger, she towered over Marie (an anomaly of nature I was all too familiar with myself).

When Marie tried to purchase her ticket, she was immediately escorted backstage to see Ike Rose, who was quite taken with her. Because of her size and singing ability, he offered her a job with the troupe. Seeing other little people for the first time in her life had enchanted Marie—as it had me at the Chicago World's Fair—and the opportunity to travel the country was too tempting to turn down. But Mrs. Hartline told Marie that she couldn't join Ike's troupe until she graduated from the eighth grade, at least.

When Marie graduated from the eighth grade a year later, she waited for the troupe to pass through Chicago, the nearest stop to Akron on its vaudeville circuit. At that time Mr. Hartline was out of work, so he contacted a brother

Cliff Thompson, a giant, holds me for a publicity photo that appeared in the February 29, 1940, edition of The Illinois State Journal—*"leap day." Well, I had to leap to get up there, since Cliff was eight feet, seven inches tall; he weighed 460 pounds. That was twice my height and six times my weight! Cliff was a salesman for Blatz Brewing Company. He was the tallest salesman in the country, and I was the shortest. To this day, I have not met anyone taller than he was.*

living in Chicago, hoping to locate a job there. When the brother found Marie's dad a job, father and daughter headed to the Windy City. Marie made the transition from school to living in Chicago with great ease, and she visited Ike and the midget troupe during their second-to-last show in town. Ike was happy to see her again and immediately offered her a spot in the troupe.

Marie traveled with Rose's Royal Midget Troupe from 1927 until 1932, as part of a group song-and-dance act. The troupe played many of the biggest cities in North America. It was the most famous American midget company at the time, second worldwide only to Singer's Midget Troupe.

It has always interested me how certain paths intersect at the appropriate times. If I had only worked at the Chicago World's Fair and done nothing else, then I would have met the Singer midgets but would never have been a Munchkin. If Marie had stayed with the Ike Rose troupe two years longer, I would have seen her at the fair, too, but she returned home at seventeen to finish high school. Due to her time in the troupe, she did not graduate until after her twenty-first birthday.

The Rose troupe (billed as the Ike Rose Midgets) was used to augment the number of little people in the Chicago World's Fair Midget City, which surpassed 150 the year I worked there (1934). To my knowledge, that city within a city in Chicago, created nearly three-quarters of a century ago, still holds the record for having the most little people working in one place.

The next time I swung through Akron in the Wienermobile, I immediately contacted Marie. This time she kindly invited me to her parents' home for a Sunday dinner. Both of them were of average size, as were her two siblings—she had a younger brother and sister. Her father was Edward Hartline, a successful interior decorator and painter. His specialty was painting very high objects, such as the outsides of tall buildings or fixtures such as flagpoles. Her mother, Jennie Elmore Hartline, had been a seamstress before she met and married Edward, and this skill proved very useful for "tailoring" to the needs of her children—especially Marie (whom she taught to sew her own clothes).

Like my parents, Marie's were quite supportive of their children and did not consider her lack of stature to be a handicap. Her father taught her how to paint home interiors and she was quite an apt pupil. Even at less than four feet in height, she could paint a full-sized room in the same time as anyone else. Of course, she had to run frantically up and down her ladder to do so, but she was an agile little Aphrodite in her youth.

The dinner with Marie's family went well, and they genuinely seemed to take to me. Her dad gave the clue that I was welcome by telling me to be sure to visit any time I was in the area. Marie and I were both in our late twenties by then—she was six months my senior—and I'm sure both sets of parents hoped to hear wedding bells (and the pitter-patter of very tiny feet).

Marie had not been seeing anyone seriously at the time, although one acquaintance thought otherwise: A little person named Jake Smith had recently claimed to people in town that he was going to marry Marie. Jake was employed with Ringling Brothers as an acrobat and courted her whenever the circus came through Akron. Luckily for me, Marie was only interested in one ring—not three!

Marie's vaudeville stories intrigued me, and she was interesting to listen to. Her experiences were just as exciting as my past exploits, and I think we appreciated our mutual worldliness (and possibly my wordiness, too). She told me about hearing all of the big bands of the era when they came through Akron. The Mayflower Hotel, where she worked, was a popular place for the performers to stay, and she saw every one passing through, from Artie Shaw to the Andrews Sisters.

Marie's favorite story was of an encounter during World War II, a few years after we met. It centered on an average-sized attractive young man who was staying at the hotel one evening. This blue-eyed fellow seemed very intent on speaking to her while she was working, and bought many of her cigarettes—which were a luxury and in limited supply during those wartime years—before going onstage. Later he summoned Marie to his suite; he said he needed more cigarettes. He and his entourage were having drinks and just relaxing after he had performed at a local nightclub. He bought her a Cuba Libre drink and chatted with her quite amiably and pleasantly. She received a large tip and a kiss on the cheek that she never forgot. That blue-eyed young man was none other than Frank Sinatra.

It was wonderful meeting Marie, and soon she became all I could think about. I was going to see her after I made one of my longer East Coast sales trips, in December of 1941, but plans soon changed—for everyone.

On Friday, December 5, I was in Baltimore, Maryland, with the Wienermobile, ready to attend a big food share meeting (a kind of sales convention for food brokers) on Monday, where I would be pitching Oscar Mayer meats. I stayed at the home of a local-area sales representative and

was enjoying the weekend break. I went sightseeing in downtown Baltimore on Saturday and stopped to view the Navy frigate the U. S. S. *Constellation*. The sad irony of visiting that majestic warship would come to light the following morning, Sunday, December 7, 1941, when our Pacific fleet was attacked at Pearl Harbor. It was a day that will never be forgotten.

I listened in horror to the news unfolding on the radio and realized things would never be the same. On Monday my host gave me a telegram sent by the Oscar Mayer corporate headquarters in Madison, instructing the Wienermobile driver and me to return to home base at once.

Upon arriving at the Madison office, I found out that the army had requisitioned all of our canned meats, and I was out of a job. I was not canned, however, and continued to work around the office, performing various clerical jobs. I kept in touch with Marie by writing her often, and I told her how much I missed her and that I hoped to see her soon.

In the corporate office I overheard that there was a territory in upper Michigan where Oscar Mayer had never had a sales representative and that company executives were anxious to send someone up there.

Seeing this as an opportunity to get out of the office, I asked if I could open up the territory. They told me it was quite a rough deal up there to start from scratch, and that it might not be something I wanted to do. I replied that I would rather be the first one in the area and make my own mistakes than follow someone else's failure and have to live down his mistakes.

Once again to Oscar Mayer's credit, they gave me a shot at the job. In January 1942, after getting detailed instructions from the sales and credit managers on how to open up accounts in the area, I headed off to Michigan's Upper Peninsula—to Escanaba, on Lake Michigan, a town so far "up north" (250 miles northeast of Madison) that it is above the Canadian border. Growing up on a somewhat frigid farm would prepare me well for the extreme cold of that winter.

Upon arriving in Escanaba, the central point of my new territory, I purchased a car, had it outfitted with pedal extensions, obtained ration cards for gas and food, and rented a small apartment.

It was a little daunting to learn that five different meat-packing companies were represented in the Upper Michigan region, among them Swift and Armour. The reps were not very professional and often ridiculed me—most often behind my back, or with my customers. (If they ever did it in front of me, it must have gone "over my head.")

These salesmen were not happy about such a little squirt trying to bust into their territory, and they made bets that I

(TIMES Photo)

Lieut. David N. Goldenson and Meinhardt F. Raabe

Lieutenant junior-grade David Goldenson and I met at the navy recruiting office in February 1942. I was four feet six inches tall. None of the regular services would let me enlist, but the navy was at least gracious in how they told me.

wouldn't last very long. Their bad-mouthing backfired, however, because by making fun of me to our customers, they became my advance men. Every time I made a call, the prospective customer would say, "Oh, yes, you're the fellow those other meat salesmen have been telling us about. They've been laughing about a midget trying to compete with them!" Then they usually called their wives and said, "Come, Ma; come, kids. The midget we've been hearing about is here." They may have gazed and gawked, but in the end I was the salesman with the tallest orders.

The Office of Defense Transportation ruled that all companies' orders had to weigh more than twenty thousand pounds or else we couldn't ship them, since shipping an underweight load would be a waste of gasoline. Soon my competitors—these rugged, experienced salesmen—started dropping out because they could not make the weight. Their former customers asked me to supply them, and as my orders kept stacking up, the rest of my rivals went home packing. Eventually I became the top—and only—seller in the region.

I was proud of my accomplishment, but I would not be able to enjoy my laurels for long. A few months later I received my draft notice in the mail. When I went to the local draft board, the secretary took one look at me and asked, "Who in the world sent you in here?" as if I should feel bad for doing my duty. Unabashed, I told her I had received the notice in the mail and "Here I am." She replied that there was no use in wasting the doctor's time by sending me into his office; then she simply stamped a big 4-F on the card and sent me on my way. I thought they were making fun of me with the 4-F, referencing my height of about four feet—but that was simply the draft designation for a candidate considered "medically unfit."

I was twenty-six years old by this time, and too full of vim and vinegar to settle for that answer. My next stop was the army recruiting office, where I asked if I would be a good candidate for an interpreter. I thought my ability to speak and write German fluently would be an advantage on the European front. At the time, though, they were quite picky and only took interpreters who could speak four languages. The colonel I spoke to quickly declared there would be no place for me—unless the army "started enlisting mascots." Well, I knew the army's mascot was the mule—and the colonel was filling that profile quite nicely.

The navy recruiting office staff was much nicer and more accommodating. I spoke with a Lieutenant junior-grade Goldenson and a chief boatswain's mate who worked in the office. I told them that I knew they needed chefs (mess cooks) on the submarines, and that I could easily fit in all of those small spaces. I could cook quite well with minimal ingredients, and being rather fond of cleanliness figured I could clean up any navy mess!

The chief appreciated my enthusiasm but explained that everyone on board also manned a battle station—I'd have to be able to reach everything to be effective when the general quarters alarm was sounded. The chef's battle station also served as the torpedo room. I asked about the small mosquito boats, but they said the gun mounts would also be too hard for me to reach. Of all the services I tried to enlist with, though, the United States Navy was the most empathetic and courteous. They even suggested other areas in which I could help out in the war effort. I guess that is why, more than sixty years later, I chose to work with the navy again— for this book, anyway.

One of the navy's suggestions was that I try the various factories that were building bombers. Many of my friends who were little people, such as Munchkin Soldier Lewis Croft, were working in such factories, where they could get into small places that the larger men could not. I was determined to find something I could do to help out.

Gas rationing was in effect throughout the war, and its impact could be felt in all aspects of life. Many people chose to walk to work instead of driving (today it is called "exercising") and long-distance traveling was usually out of the question. I did not have enough gas to finish my weekly sales route, so I covered one half in one week and the remaining half in the following week. The intervals between the routes gave me time to write Marie more frequently. The best part of any week, or day, would be receiving correspondence from her. One of her kind and sweet letters was worth more to me than a hundred rations of sugar!

I found another way to utilize my free time after a visit to the Escanaba airport. I learned that, due to the war, flying instructors were willing to give lessons to anyone who applied. It was not too hard for me to sign up for one of the available slots, and they welcomed my tuition. Before I knew it I was fulfilling my boyhood ambition; I was hooked and started taking as many lessons as I could.

The plane I flew was a small two-seater, and though my short stature made operating a car more difficult, here the opposite was true. At that time pilots were required to wear parachutes on every flight, just as sportsmen are required to wear life vests on fishing boats. Most private planes did not have room for strapping on the parachute like a backpack, so standard procedure was to sit on it. This just made things easier for me, giving me a full, unimpeded panoramic view out of the windows. Another stroke of luck was that most of the aircraft's controls were on the throttles, so I had no cumbersome pedals to worry about.

MEINHARDT RAABE—"I'm a rattling good territory opener. After a single call customers recognize me years later. Do you know any salesman who's sure of being remembered that long?"

This is the single-engine plane I used to open up new territories in Escanaba, Michigan, for Oscar Mayer during World War II.

I continued making my normal runs for Oscar Mayer by car during the week, while honing my flying skills on the weekends and thinking that the plane would certainly speed up certain runs for the company. The planes burned fuel, too, but they did not need nearly as much as my car did to cover the same ground. I figured I could not only better my time on my existing runs, but extend my territory even farther.

One of the happiest days in my life was when I had accumulated enough flight hours to qualify for my private pilot's license. Getting that license would mean that I could fly solo anytime I liked. It would be one area in which I would not have to live by anyone else's leave. I felt I was on top of the world—and, in a way, I was. It would be a lie to say I didn't feel a sense of irony when I was able to soar far above—and then look down upon—the society of the mid-twentieth century that had, for the most part, always looked down upon me. I do not believe in poor winners; I just wanted to be productive and gain respect for doing a man-sized job.

This is not as nice as the planes I flew during the war, but it still fits me just fine.

Legally, however, I wouldn't be allowed to soar solo until I'd actually obtained my private pilot's license. Getting my driver's license had been difficult, but that was nothing compared to what I was in for now. When my instructors felt I was ready, I set up an appointment with a Civil Aeronautics inspector for a test flight. The inspector, Mr. Crites, met me at the Escanaba airport, and without too much ado we headed out for an assortment of test sorties. I did everything he asked, yet when the day was done he did not sign my ticket—nor did he give me any indication of what I might have done wrong.

Undaunted, I kept up with my weekend lessons and set up another test a few months later. Mr. Crites returned, and still seemed to be a rather deadpan type of person. "Ready?" he asked rhetorically, then we headed out. It was winter and a foot of snow had recently fallen; though the airport had been plowed, we had to take a plane equipped with skis for landing. During the flight, Mr. Crites told me to demonstrate an emergency landing. The protocol in the Upper Michigan woodland area was to look for a body of water, because you

can always plunk down in a lake without wrecking the plane or yourself, as you would by hitting trees, for example.

I sat the plane down without any trouble on Lake Michigan—which, like an ocean, is so large that you cannot begin to see across it. Flying off the frigid lake was pretty easy, since all I had to do was point into the wind and push the throttle forward—no waiting for a plane ahead of me on the runway or an all-clear from an air-control tower.

Our airport was only five blocks from the lake, and as we flew back to the runway Mr. Crites diverted me to make a spot landing—to come down with all three wheels inside a 300-foot circle painted on the runway. No hops or jumps are allowed. It was the ultimate, and final, test.

Mr. Crites made me sit around for three hours before finally signing my ticket. However, he did admit that the first time we had flown together he did not have the security of mind to sign a license for someone so small. In the following weeks, he had done his research, but he had found no rule or hindrance against my height. I respected his honesty and thought it took a lot of integrity to not only admit his original bias, but to have an open mind once he had learned that my height did not prevent me from obtaining a license. So, shortly before Thanksgiving 1944, I became "properly qualified to exercise the privileges of a private pilot" and to fly high with all the other turkeys.

Once I had obtained my license, I immediately cut down on my weekend flights, to save my fuel rations. My rationale was that when I had saved enough of them I could fly down to Akron and surprise Marie for Christmas—and that is exactly what I did.

The trip took two legs and a lot of planning, but it was all worthwhile when I touched down and saw Marie standing outside the little airport waiting for me. She warmed me up with a little hug and her big smile . . . ahhh, Christmas really did seem like the most wonderful time of the year!

Marie was still working as a cigarette girl at the Mayflower Hotel. She met a lot of young servicemen who were going through Ohio on leave or heading back to their bases. It seemed that one of these young men, not having close friends or family himself, had timidly asked Marie whether he could write to her when he was overseas, so that he would have some connection to the States. She felt genuinely moved by his request and told him to send her his address once he finally got wherever he was going. She could see how that made a difference in his face as he said good-bye and prepared to ship out.

Not too long after she started writing the first soldier, another one asked her to do the same thing; she accepted again. Each time I wrote her, it seemed her list of soldier and sailor pen pals had increased. She later told me that at one time during the war she was corresponding with no fewer than eighteen servicemen. "I just could not turn any of those brave boys down," she told me. "I would have written every sailor and soldier if I could have. Many of them would stop writing abruptly, and after a few weeks I knew what had happened. Those were the bad days, and I would read their old letters and cry, thinking about them." Marie's great capacity for love and friendship toward everyone was just one of a million reasons I found myself falling deeper in love with her every day.

Christmas ended, and I headed back up to Michigan just in time to see 1945 begin. Around the second or third weekend in January while at the Escanaba airport, I overheard the manager talking to someone about the local Civil Air Patrol station. I had not heard of the Civil Air Patrol, or CAP, until that moment, but I became very interested in it. The organization is equivalent to the National Guard and provides coastal defense along with performing inland rescue missions. During the war the CAP also prepared a lot of

I was dashing in my Civil Air Patrol uniform.

young men for their eventual entry into the Army Air Corps, and these instructing jobs really interested me. Back then *everyone* helped out and supported the war effort, but this might finally enable me to help out in a somewhat more official capacity.

I decided to visit the Wisconsin chapter CAP station and inquire about any positions. It was a long shot and I was not looking forward to another rejection, but my twenty-nine-year-old skin was thicker than an elephant's.

To my surprise, my experience at the CAP station was far different than my other job applications. Many of the local pilots had already heard of me, and I was welcomed right away. I was accepted in the position of ground instructor and immediately began teaching navigation and meteorology to the young students. Most of these kids either felt their army draft numbers were coming up or were volunteers who wanted to have a little choice in which service they joined.

These youngsters often looked at me quizzically, probably wondering, "Why is a child teaching us these subjects?" I joked that I was their ground instructor by virtue of my proximity to it—and that seemed to break the ice a little bit for them. These students were determined to soak up as much information as they could and did not care if their instructor was *wunderkind*, waif, or what-have-you.

I learned that the CAP had begun to form back in 1938, when I was still in the Land of Munchkins. The dominance of the German Air Force, the *Luftwaffe*, worried many Americans, and a better air-defense force was needed to protect our borders. The Civil Air Patrol officially came into existence on December 1, 1941—a week before the Japanese air attack at Pearl Harbor. The Office of Civilian Defense that was headed by former New York Mayor Fiorello La Guardia first controlled the organization.

Members of the CAP were known as the Flying Minutemen—so maybe that meant I was a *minute* minuteman? The missions were broken down into coastal patrol, search, and rescue within the United States; cargo flights to transfer critical material to military personnel; and even towing targets for the Army Air Corps' practice shooting— not exactly the safest mission, since the gunners were all novice shooters.

Our insignia—a blue disk behind a superimposed isosceles triangle with a red, three-bladed propeller inside—was placed on the wings and fuselages of our aircraft and was worn on our uniforms. The coastal patrol division omitted the red propeller from its insignia, to avoid confusion with the Japanese emblem of the rising sun. (If the wrong person thought a CAP plane was a "Jap" plane, then it would probably end up a scrap plane!)

Although I was not a flight instructor for the students, I did take a few of these kids up in the air on the weekends, in the private plane I sometimes rented. Their insatiable curiosity and love of the air was contagious. I was happy and proud to have the honor of working with these bright young men.

The knowledge that these students gained in the CAP gave them a leg up with the army recruiters. Since the prospective recruits could speak the lingo, instead of going directly to the ground-pounders (infantry), they would have a good shot at flying in the Army Air Corps. *All* of my students were successfully placed in the Army Air Corps when they volunteered or were officially drafted. That has always given me a deep sense of satisfaction, and I'm so thankful that I was able to help in the war effort in even the most nominal way.

Not long before I had joined the Civil Air Patrol, it had been officially placed under the tactical command of the War Department, on April 23, 1943. This was a few years before the United States Air Force was officially established as a separate branch of the armed forces, on September 18, 1947. Prior to this time, the only military combatant air force had been the Army's Air Corps branch. The huge build-up of American aviation personnel and planes during the war and afterward, and the remnants of the Army Air Corps, formed the new Army Air Force.

The Civil Air Patrol became an auxiliary of the Army Air Forces in no small part due to CAP's exemplary record. The organization flew more than half a million hours and rescued hundreds of plane-crash victims. It sank two German submarines and deterred many more— first with mock attack formations (before the planes were

This is my original CAP patch from the 1940s.

My Civil Air Patrol membership card showed that I was a member of the Camp Sauganash Squadron in Chicago.

outfitted with weapons) and later with real attacks and armament.

Civil Air Patrol historian Robert E. Neprud's book *Flying Minute Men* explains why the German U-boats withdrew from the U.S. coastal waters early in 1943. The book includes a translated quote from a high-ranking Nazi naval officer who declared, "It was because of those damned little red-and-yellow planes!" Believe me, this sounds more formidable out loud and in German.

Not long after signing up with the Civil Air Patrol, I received a federal identification card. All members of the armed forces were required to carry these at all times. Having the card allowed me to enter any military base in the country.

The only problem I encountered was that government personnel were also required to be in uniform when entering the installations. Unfortunately, the army, navy, and marines didn't make a uniform in my size—this was long before "big and small" stores were thought of. I finally bought a Boy Scout uniform so I could "be prepared" and affixed my insignia to that new G.I. garb. My idea worked, and I was able to enter military bases frequently throughout the war.

During the war, our Escanaba Civil Air Patrol station was pinch-hitting for the Forest Patrol and Coast Guard search-and-rescue units. (The Coast Guard is normally part of the Department of Transportation but becomes part of the Department of Defense during wartime.) We were in charge of taking care of local search-and-rescue emergencies, on land or sea. Since I was still working for Oscar Mayer during the week and the CAP was a volunteer force, I could only dedicate my weekends to the unit.

The only rescue mission in which our unit participated happened one spring. Ice fishing is a common wintertime activity in Michigan. A hole is dug through the ice with an auger, then a shanty structure is built around the hole for protection from the elements. A group of men and a boy were ice fishing on the Bay de Noc, the bay closest to Wisconsin, the Michigan Upper Peninsula's western neighbor. They became stranded when the chunk of ice where they were fishing broke off and started floating out into Lake Michigan, propelled by a strong eastern wind.

An older member of our unit owned his own plane, and when I received the mayday call over the emergency radio circuit we were required to monitor, he was the first, and only, person whom I contacted. He was able to land on that iceberg and pick up the fishermen, one at a time—starting with the boy. It was a good catch for us that day, and the only "one" that got away was the iceberg itself.

Everyone has a big-fish story and I am no exception. Michigan is an angler's paradise, and I occasionally went fishing during the nonwinter months when I lived in Escanaba. One such trip even made the headlines in the local paper, *The Escanaba Daily Press*. While fishing in the Garden Bay with the twelve-year-old son of one of my local customers, I got a bite from a twenty-two pound northern pike.

Landing him was hard—and picking him up was even harder when we were finally *on* land. I was roughly fifty-four inches tall at the time and the pike was forty-two inches long! Just to lift him up off the ground took every ounce of strength I had. It would have been merely another tall tale by a short person . . . if I had not had the photo in the paper to prove it. My catch was entered in the *Daily Press* fishing contest, but it didn't win. I guess that proved the old adage (one that I knew very well): There is always a bigger fish!

I liked living in Escanaba but was relieved when the company transferred me back to Chicago. With the war still raging in the Japanese theater, gas rationing had kept me from seeing Marie, and it was becoming harder and harder to be away from her. Our separation due to the war made me realize how much I truly loved her, and that something would need to be done soon in order not to lose her.

The one that didn't get away!

In Chicago I joined the local Civilian Air Patrol squadron at Camp Sauganash, in April 1945, volunteering as a part-time ground instructor in the evenings while working for Oscar Mayer during the day. One day the commanding officer, a navy rear admiral of the Glenview Naval Air Station, stopped in at our unit unannounced. Everyone scrambled to attention and fumbled around in the way that is common when a flag-level officer visits your command. Luckily, he was bearing only good tidings: "Any of you gentlemen who has a license and is serving as an instructor is welcome to come up to my base to use the Link trainers," he offered. These were used for "blind" flying instruction (flying by instrumentation only) and were operated by the WAVES (Women Accepted for Volunteer Emergency Service) on the base. I headed up there, eventually logging more than twenty-five hours of flight time in the Link trainers, courtesy of the wonderful WAVES and the United States Navy.

A significant tidbit about my role in the Civil Air Patrol is that it gave me the distinction of being the smallest pilot in uniform during World War II. I ended up flying every type of single-engine airplane made at that time—on wheels, skis, and floats!

The Wienermobile driver, Bill Dozier, and I visited a Philadelphia fairground and many other hot spots.

On August 6, 1945, a single American plane ended the war started by many Japanese aircraft: Colonel Paul Tibbits and his crew on board the *Enola Gay* dropped the atomic bomb on Hiroshima. The war that had begun on one island ended on another, with one "Little Boy" bomb.

A shock wave of relief that the war was over rippled throughout the United States.

Service members came home by the bus-, car-, and plane-load, looking like the arrivals section of an airport—times infinity. I was relieved to read about the plans for tickertape parades and various homecoming and victory celebrations; our boys would be coming home safely. I was extremely happy for those who made it home and sad for those who had paid the ultimate sacrifice for our freedoms. All of the tearful reunions brought my thoughts drifting back to Marie. I knew then and there that I would marry her.

I was sent back out in the Wienermobile with my new driver, Bill Dozier, who had served as a marine in artillery during the war. He was nice as could be but did not know north from south, so I helped him navigate as we started hitting the big cities, looking for wholesale grocers who might be interested in our shelf item. (The first product that Oscar Mayer started to promote was the canned wieners.) Our route took us to the major food brokers in New York, Pittsburgh, Boston, Cleveland—and, best of all: Akron! During this initial postwar run, I was able to see Marie for the first time since our Christmas together in 1944. It was as if we had never been separated, and we saw each other on a regular basis from then on.

In September 1946 I asked Marie to marry me. I was living in Escanaba again and proposed when she came up to visit me one weekend. She seemed happy but did not give me her answer until she got back to Akron. I was extremely nervous when she gave me a call just after my thirty-first birthday—but all trepidation and fears melted with the sound of her simple and sweet, "Yes." Marie arranged the entire wedding by herself and I began to get the idea that my days of controlling most of the aspects of my life would soon be over—but she was worth it.

We were married in Marie's hometown church in Akron, on December 15, 1946. Our wedding went off without a hitch—except for the two of us—and it was just a great day in every way. The ceremony was not large in numbers, but all of our close family members attended. Both sets of parents were present, as were Marie's brother and sister, and my sister, Marion, and her husband, Clifford. (They had been married before Marie and I met, and I had been one of their groomsman. My Munchkin friend Ruth Duccini had been a bridesmaid.) Marie's father gave her away—luckily, to me—and both of our mothers cried profusely.

December 15, 1946, was a wonderful day.

Our Tom Thumb-themed (or so it must have seemed) wedding had one other pair of little people in attendance: Victor and Gladys (née Farkas) Bump, who were mutual friends of ours from way back and lived in Cleveland at the time. Gladys had been Marie's first little-person friend when they worked for Ike Rose's midget troupe. Victor and I had performed together in the Chicago World's Fair (he was the Good Humor man) and in Cleveland for the Great Lakes Exposition. His specialty was the cornet. Later Leo Singer had asked the Bumps to perform in *The Wizard of Oz,* but they had declined. I've lost touch with them over the years. Eventually, they retired and moved to Austin, Minnesota, and I believe Gladys is still alive and well.

I would never have been able to foresee that Victor, with whom I had first worked more than a decade before in the midget bands, would make our *wedding* bands, but he did just that. He owned a jewelry and watchmaking shop in Cleveland, and knew that Marie and I would love to have specially designed and forged bands for our wedding. Our

rings were simple gold bands, each with a little twist and a little protrusion, a tiny half-heart that when joined with its partner formed a complete heart. This was very special to me because it was Marie who completed me.

Marie and I stayed in the best suite at the Mayflower Hotel before leaving Akron the following day for our honeymoon to Niagara Falls. It was hard to believe that the beautiful cigarette girl who had caught Frank Sinatra's eye was now my wife. As Fred Astaire notes of dancing cheek-to-cheek: I was in heaven!

Marie and I started driving toward New York State the next day. We had a wonderful time heading up there and occasionally stopped for a picnic or just to visit local attractions along the route. When we first saw the expansive panorama of Niagara Falls we were enamored with the splendor of the majestic river and rapids. When we crossed the aptly named Rainbow Bridge, I could not help thinking that Marie and I were in paradise over the rainbow, and any troubles we might have had before melted like lemon drops.

Just married!

Later we headed south to New Orleans, where we spent New Year's Eve. We then moved into a small cottage in Escanaba. This was our first home, though only for our first year of marriage

Late in 1946, just before marrying Marie, I had left the Oscar Mayer Company. After eight years I was weary of constantly being on the road and had been busy courting Marie. Having made good contacts while working in Escanaba during the war, I was offered an executive salesman job by the Chicago-based A. W. Nygren & Associates food brokerage house. I accepted. I ended up selling many products from their food line, but by peddling their midget pickles I became known as the Petite Pickle Peddler.

I did not peddle pickles for long, though, and left the company after less than a year. Wanting to keep traveling, Marie and I spent our first wedding anniversary in Duluth, Minnesota—thanks to a snowstorm we encountered on our way west. We found we liked Duluth so much that we hung around even after the storm had abated—for thirteen months, to be precise!

In 1947 we moved to Wausau, Wisconsin, a city about two hundred miles south of Escanaba. I worked at a local food brokerage and found I was flying less and less—Marie was always worried when I flew and permanently grounded me after a while. . . . Well, that really is not true. Priorities

had simply changed in our new life as a married couple, and we enjoyed spending as much of our free time together as we could. She always made me feel that I could walk on air anyway, so I considered it an upgrade in flight status—not a demotion.

Living closer to Watertown (175 miles to the south) meant that Marie and I could alternate our visits to our respective parents each year during the holidays. I particularly enjoyed visiting Marie's nieces and nephews in Ohio. These average-sized children had an especially close relationship with their little aunt and uncle Raabe, as many children seem to have with little people.

It was not too long before Oscar Mayer offered me another job: to work exclusively as the East Coast Little Oscar, based in Philadelphia, Pennsylvania. Marie figured that without any flying Wienercraft this would be fine, and the move would give us a chance to see more of the East.

Just before leaving Wausau, in 1950, Marie and I attended a unique wedding. Joe Kotalik was another little person whom I knew from the Chicago World's Fair. He was marrying Odette Myrtle Pilkerton. Originally from Tennessee, Odette had worked with Marie in Rose's Royal Midget Troupe and with me at the Chicago Fair—where she first met Joe.

Joe and Myrtle's wedding was big news.

Joe and Myrtle's wedding, at the Holy Rosary Church in Ashley, Pennsylvania, boasted more than two thousand spectators and made all the local papers. Fourteen midgets attended, eight of whom (four couples, including the bride and groom) were members of the wedding party. Marie and I were one of these couples.

The church was filled to capacity, with at least three hundred more watchers lining up on the steps outside the church. Myrtle and Joe didn't seem to mind the fanfare and enjoyed knowing that their wedding would appear not only in local and national newspapers, but in national newsreels.

Odette had toured with the Ziegfeld Follies in 1936 and as an entertainer during the war, performing for our troupes at home. At one time Joe had been a bellboy on a luxury liner that sailed from New York to the West Indies and Central America. During the war he had worked at an aircraft plant in Louisiana. After the war he moved back up to his hometown of Ashley, Pennsylvania, near Wilkes-Barre.

I knew two of the little-people couples: Victor and Gladys Bump, and Eddy A. Kozicki and his wife. Eddy and I were the only former Munchkins at the ceremony. He had been one of the five Fiddlers in *The Wizard of Oz*, and I had not seen him since the film. We enjoyed our unofficial reunion and shared fond reminiscences of the parts we had played more than a decade before.

Not long after the wedding, Marie and I moved to Philadelphia. I was happy to be back with Oscar Mayer because my favorite part of my job had always been being Little Oscar and traveling around in the very striking Wienermobile. Marie wanted to work also, and she signed on with the W. T. Grant clothing store as a cashier.

Marie worked in the Grant store for many years, and one of her more interesting jobs was to watch for shoplifters. Part of her ruse was to rummage through the clothes as if she were a customer, all the while keeping an eye out for suspicious activities. If she thought someone might be stealing, she followed the possible culprit to be sure. The would-be thieves weren't likely to suspect the diminutive detective, and if they did not look at her closely, they most likely thought she was a young girl shopping for clothes. Marie had less-exciting sales positions in the store, but sleuthing was her favorite.

I rejoined Oscar Mayer at a good time. The Wienermobile had been generating a lot of publicity and boosting sales. This encouraged rapid expansion, so the company built additional Wienermobiles, which in turn required more Little Oscars. George Molchan was hired in 1951, and Joe White and Munchkin Jerry Maren in 1953. All were little people. I spent a lot of time working with George and

enjoyed having a protégé. He ended up working more consecutive years than any of the seven other Little Oscars—just shy of twenty-five. That topped me, though I had accumulated a total of twenty-nine years in my two stints with the company.

The Wiener Guild: I'm posing with Joe White, George Molchan, and Jerry Maren, all of whom I trained to be proper Little Oscars. I stayed on the East Coast, Jerry took the West Coast, and George and Joe traveled across the country.

Today's Wienermobile can travel up to ninety miles per hour— but only if there's enough ketchup in the tank.

This was the first time I had seen Jerry since *The Wizard of Oz*, and I had a good time showing him the ropes. Jerry was not in Philadelphia too long before he was sent out to the newly opened Oscar Mayer plant in California, where he had lived since making the film. It turned out to be a great location for publicity, and Jerry hobnobbed with many movie and entertainment stars in the Hollywood area, including my wife's favorite Frank: Sinatra.

With the advent of television as a mainstream medium, I found myself in demand at the local stations, doing promotional spots and commercials. It was fun and was not too hard. I had been doing demonstrations for so many people for so long that the commercials just came naturally to me. When I traveled outside the Philadelphia area in the Wienermobile, I also provided television spots to local stations along our East Coast route.

My most famous Little Oscar publicity picture is still remembered by many, many people.

In the early sixties Marie and I decided we would like to travel more. We purchased a small motor home that was fully equipped with a kitchen and bathroom. The motor home was white with a blue stripe along the side and about twenty-five feet in length. Average-sized people might have found the scaled-down accommodations a slight inconvenience, but for us it was like having a custom-made home that fit our slightly smaller sizes. Everything was within reach for a change—including the apparatus on the driver's side of the vehicle, where I did not need any foot pedal extensions or extra seat cushions.

During our vacation time we packed up the motor home to head out West. We visited Marie's sister in Montana and the Seattle World's Fair in 1962. There was no Midget City, but we enjoyed seeing the new Space Needle and the country's first world's fair since the end of World War II.

Marie and I had a nice life together in Philadelphia. We enjoyed the city and the traveling during our vacations. I decided to further my education and enrolled at nearby Drexel University, working at Oscar Mayer during the day and taking classes in the evening. In 1970, in under two years, I graduated with a master's degree in business administration—go, Drexel Dragons!

Things were going great—or so I thought.

It was during the early 1970s that I began wondering if I was turning into a klutz. I bumped into doors and other objects, but only occasionally, so I did not pay much attention. My clumsiness continued, however, and I noticed that I was having trouble seeing with my left eye. I stubbornly ignored the problem, and eventually my right eye seemed to compensate for the problems in my left—but I had lost my depth perception.

One morning I felt very strange upon waking, as if I had slept on the right side of my face all night, and my right eye was bloodshot. At work I noticed that I was having some trouble with my eye and asked if I could take time off to get it checked out at the hospital. Marie was a little scared because of the problem I had with my left, which had worsened in just a few months. I was extremely sensitive to changes in my good eye, which is why this time I didn't hesitate to see an eye doctor right away.

I called the chief of the ophthalmology department to schedule an appointment that day. The doctor didn't look at my eye for more than two minutes before quickly telling his nurse to call the hospital to reserve the first bed available. Knowing instantly that something was seriously wrong, he arranged for a surgeon to visit me immediately.

The surgeon told me that I had a large tumor in the right side of my head that was pushing on the optic nerve. He said that if it was not removed very soon, I would lose my sight in that eye permanently. I called Marie to break the news; she was soon at my side, and we headed to the hospital together. The following morning they opened up the right side of my skull like a clamshell, excising a large, but benign, growth. The surgery immediately reversed the problem; within a few months the swelling had gone down completely and the vision in my right eye returned to normal. Wearing the puffy Little Oscar chef's hat helped cover up the site of the operation.

I was not so lucky with my left eye. The problem there had been caused by pressure from another tumor, which had subsided on its own—but not before causing permanent damage. At first I was able to discern shapes, then light and dark; but over the years my vision in that eye became worse and worse until I lost sight in it completely, in the early 1980s.

At the time of the surgery, I was fifty-six years old, and I decided to retire from Oscar Mayer. General Foods had just bought out the company anyway, and they didn't really appreciate the value of the Wienermobiles. Most of the older Oscar Mayer employees were laid off or took retirement.

This was not a sad time for me, because I was ready for a job that didn't keep me on the go so much. The Retired Service Personnel (RSP) group, in Philadelphia, assisted retirees who were seeking employment, so I joined the organization and decided to work as a librarian at the state medical hospital. The RSP group paid for my transportation costs, which gave me a nice little boost.

At sixty-five I started working in the Philadelphia school district as a teacher's assistant. I had applied for a regular teaching job but didn't have the teaching certificate that was required. Since it was a little late in the game for me to go back to school all over again, I simply decided to do what I could to help out.

Once I was called into a school by the principal to fill in for a German teacher. They never asked if I had a teaching certificate, and I taught that class for two months. The principal thought I was doing an excellent job; but the school was required by law to provide a licensed teacher, so he gave me a glowing recommendation, suggesting that I help out in the special education program.

I spent the next four years as a special ed assistant and had a wonderful time working with the children.

This was in the early 1980s, when I first started to realize how popular *The Wizard of Oz* film had become in America. I used that to my advantage and brought in pictures of the Lion, Scarecrow, and other characters for the kids to practice coloring. The idea was well received, and parents came to visit me after their kids told them that the Coroner had shown them how to draw *The Wizard of Oz* characters. When the adults first arrived, I thought they might be upset or something—but they wanted my autograph because they had grown up with the film themselves. I felt very flattered, but somewhat old, too! Unfortunately, I hit the mandatory retirement age of seventy in 1985 and was not able to help out at the schools anymore.

Deciding to take an overseas trip, Marie and I flew to Frankfurt, Germany, that summer. We went on to Athens, Greece, for a few days before arriving in Egypt. It was amazing to see the Great Pyramids.

Traveling to Jordan proved to be the highlight of our trip. We visited the ancient ruins of Petra, a city that was carved out of stone in the first century and is located at the bottom of a steep canyon. Many tourists rode camels to the bottom of the gorge, but after Marie saw one woman fall off her mount, she declared, "No, not for me!"

Abiding by her wishes, we walked. As we made our pleasant descent down the canyon, we could see the layers of colored rock. The buildings were fascinating to view, and quite advanced for a civilization of that time.

Marie and I had barely returned home from our overseas trip when we packed up the motor home to head for Idaho. The Little People of America was holding its national convention out there. I liked to attend those gatherings whenever possible, to see my old friends and hopefully make some new acquaintances, too.

However, not long after arriving in Idaho we were still on the freeway when a moose jumped out in front of our motor home. I slammed on the brakes, but could not avoid hitting him. Marie and I were okay, but I was not sure about the moose. As I got out, I saw him limp off the road, and I was glad he was not seriously hurt—but that was more than I could say for our motor home.

The entire front of the vehicle was dented and the engine was no longer operable. We had to be towed to town to see what the mechanic would say. The cost of repairs turned out to be more than the motor home itself was worth.

We were able to attend the convention for a day, thanks to some friends at the event who gave us a ride, but we left as soon as arrangements were made to have our vehicle shipped back to Philadelphia on a flatbed truck. We took a bus home to Philly, and that was the end of our motor home—and of our days exploring nature.

Marie and I posed in the 1950s, just before we got our motor home.

CHAPTER ELEVEN

Return to Oz

ZOOMING AROUND THE COUNTRY IN OUR motor home had been a lot of fun, but as we advanced in age we decided to move away from Philadelphia and return to life on the farm—not the kind of farm I had grown up on in Wisconsin, or Dorothy Gale had called home in Kansas, but a retirement community in the village of Penney Farms, Florida.

Marie and I had visited Penney Farms before our overseas vacation and had decided it would be the ideal place to retire. Retail store magnate J. C. Penney had founded the community in memory of his parents, back in 1926, and its residents made up the majority of the village's population. Because J. C.'s dad had been a minister, it had originally catered to Christian laypeople, or to those who had previously served in the ministry. That was not a requirement when we moved in, but a lot of people living there had formerly worked as priests and ministers.

Part of the deal with the retirement community was that members would help out in certain areas on a volunteer basis if they were physically able. Marie and I took horticulture classes at a local school and were able to obtain our degrees as master gardeners. I had also studied horticulture at Drexel University, but I enjoyed going to classes with Marie. She was very happy when she got her horticulture degree—because then she knew how to both sew *and* sow!

We used our love of plants to help out with landscaping the community grounds, which were fairly expansive. Marie worked mainly with the flower beds and I worked on landscaping the trees and shrubberies. We were called on many times for our services; though Marie might have been slightly mature for a flower child, at least she was not known as the Wee Tree Man like I was!

When Marie and I moved into Penney Farms in the spring of 1986, we immediately knew we had made the right decision. Everyone was very polite, and the community had a nice tucked-away quality—not unlike Munchkinland. We chose a low-roofed, single-story bungalow, on Studio Road (an appropriate choice for me, I suppose), and lived there for more than a decade. Visitors would often note that the thigh-high peephole in our front door gave our identity away, but I did not post any telltale exterior *Oz* memorabilia.

We made ourselves right at home, and before growing any permanent roots of our own, we made sure to plant seeds in our backyard so that a nice garden would be ready by the summertime.

Marie was well known for her brisk early constitutions around the community grounds. Despite her lack of height she would fly by average-sized residents, but always offered a kind word or two before leaving them in the dust. I went with her sometimes, but mostly stayed in and read the latest newspaper headlines. I would be sure that her tea was ready by the time she returned.

Marie and I kept up to date about the ever-growing *Oz* fervor and fan base. We occasionally saw the film on its annual television airing, but we were unprepared for the *Oz* storm that began to hit the country, and the world, full force, in the late 1980s. The events that led up to the annual viewing of *The Wizard of Oz* had been set in motion years before.

I did not work in any world's fairs after *The Wizard of Oz*, but I did visit the New York World's Fair in 1939 (so did Judy Garland and Mickey Rooney, though I did not see them), where I first noted a fairly new invention, the television.

These panels are from a special oversized comic adaptation of The Wizard of Oz *by Marvel Comics and DC Comics—their first collaboration. It was published in 1975. The illustrations of me are by comic-art legend John Buscema.*

19

President Franklin Delano Roosevelt conducted the opening ceremonies on April 30, which were caught on film, making him the first president to be televised.

Television really took hold in the late 1940s and was a common household accessory by the 1950s. CBS had approached MGM Studios about leasing some of its films for national broadcasting. The number-one pick was *Gone with the Wind*, but MGM refused to lease or release it. The studio did, however, let CBS have its second choice: *The Wizard of Oz*. MGM agreed to temporarily lease the rights

to that movie, and CBS first acquired the contract on July 25, 1956.

Oz had just been rereleased in the theaters for a second time the previous year and had not fared quite as well as the studio executives thought it would. Still, it brought in close to a half million dollars. Adding that to earnings from the first rerelease, in 1949, brought the grand total to two million dollars.

The deal with CBS made *The Wizard of Oz* the first MGM film to be sold to a television network and netted

MGM a quarter million dollars. The Cowardly Lion himself, Bert Lahr, and Judy Garland's older daughter, ten-year-old Liza Minnelli, hosted the TV world premiere. Overall, more than 50 percent of the nation's households that were watching television during that time slot tuned in for the film. Its incredible run had begun.

The movie had nine annual showings on CBS, hosted by the likes of Dick Van Dyke and Danny Kaye, before NBC outbid it for the screening rights. The film's ability to command more and more money for exclusive screening rights was another sign of its growing popularity—and this was when it was only shown on black-and-white TV!

The death of Judy Garland, on June 22, 1969, prompted numerous tributes to the late actress, and that year's *Oz* telecast was made extra special out of respect for her memory. The Singer Company (the sewing machine manufacturer—not Leo's famed midget troupe) joined forces with NBC as the sponsor of *The Wizard of Oz*, creating a campaign program that was more aggressive and costly than those of the original 1939 release and 1949 rerelease combined: just over two million dollars.

The film gained worldwide popularity as it was translated and played in more and more overseas theaters. CBS recaptured the screening rights in 1976, holding them until the advent of videotapes and players in the late 1980s. MGM released the movie on video in 1980, then in 1985, and again in 1988. The biggest surge in videotape sales was a year later, during the film's fiftieth-anniversary commemoration.

In 1989 I was at the Culver City Filmland Center Building with Jack Haley Jr. to kick off the MGM/United Artists home video release of *The Wizard of Oz*. This golden jubilee was unbelievable; the film seemed to pop out of the past, into the realm of pop culture, overnight. The fiftieth-anniversary videotape was the first to show the film as it originally had appeared in 1939. Restored from a Technicolor print, the video contained an original theater trailer and other rare footage. My personal friend author John Fricke wrote an elaborate thirty-two-page illustrated booklet that accompanied the videotape. This became the fifth-top-selling video in 1989—a time when videotape sales were at their peak.

Oz-related events were held all over the country that year, and Marie and I made no fewer than sixteen separate trips during that period. Some festivals had been occurring for years and others were in their infancy.

The International Wizard of Oz Club had been holding regional festivals for more than twenty years by 1989. These celebrated all things Oz—related to the book as much as to the film. In 1970, I attended one of these conventions in

Pennsylvania. It was advertised as the International Wizard of Oz Club's annual Munchkin Convention. I showed up mistakenly expecting to see a lot of other Munchkins from the film. I have never read the original *The Wonderful Wizard of Oz* book, but at the convention I quickly learned that the fantasy land is divided up into four main quadrants based on the cardinal directions of north, south, east, and west.

The convention was named after the region in Oz mythology, not after the little people who inhabit it. Munchkinland was in the east of Oz, and Pennsylvania is certainly pretty far east in the U. S. The International Wizard of Oz Club holds several annual gatherings—such as the Winkie Convention, out west in California. (The Winkies were the Wicked Witch of the West's loyal guards. They all lived in Winkie Country—located, naturally, in the western section of Oz.) This geographic division made sense to me because I was able to make the connections with the witches in the film. Now I finally knew why the Wicked Witch of the East had been killed by Dorothy's fallen farmhouse in the eastern land of the Munchkins.

The Madame Alexander Doll Company created this eight-inch-tall version of my Munchkin Coroner character, as well as a five-inch version.

Jeane LaBarbera, Nita Krebs (seated), Karl Slover, Gus Wayne, Tiny Doll, and I pose like elves inside the trunk of this tree for People *magazine. We were all of the surviving "Florida Munchkins," celebrating the fiftieth anniversary of the movie.*

In spite of my initial confusion, everyone was very happy to see me at the convention. To the best of my knowledge this was the club's third or fourth annual assembly, and I was the first real Munchkin ever to attend. In July 2004 I attended the thirty-seventh annual Munchkin Convention, with fellow Munchkin Lewis Croft, a Soldier in the *Oz* film.

Along with being the first group to hold annual *Wizard of Oz*-themed conventions, the International Wizard of Oz Club publishes a quarterly magazine, completely dedicated to everything Oz, titled *The Baum Bugle*. I became the first card-carrying Munchkin member of this club and subscriber to the periodical.

Newer Oz-themed festivals began springing up in the late 1970s and early 1980s, in such cities as Chittenango, New York (L. Frank Baum's birthplace), and Chesterton, Indiana. They have a common thread of celebrating Oz and have grown into annually held events. I use the term "newer" loosely, since most of these are past the quarter-century mark already!

My favorite photo shoot was for *People* magazine, in 1989. It reunited all of the Munchkins who lived in Florida for a feature story about the film. Tiny Doll, Nita Krebs, Jeane LaBarbera, Karl Slover, Gus Wayne, and I were positioned inside the mouth of a large fiberglass tree that was a prop on a miniature golf course in Sarasota. Sadly, Karl and I are the only surviving Munchkins from that picture.

Later that year members of an Orlando area community college theater company contacted me. They had just finished their stage production of *The Wizard of Oz* and offered to give me their Munchkin Coroner's costume. It had been made for a child and fit me perfectly when I tried it on. I accepted their kind offer, becoming one of the first Munchkins to wear a replica of his or her original *Oz* costume to public appearances. The response was so overwhelmingly positive that I still wear a replica of my costume to conventions and for appearances.

Since 1975 the Judy Garland Festival, or JudyFest as it is commonly called, has been held every June in Grand Rapids, Minnesota. This, her birthplace, is also the location of the Judy Garland Museum. Attached to the museum is the Garland house, which was moved to its current site in 1994 and fully restored in 1996. The museum, which boasts the largest collection of Judy Garland memorabilia in the world, features the carriage that carried Dorothy and company through the Emerald City in *The Wizard of Oz*. But before it helped them "laugh the day away" there, it had been owned by none other than Abraham Lincoln—honest!

The first Munchkin reunion was held at the fifteenth annual JudyFest, in June 1990. All told, we numbered thirteen—the largest group of Munchkins that had ever been assembled since 1938. In most of the photographs taken during this event, I was in the anchor position at the end of our lineup as number thirteen. Whether this was due to my being the tallest or was just a serendipitous (or superstitious) placement of the Coroner, I am not sure!

What I *am* sure of is that the JudyFest reunion tally was surpassed just four months later, at the Oztoberfest held in Liberal, Kansas, with the addition of Munchkin Nels Nelson to our group. That record can never be broken, since only nine Munchkins remain on this side of the rainbow.

Liberal boasts its own yellow brick road, leading up to a full-sized replica of the Gale family farmhouse, copied from the film. Many of the bricks were personalized with names of the munificent donors, and all of the Munchkin actors had bricks named in their honor. Mine is not too far from the entrance to the farmhouse—which is fitting since, to the best of my Munchkin medical knowledge, it was the *house* that killed the Wicked Witch of the East.

L. Frank Baum's boyhood home, Chittenango, New York, has held its annual OzFest since May 1979 (he was born and died in May). I read about the festival just after Marie and I moved to Penney Farms, and I wrote the area chamber of commerce inquiring whether I could visit as a guest. I did not get an answer in time to attend that year's convention. But as fate would have it, hearing that I had written to Chittenango, the Syracuse Chamber of Commerce asked if I would like to be a guest in the St. Patrick's Day Parade the following year. Chittenango, fifteen miles east of Syracuse, was sponsoring an *Oz*-themed float, which I did, indeed, ride on. The Chittenango Oz festival organizers invited me the following year with open arms, and have extended their invitation annually since. I was OzFest's first authentic Munchkin guest and religiously attended the festival for sixteen years, until in May 2003 my own broken arm broke my streak of seventeen consecutive appearances. (I returned in 2004.)

The Mayor of Munchkinland had been a friend of mine, of course, but it was the mayor of Chittenango who

Thirteen of the surviving Munchkins gathered in Grand Rapids, Minnesota, the birthplace of Judy Garland, for the 1990 JudyFest. Here are Jeane LaBarbera, Nita Krebs, Margaret Pellegrini, Ruth Duccini, Karl Slover, Jerry Maren, Emil Kranzler, Fern Formica, Betty Tanner, Gus Wayne, Clarence Swensen, Lewis Croft, and me.

Karl Slover, Ruth Duccini, Clarence Swensen, Margaret Pellegrini, Jerry Maren, and I in Chittenago, New York. We're posing in the Meinhardt Raabe Garden, which the city named for me and my interest in horticulture.

honored me by naming the garden behind the village hall the Meinhardt Raabe Garden. Luckily, no one thought it strange to name such a beautiful little land of the living after a coroner.

None of the stars from *The Wizard of Oz* lived long enough to participate in the movie's fiftieth anniversary. However, I was able to see Margaret Hamilton a second and final time, a few years before her death in 1985. When I was living in Philadelphia, a local museum mounted a series of programs about costume and makeup. The organizers invited Margaret to be their featured guest and asked me to be the second onstage speaker.

The questions quickly became more and more geared toward specific events from the filming of *The Wizard of Oz*, rather than the general topics of costume and makeup. The emcee and standing-room-only crowd asked us about everything *Oz*-related, and we took turns answering the questions. Margaret and I had a great time catching up, and

the audience thought the pairing of the Wicked Witch and the Munchkin Coroner was very funny. It was a great event, with Margaret proving to be just as kind and thoughtful as she had been more than forty years earlier.

In May 1989 the Disney-MGM Studios theme park debuted in Orlando, Florida. The centerpiece of the park was a recreation of Grauman's Chinese Theatre, complete with cement handprints from real, contemporary stars of Hollywood. Inside the theater was the Great Movie Ride, with the world's only animatronic Munchkinland, complete with our little houses and even the Sleepy Head nest. Disney also had one of the pairs of ruby slippers that were worn in *The Wizard of Oz*, on loan from a private collection. A few of the Florida Munchkins were given a special tour of the ride in conjunction with their *Oz* exhibit and were able to hold the ruby slippers. Disney's Munchkinland was not as large as ours had been at MGM, of course, but the mechanical Wicked Witch certainly looked green and mean!

In 1990 Olive Brasko-Wayne, Karl Slover, Jeane LaBarbera, and Marie and I posed in front of the Disney-MGM Studios Great Movie Ride. The ride has a minimuseum inside, and this original pair of ruby slippers was on display there.

These authentic prop ruby slippers were worth a pittance compared to the pair made by the House of Harry Winston in 1989. Those featured more than fifty carats of diamonds and 4,600 rubies. Valued at more than three million dollars, the shoes would tap out many a fortune; the magical three taps would certainly spirit home the wearer in style!

The fiftieth-anniversary celebration continued through 1990. In that year the United States Postal Service unveiled a series of four first-class stamps commemorating classic MGM films from 1939: *Gone with the Wind, Beau Geste, Stagecoach,* and, of course, *The Wizard of Oz.* The stamps were all painted by Thomas Blackshear, who perfectly captured the emotion behind Judy Garland's famous pose as Dorothy holding Toto in her arms.

The last of the movie's golden-jubilee events occurred on December 10, 1990, when the L. Frank Baum biography *The Dreamer of Oz* debuted on television, starring John Ritter as Baum and Annette O'Toole as his wife, Maud. It was a wonderful life history and featured a former Munchkin—Jerry Maren—whose wife, Elizabeth, also appeared. Dr. Robert Baum, L. Frank Baum's great-grandson; his wife, Clare; and their two daughters, Carolyn and Christine, all played townspeople. Dr. Baum lent many of his family's original books for the film—including a rare first edition of *The Wonderful Wizard of Oz.* All copies of this edition are rare, of course, but this one was especially so since it had belonged to the author himself. Talk about authentic props!

Marie and I celebrated our fiftieth wedding anniversary at the Penney Farms Memorial Chapel on December 15, 1996.

We had walked beside each other for many miles in life, with both of our little half steps making up a whole. We renewed our vows that day and looked forward to another fifty years together. I knew we might fall a little short of that goal—but I did not know we would fall forty-nine years short.

A collision on a frigid October morning in 1997 ended that dream. Our station wagon and a large van collided at a stop sign near Penney Farms. Everything happened so quickly that I did not have a chance to say good-bye to Marie before the paramedics rushed her thirty miles north, to the University Hospital in Jacksonville, which was better equipped for serious trauma. I was taken to a closer hospital in Green Cove Springs.

I had suffered a large gash on my head, so was in and out of consciousness for the first day. I didn't know where Marie was or how she was doing, and was growing anxious and irritable. At last I received the fateful call from one of her doctors: He told me she had died the day of the accident. My wife was my life, and in a way both of our hearts stopped beating on that cold, empty Wednesday.

Weeks of physical therapy prevented me from even having the closure of attending Marie's funeral services. She was buried in our family plot up near Watertown, Wisconsin, and my sister, Marion, made the arrangements.

Vera S. Boyd, a good friend of ours at Penney Farms, delivered a eulogy at "our" chapel there. This is what Vera said about my lovely Marie:

"Little person Marie Raabe, wife of our *Wizard of Oz* Munchkin, will be greatly missed at the Penney Retirement

Community. She and her husband, Raabe, were intelligent, courageous, and greatly enriched our community. Marie had long overcome prejudice against her size, and she sparkled with love and joy as she walked briskly around the campus early each morning.

"She had a sweet and melodious voice, and our exceptionally fine choir will miss her singing as she sat on the front row each Sunday. Dr. Tappan, music director, had two small robes custom-made for her. She was a behind-the-scenes person, needing no praise, just willing to do with all her might that which her tiny hands found to do. She took charge of selling shoes at rummage, acted in many plays and skits, helped with the Tender Loving Care work, and ordered and delivered pecans for all of us.

"The postmistress stated that Marie made her feel good every time she came in the post office. She just never lost her enthusiasm, and at age eighty-two delighted in whatever she did. She and Raabe gave many, many hours to the schoolchildren in the county, and the children wept at the news of this tragedy. Because of her gigantic stature of character and goodness, we, who were much taller, had to look up to her—a lovely, miniature child of God and example of His grace."

Life without Marie has been the hardest road of all for me to follow. But another road—one made of yellow brick—gave me at least one reason to keep going. The fans of the The Wizard of Oz, especially the children, really provided me with a lot of comfort, so I decided to attend Oz festivals in Chittenango and Chesterton the following June and September 1998. That year marked the sixtieth anniversary of the movie's initial release, and it was once again in theaters across the country.

The film had been digitally remastered, and the clarity and color of the final version were breathtaking. When I saw this crisp and vivid film version on the big screen with state-of-the-art surround sound for the first time, I felt as if I were back on the Munchkinland set. The movie was released on November 6, 1998, right before the Thanksgiving and Christmas holidays—promoted by a new theater poster.

If you have never seen this Warner Bros. DVD, then you have not really seen The Wizard of Oz! Its extra features include The Wonderful Wizard of Oz: The Making of a Movie Classic, hosted by Angela Lansbury and originally shown in 1989; interviews with Jerry Maren and me; and Buddy

Ebsen's rendition of "If I Only Had a Heart." It also shows the 1940 Academy Awards ceremony that was emceed by Bob Hope. He introduced Mickey Rooney who, in turn, presented Judy Garland with a miniature Oscar for her "outstanding performance as a screen juvenile during the past year." This was the only Academy Award that Judy won during her entire career (though she was later nominated twice), and she often playfully quipped that it was her "Munchkin award."

Not many Munchkins survived for the film's sixtieth anniversary, but those of us who were physically able promoted Oz in various theaters. I was contacted by a theater owner in Cherry Hill, New Jersey, to appear as a special guest on the opening night of that 1998 rerelease. The theater was old-fashioned in decor, and the fans were very supportive and appreciative of my appearance.

What has amazed me the most about The Wizard of Oz is that it still continues to grow in popularity. I made an impromptu appearance in October 2003 at the Sing-A-Long Wizard of Oz show at the Enzian Theater, located just north of Orlando, to commemorate the sixty-fifth anniversary of the filming of the Munchkinland sequence. At this interactive show, which began touring the country on December 12, 2002—and at the time of this writing is still on the road—fans dress up as their favorite Oz characters and sing along with the songs in the film. I sat in the balcony next to my coauthor and recited my lines when the show's emcee—who is always dressed in a replica of the Wizard of Oz's costume—came up to introduce me to the audience. It was very enjoyable to see

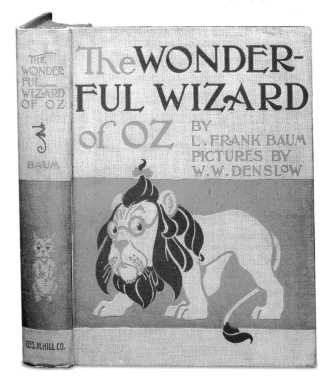

The first edition of The Wonderful Wizard of Oz is a cherished rarity.

the fans' delighted reactions, echoing those of their parents and grandparents back in the 1930s. They seemed very enthusiastic about my coming to the theater that night, and enjoyed being able to see my character up on the big screen—and little old me in my balcony seat watching with them.

The prestigious American Film Institute (AFI) has compiled lists of top films in several categories. These were voted on by a jury of leaders in the creative community: directors, actors, editors, cinematographers, screenwriters, critics, and historians. The AFI 100 Years 100 Movies list was announced in 1998 and contains the top 100 American movies of all time. These were selected from a list of 400 nominated films produced between 1912 and 1996. *The Wizard of Oz* was voted sixth and *Gone with the Wind* came in fourth—these are the only two films from a single year making the top ten. The Institute's list of 100 Heroes & Villains, which ranked the top fifty film heroes and villains of all time, gave the Wicked Witch of the West fourth place. (She trails only Dr. Hannibal Lecter from *The Silence of the Lambs*, Norman Bates from *Psycho*, and Darth Vader from *The Empire Strikes Back*.)

In June 2004, the Institute turned to the top 100 film songs of all time. Judy Garland's immortal "Over the Rainbow" blew away the competition to become the undisputed number one. The Munchkins are also represented at number eighty-two on the list, with "Ding-Dong! The Witch Is Dead." Which old witch? The Wicked Witch of the East, of course—my witch!

I am enjoying *The Wizard of Oz* at its sixty-five year mark, and hope to be around for its seventy-fifth anniversary celebration in 2014 . . . although I will be ninety-eight years old then! I know the movie will still be loved at its centennial celebration in 2039, and even in 2096—the bicentennial year of cinema itself.

I hope that there will be an *Oz* centenarian among the handful of surviving cast members and crew who are around today. At this writing, only nine little people from the film survive, and one of us will have the sad distinction of being "the Last of the Munchkins." I am the oldest of the group, so I doubt it will be me. As Coroner, I have averred enough of us over the rainbow as it is, and I don't care to be the last one standing when the music stops.

Yet with *The Wizard of Oz*, the music never stops. It's safe to assume that somewhere in the world the film is playing at any given moment—so in a way, we will always be alive in the Land of Oz. Ray Bolger thought so: "We do not get any residuals," he explained in a 1979 television interview with fellow cast member Jack Haley. "But we have a better thing than residuals—we have a kind of immortality. And a great pride in being part of an American classic."

The word "Munchkin" has always seemed like knighthood to me. *The Wizard of Oz* filming not only benefited those of us who were there, but all little people throughout the country. The terms "midget" and "dwarf" virtually disappeared, and all of us, regardless of race, sex, or size, were accepted as "Munchkins," period.

Reminiscing about my small association with this American classic has been a journey enjoyable beyond words. I am thankful to every fan who has had a kind word to say about the movie or me. These wonderful people of all ages who remain "young in heart" are those to whom the film's preface is dedicated. I have always striven to live by "kindly philosophy," and that is why this Munchkin Coroner still is excited by the prospect of what lies around the next bend of the ever-winding, never-ending yellow brick road of life.

Marie and I in the early 1990s.

PART TWO

Munchkin Marketing

F ALL THE FILMS MADE IN 1939, *THE WIZARD OF OZ* WAS ONE OF the most costly—so costly, in fact, that the studio executives at MGM occasionally roared at producer Mervyn LeRoy for spending more than $2.75 million to complete the film. Still, the studio, along with its parent company, Loew's Incorporated, was intent on recouping its investment. As a result, MGM spent another $250,000 on the publicity campaign for the movie—an unheard-of figure back in the 1930s.

Howard Dietz, the head of the studio's New York publicity department, spearheaded the overall publicity campaign for the movie. Dietz came up with imaginative poster art and marketing ideas for *The Wizard of Oz*. As was usual in those days, all the promotional material was displayed in a full-color "campaign book," the forerunner of today's press kit. This book showcased all the posters, lobby cards, hangers, stand-ups, and other items available to promote the new movie. Campaign books were issued to theater managers, who then selected the items they would use to market the movie in the theater.

By the 1930s, Al Hirschfeld was a well-established movie artist. (Later, of course, he become the most renowned caricaturist of the American theater.) Hirschfeld, born in 1903, had been named art director of Selznick Pictures in 1920. Throughout the 1920s and 1930s, he had created whimsical art for many movie studios, including First National, Goldwyn Studio, RKO, and especially MGM. By a wonderful stroke of luck, and because *The Wizard of Oz* was one of MGM's prestige projects for 1939, he was hired to create the lion's share of the film's promotional artwork.

For *The Wizard of Oz*, Hirschfeld created sketches, paintings, and watercolors of the principal characters, which were used on the film's posters, as well as the title and jumbo window cards and even the glass slides that served as a preview for the movie. Additional promotional items, such as the Loew's Palace pins worn by ushers, all feature art from Hirschfeld's hands. So did the film's sheet music and even the personal letterhead of L. Frank Baum's widow, Maud Gage Baum.

This section of *Memories of a Munchkin* presents the most complete collection of promotional material for *The Wizard of Oz* ever published. Among the rarest pieces are a never-before-seen jumbo window card from the film that was originally displayed in Mr. Raabe's hometown theater in Watertown, Wisconsin.

Perhaps the prize of the collection comes from the distinguished *Wizard of Oz* collector, author, and friend Willard Carroll. He provided an image of a beautiful watercolor that was painted and signed by Al Hirschfeld at the request of Howard Dietz. But this watercolor was never used on any of the original promotional material for the movie, and it has remained unseen by the general public for more than sixty-six years. We are extremely pleased to show it here for the first time, a tribute to the late Al Hirschfeld—a great artist and a great friend.

The "campaign book," distributed to theater owners, was the press kit of its day. It showed all the promotional materials available on the movie. The book for The Wizard of Oz, an important and prestigious project for MGM, was particularly elaborate. These images show the front and back of the book, covered with images of available posters.

◀ This jumbo window card, direct from the Classic Theatre in Watertown, Wisconsin, is shown here for the first time since 1939! It was used to promote The Wizard of Oz for the advance screening near Meinhardt Raabe's hometown. The card measures 22 x 28 inches and features the intricate lettering artwork by Al Hirschfeld.

◀ This 14 x 22-inch window card spotlights the stars and leaves room for the individual theater to fill in dates.

▼ Scenes from the movie draw customers to this "midget window card," measuring just 8 x 14 inches.

This 11 x 14-inch title card features the special letters Hirschfeld designed for the movie. Each letter is packed with tiny scenes and characters from the movie, distinctive and stylish.

AN * Ray BOLGER * Bert LAHR * Jack HALEY

Gaiety! Glory! Glamour!

...DWYN-MAYER'S TECHNICOLOR TRIUMPH!

A VICTOR FLEMING production
Produced by MERVYN LE ROY

(T)

The Coroner is front and (almost) center in this 11 x 14-inch lobby card, the only one that features the Munchkins. Lobby cards date back to the earliest days of movies. Originally they were 8 x 10-inch black-and-white cards, placed in the theater lobby to create interest in current and coming attractions. Later the cards were hand-colored, and still later they began to be printed in color. By the 1930s, the cards generally measured 11 x 14 inches and were offered in sets of eight, including one title card and seven images from exciting scenes in the movie. (The title card from this set is shown on page 182.) When all the cards were displayed together in order, moviegoers could understand the basic plot of the movie.

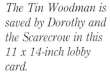

The Tin Woodman is saved by Dorothy and the Scarecrow in this 11 x 14-inch lobby card.

Dorothy, Toto, the Tin Woodman, and the Scarecrow parade down the yellow brick road in this 11 x 14-inch lobby card.

The *"Crying Scene"*
card, with Dorothy
wiping the Cowardly
Lion's tears, is very
popular with collectors.

The *Tin Woodman,*
the Cowardly Lion,
and the Scarecrow
pose as Winkie
Guards. Remember
the Lion's tail flapping
under his coat?

▲ Dorothy and her friends return to the Emerald City in triumph, bringing the broom of the Wicked Witch of the West. Doesn't look familiar? That's because the scene ended up on the cutting-room floor. This fascinating lobby card, measuring 11 x 14 inches, is one of the few surviving images.

◄ The last in the series of lobby cards shows the Wizard taking off in his hot-air balloon without Dorothy and Toto. Fortunately, the ruby slippers will save her.

This twenty-four sheet poster, measuring an impressive 9 x 24 feet, was intended for use on a billboard. The artwork is by Armando Seguso.

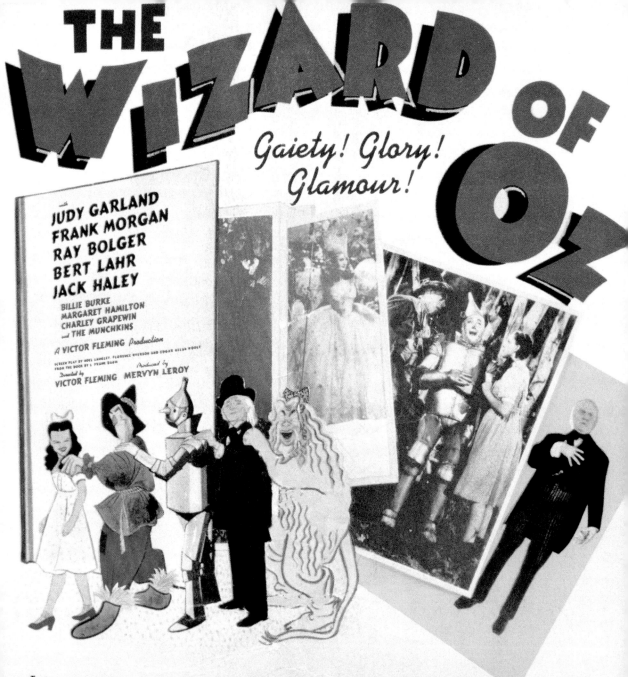

◀ *Three-sheet posters measure 41 x 81 inches. This is style B; the center art is by Al Hirschfeld.*

▼ *In autumn 1969,* The Baum Bugle, *published by the International Wizard of Oz Society, included this watercolor painting by Al Hirschfeld—the original art for three-sheet poster style B. Since then the painting has been lost.*

◀ *Style A, the alternate three-sheet poster, also measures 41 x 81 inches.*

▼ *Insert cards, generally printed on card stock for durability, were used throughout the theater lobby and in outdoor displays. This one, measuring the standard 14 x 36 inches, features Hirschfeld lettering.*

▲ Two-sheet posters, measuring 40 x 60 inches, were printed only for major releases; of course there was one for The Wizard of Oz. However, few of the two-sheets survived. This black-and-white image shows that the two-sheet looked similar to other posters for the movie.

▶ Al Hirschfeld's lettering appears on this one-sheet, style C. One-sheet posters, with their manageable yet still-impressive size of 27 x 41 inches, are popular with collectors. And unlike many of the old size formats used in the days when a theater promoted just one movie at a time, one-sheets are still used in modern multiplexes.

Gaiety!
Glory!
Glamour!

with
**JUDY GARLAND
FRANK MORGAN RAY BOLGER
BERT LAHR   JACK HALEY**
BILLIE BURKE MARGARET HAMILTON
CHARLEY GRAPEWIN and THE MUNCHKINS
A VICTOR FLEMING Production
SCREEN PLAY BY NOEL LANGLEY, FLORENCE RYERSON AND EDGAR ALLAN WOOLF
FROM THE BOOK BY L FRANK BAUM
Directed by
VICTOR FLEMING· Produced by
MERVYN LEROY
It's **METRO-GOLDWYN-MAYER'S TECHNICOLOR TRIUMPH!**

LITHO IN U.S A   *3685   TOOKER LITHO CO N Y

This never-before-seen artwork, painted in watercolor by Al Hirschfeld in 1939, was not used to promote the movie. This black-and-white photograph of the painting is the only known record of its existence; the original watercolor is now lost.

◀ *Another one-sheet poster, style D; like the other one-sheets, this one measures 27 x 41 inches. "Gaiety! Glory! Glamour!" was a recurring selling line for* The Wizard of Oz *and appears on many of the posters.*

Hirschfeld's caricatures are prominently featured on this 27 x 40-inch one-sheet, previously unpublished, that was created specifically for the Australian market. Note the similarities between this and Maud Gage Baum's personal stationery on page 202.

Half-sheet posters, measuring 22 x 28 inches, were usually printed on card stock and were displayed inside the theater.

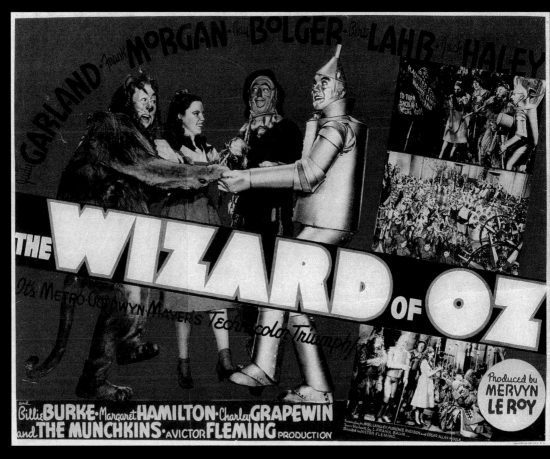

*This half-sheet style B, in bright red,
features scenes from the movie.*

Glinda stars on this fabulous standup. This was probably cut out of three-sheet stock, measuring 41 x 81 inches. The movie information plus a life-size Billie Burke, in sturdy cardboard with a rear support to make the picture stand alone, makes for an impressive display that would tower over most moviegoers, especially Munchkins.

This cutout of Frank Morgan as the Wizard was probably much smaller than the Glinda standup; it was a hanger, intended to swing from the ceiling of the movie lobby. The Wizard was one of a set of six that included Dorothy, Glinda, the Scarecrow, the Tin Woodman, and the Cowardly Lion.

Maud Gage Baum used Hirschfeld's promotional artwork on her personal stationery. The studio may have created this letterhead and printed it for a number of different Wizard of Oz VIPs.

Hirschfeld's art appears yet again, this time on the sheet music for "Ding-Dong! The Witch Is Dead."

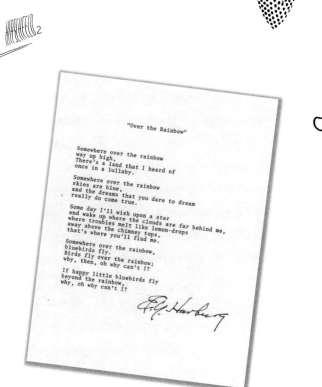

E.Y. "Yip" Harburg wrote the lyrics for the songs from The Wizard of Oz, as well as a good deal of the dialogue-including the rhyming patter spoken by the Munchkins. Harburg wrote the lyrics to many, many standards, including "April in Paris," "It's Only a Paper Moon," and "Brother, Can You Spare a Dime?" Al Hirschfeld drew him several times during his long career.

"Over the Rainbow"

Somewhere over the rainbow
way up high,
There's a land that I heard of
once in a lullaby.

Somewhere over the rainbow
skies are blue,
and the dreams that you dare to dream
really do come true.

Some day I'll wish upon a star
and wake up where the clouds are far behind me,
where troubles melt like lemon-drops
away above the chimney tops,
that's where you'll find me.

Somewhere over the rainbow,
bluebirds fly.
Birds fly over the rainbow;
why, then, oh why can't I?

If happy little bluebirds fly
beyond the rainbow,
why, oh why can't I?

E.Y. Harburg

Hirschfeld captured Ray Bolger as the Scarecrow in the 1940s . . .

. . . as well as Judy Garland as Dorothy.

HIRSCHFELD

In 1989, Hirschfeld commemorated the fiftieth anniversary of The Wizard of Oz *with this wonderful drawing of the principal characters.*

The WIZARD of OZ Comes to Life

PROGRAM...GRAUMAN'S CHINESE THEATRE
TUESDAY EVENING, AUGUST FIFTEENTH, NINETEEN HUNDRED AND THIRTY NINE

◄ Most of the movie's stars attended the gala West Coast premiere of The Wizard of Oz, *held at Grauman's Chinese Theatre. Each one received a copy of this lavish illustrated program. Judy Garland missed the premiere; she was already in New York with Mickey Rooney, rehearsing for the East Coast showings.*

On the East Coast, the premiere engagement of The Wizard of Oz *featured a live show by Judy Garland and Mickey Rooney after every screening at the Capitol Theatre.*

The souvenir program from the West Coast premier included this charming color vignette of the Munchkin Coroner in the Hirschfeld style—unseen since August of 1939.

Glass slides were used in movie theaters to advertise
upcoming movies. During intermissions and before shows,
the slides, about 3 1/4 x 4 inches, were shown using special
projectors called Magic Lanterns. Delicate and fragile, these
slides are among the rarest of movie memorabilia. This
Australian slide, never before published, shows the major
players standing on a prop book.

Another unpublished Australian slide from the movie's original 1940 run in Australia. This one shows Dorothy reading The Wonderful Wizard of Oz.

Glass slides had a blank space where the theater manager could write in the dates of the movie's engagement. This slide was used for the first United States release of the movie.

PART THREE

An Illustrated Walk Down the Yellow Brick Road

EBRAS DO NOT LIVE IN OZ . . . BUT THE HORSE OF A DIFFERENT color does. When you think of *The Wizard of Oz*, countless colorful images come to mind: red ruby slippers, the yellow brick road that leads direct to the capital, lush Emerald City buildings and streets packed with green-garbed inhabitants, bold masses of Winged Monkeys, a green witch, a girl in a blue dress—and of course the magnificent, colorful land of the Munchkins.

Before we sat down to write Mr. Raabe's Munchkin memoir, we had noticed a disturbing pattern in biographies and autobiographies: Very few of them contained any pictures—and those that did were mostly black-and-white.

In fact, while the children's versions of L. Frank Baum's *The Wonderful Wizard of Oz* were packed with color and innovation, the adult books on the making of this brightest of all Technicolor movies, and on its stars and creation, were almost all plainest vanilla. We realized that combining the best of two genres, illustrated children's books and narrative memoir, would be a great place to start a book geared toward the "young in heart."

Only a handful of color Munchkinland photographs exist, so to augment this we commissioned artists to create new renderings of select scenes from the film, especially those containing the Coroner character and Munchkinland. The response from these great artists was unbelievable—and not only did they really love the movie, they all genuinely had *fun* working on the various pieces. In fact, many of them wanted to share their warm feelings about this classic movie with words as well as art.

So as Coroner (and coauthor), we do aver: This gallery contains more than fifty pieces of art, all inspired by the Munchkin Coroner and *The Wizard of Oz*. We hope you enjoy turning page after page, uncovering the next insightful quote, the next fabulous illustration, discovering intriguing new ways to look at a beloved favorite.

Ray Alma

In order to research the illustrations, I watched the movie again on DVD for the first time in years. I watched it with my five-year-old twin nieces, Robyn and Jenna, who had never seen it before. Being so familiar with the movie, I was jaded to all the emotional content of the film. It was fascinating and so moving to watch it with children experiencing it for the first time. They were so into it. They were scared, sad, happy, and otherwise completely amazed. Watching it with them allowed me to experience it again for the first time vicariously. It made me appreciate, all over again, what a truly magical film it is.

RAY ALMA

Ray Alma, who drew the flying monkeys in Part One and the picture on page 283 as well as these pieces, is a frequent contributor to MAD magazine. His work has also been seen in Golf Illustrated, Field and Stream, and many other publications. He lives in New York.

Sergio Aragonés

I was living in Mexico City, where I grew up, when I saw *El Mago de Oz* for the first time. I remember it vividly because up to that day, all the drawing I was doing in my schoolbook and any white sheet of paper I could get my hands on was about war, planes, and tanks. So vivid was my memory of the second world war that that was all I drew. But after *The Wizard of Oz*, my imagination drifted to fantasy, magic, and other worlds—and yes, we can say it made an everlasting impression on me. I was ten years old.

SERGIO ARAGONÉS

Sergio Aragonés, the fastest cartoonist in the world, has won every major award in the field, including the National Cartoonists Society's Reuben Award and the Will Eisner Hall of Fame Award. He has contributed to every issue of MAD *since January 1963, except one (the post office screwed up). He is the cocreator of Groo the Wanderer, as well as Fanboy, Boogeyman, and Magnor, and many other comic books. He lives in California.*

Tom Luth, the colorist on this piece, is a noted illustrator and artist who has worked with Sergio Aragonés for more than two decades. He lives in California.

Philo Barnhart

In December of 1962, I watched *The Wizard of Oz* for the first time, on a small black-and-white television, with my family. To say that Oz had a profound influence on that five-year-old boy would be an understatement! I fell in love with "Over the Rainbow" and the girl who sang it. Was terrified by the Witch, charmed by Dorothy's new friends, but especially identified with Munchkinland (perhaps because I was myself a Munchkin back then?), and was quite tickled with the character of the Munchkin Coroner. *Oz* was the beginning of a dream of making fantasy projects of my own. Meeting Walt Disney at his studio (where my late father, Dale, was employed from 1944 to 1971) was a highlight of my childhood. I was seven years old, and runner-up for the voice of Christopher Robin in the first Winnie-the-Pooh movie. I didn't get the part, but I shall always remember that time fondly because of meeting Walt, one I idolized.

PHILO BARNHART

Philo Barnhart specializes in creating original characters for films, books, and products. An animator and illustrator for Disney for many years, he now works as an independent artist. He lives in California.

Tom Bunk

Tom Bunk

Growing up in Europe I didn't know nothing about
The Wizard of Oz until I flew over the rainbow to
New York. Here, thanks to my two children I must
have traveled the yellow brick road more than ten
thousand times. Since then the yellow bricks have
become the main ingredients of my Munchkin brain.

TOM BUNK

*Tom Bunk has worked for Art
Spiegelman's graphix magazine
Raw and for Topps, producing
Garbage Pail Kids, Wacky
Packages, and many more pop-
culture favorites. His work
frequently appears in MAD
magazine and other publications.
He lives in New York.*

Bob Clarke

I first began my career in advertising in an all-too-brief stint as an art director. This was also a time when art directors knew how to draw. What was presented to the clients had to look like the real thing, and thus I became adept at mimicking many styles. This evolved into work for *MAD* magazine, where they desired that illustrations not merely imitate styles but satirize them as well. Lampooning cartooning styles was one thing; however, it was just as necessary to satirize illustration, photo, and even type styles, too. The absolute genius of type styles was none other than *MAD*'s first art director, John Putnam.

I feel it is an honor to be included with some great works here drawn by many of my most admired and distinguished colleagues. I enjoyed working on this cross between *The Wonderful Wizard of Oz* and *Alice in Wonderland* illustration in crosshatch, because it brought out the essence of Tennicl and the vivid imagination of Baum.

BOB CLARKE

Bob Clarke's work first appeared in MAD *in November 1956 and has appeared in 286 issues since. His parodies of advertisements are particularly memorable for longtime fans. He lives in Delaware.*

AFTER TENNIEL
(LONG AFTER)

Paul Coker Jr.

It was entertaining to research and revisit Oz for the delightful details needed for this drawing; it reminded me of all the great things I loved about the film and had forgotten—especially the Munchkins, who are both visually impressive and endearing in demeanor.

PAUL COKER JR.

Paul Coker Jr.'s distinctive drawings have appeared on greeting cards and in magazines since the mid-1950s. He began contributing to MAD *magazine in 1962 and his work has appeared there regularly ever since. He lives in New Mexico.*

..the Wicked Witch is dead!
She's gone where the goblins go
Below...Below...Below

Certificate of Death †

As Coroner I must aver, I've thoroughly examined her and she's not merely dead, she's really most sincerely dead.

PAUL COKER, JR.

225

Sophie Crumb

My parents brainwashed me with old stuff when I was a kid: the Little Rascals, the Three Stooges, Laurel and Hardy, the Marx Brothers, Betty Boop, et cetera, et cetera . . . and it worked! I still love all of it dearly. *The Wizard of Oz* and the movie *Freaks* were part of all of it, too, especially *The Wizard of Oz*, which I watched almost every day for years and know by heart. So Meinhardt Raabe and all the others are part of what made me, in a deep deep faraway place in my being, and whenever I hear or watch any of that great old stuff, I get that weird emotional feeling that you get when childhood memories come back to the surface. You know. Sigh . . .

SOPHIE CRUMB

The daughter of underground comic artist and living legend R. Crumb, Sophie Crumb has been drawing since childhood. Her pictures have been seen in the acclaimed movie Ghost World *and on the walls of the Matthew Marks gallery in New York. She lives in Paris and New York.*

A CENTURY OF PROGRESS
CHICAGO'S 1934 WORLD'S FAIR

MIDGET CITY ——PEOPLED BY 168 MIDGET MEN,
WOMEN AND CHILDREN FROM MANY COUNTRIES, LIVING
IN HOUSES IN A VILLAGE BUILT TO THEIR PROPORTIONS.

Jack Davis

Certifiate of Death

HAUNTED FOREST
WITCHES CASTLE
1 MILE

I'D TURN
BACK IF
I WERE YOU

I am going to be eighty years old come December.
I have had a great life, some ups with some downs.
The movie *Wizard of Oz* was way ahead of its time,
a dream come true for a lot of kids. We need more
films like that—morally good and well done!

JACK DAVIS

Jack Davis worked at EC Comics in the 1950s, where his unusual style was prized on such titles as The Vault of Horror *and* MAD *magazine. He has continued to contribute to* MAD *through the years, and his work on album covers, magazines, and advertising has earned him international acclaim. In 2000, Jack Davis was the winner of the prestigious Reuben Award, given by the National Cartoonist Society. He lives in Georgia.*

Ron Dias

Whenever I am at my art board and drawing a blank—and nothing else—the one film I put in the VCR to get inspiration is *The Wizard of Oz*, because it is totally and utterly magical for me.

RON DIAS

Ron Dias is one of today's most outstanding animation artists. Over the past forty-five years, he has contributed to countless projects, from Disney's Sleeping Beauty *in the 1950s to interactive CD-ROMs today. He lives in California, not far from the Ron Dias Gallery in Monterey.*

Mort Drucker

The Wizard of Oz is one of
my favorite movies of all time.
MORT DRUCKER

*Mort Drucker is best known for his television
and movie satires in* MAD *magazine. He has
also created distinctive TV animation, movie
posters, and covers and illustrations for
magazines. In 1984, he teamed with Jerry
Dumas to draw the syndicated strip Bentley.
He lives in New York.*

Duck Edwing

HEARSE
OF A
DIFFERENT COLOR

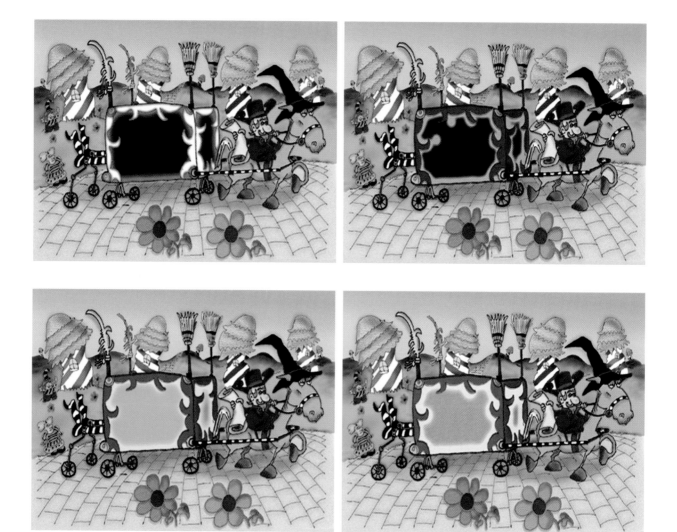

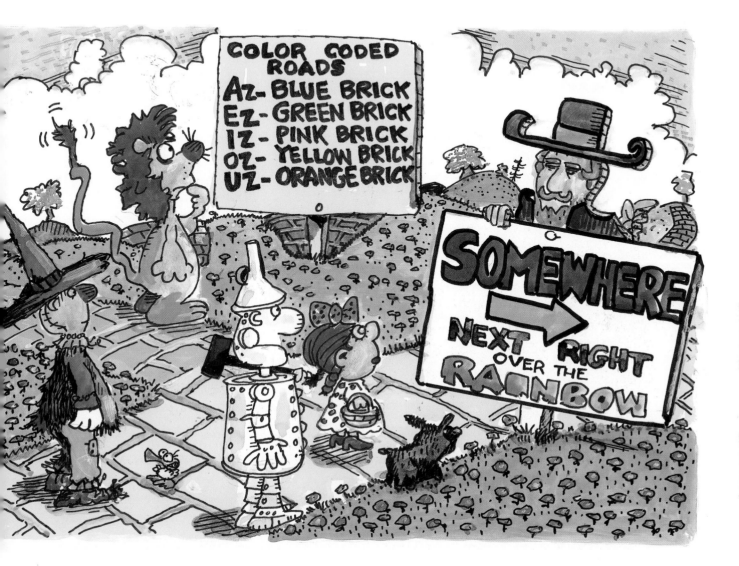

Unlike Dorothy, I never left Oz. I stayed and walked that yellow brick road and drank in all the enchantment for my entire life. The pure magic of Oz is so compelling and wondrous that I never want to leave.

DUCK EDWING

Duck Edwing is affectionately known as MAD *magazine's craziest artist. He has been contributing to* MAD *since 1961, and his cartoons have also appeared in* Playboy, Look, *the Saturday Evening Post, and many other publications. He is the creator of the comic-book heroes the Balls of Death, Super Socks, and the Super Family. He lives in Florida.*

Al Feldstein

I had a wonderful, unexpected experience—the pleasure and delight of revisiting a memorable childhood experience—when I completed the painting for this book. I had seen the original *Wizard of Oz* movie when it was first released, back in the late 1930s, and I'd fallen in love with it instantaneously.

The extensive research material for the painting brought all of the original thrills and laughter and sheer delight of that first viewing experience back to me in a rush . . . and I thoroughly enjoyed executing the painting.

AL FELDSTEIN

After contributing to many EC Comics publications in the late 1940s and 1950s, Al Feldstein was named editor of MAD *magazine in 1955. He held the job for almost thirty years. His art, with its thick lines, blocky anatomy, and two-dimensional visuals, is widely imitated and admired. He lives in Montana.*

Frank Frazetta

The special and visual effects on *The Wizard of Oz* were well done and way ahead of its time.

FRANK FRAZETTA

Frank Frazetta, a major influence on the world of science fiction art, has created seminal images for dozens of magazines and paperbacks, movie posters, and fanzines, including definitive work on Conan the Barbarian and Tarzan. He lives in Pennsylvania.

Frank Kelly Freas

1922–2005

Frank Kelly Freas, a legend in the world of science fiction
art, contributed cover art for hundreds of books and
magazines, including work s by Isaac Asimov, Arthur C.
Clarke, Robert Heinlein, Dean R. Koontz, and Ursula K.
LeGuin. In his distinguished career, he won ten Hugo
Awards; designed the cover for Queen's album News of
the World; and served as an official NASA artist.

Drew Friedman has contributed to
MAD magazine as well as Rolling
Stone, Spy, The New York
Observer, and Entertainment
Weekly. He lives in Pennsylvania.

Although I've always loved *The Wizard of Oz* for all
the obvious reasons, I have a small problem with its
ending. While it's wonderful that Dorothy finally goes
home, I can't help but assume that Miss Gulch will
show up the very next day with the sheriff's order to
remove Toto! I would have much preferred if the
screenwriters had resolved that potential menace by
having Uncle Henry inform Dorothy, upon her return,
that Miss Gulch had been flattened by the twister. With
that, Dorothy's happiness would have been secured.

DREW FRIEDMAN

Drew Friedman

Greg Hildebrandt

The Wizard of Oz was released the year my brother and I were born. I was six years old when I saw *Oz* for the first time. I can still remember my amazement when the film turned from black-and-white to color. To date I have probably seen the film 150 times. The special effects, production design, art direction, costumes and performances are among the greatest ever put on the screen. You cannot compare it to the films and special effects of today. It stands on its own! It is a classic. I admire it more as time goes by. I was extremely honored that Margaret Hamilton wrote an introduction for my illustrated version of *The Wizard of Oz* in 1985. Her portrayal of the Wicked Witch has always had an enormous impact on my art. She is one of my all-time favorite characters. Hey, everybody loves a villain!

GREG HILDEBRANDT

Greg Hildebrandt is an award-winning artist. Among many other achievements, he has illustrated fifteen classic books, including The Wonderful Wizard of Oz, Aladdin, Robin Hood, *and* Dracula. *The* New York Times *has said, "Fortunate the child or adult who receives a gift of classics richly illustrated by Greg Hildebrandt." He lives in New Jersey.*

GREG HILDEBRANDT

Al Hirschfeld

1903-2003

Fabulous!

AL HIRSCHFELD, *seeing
Meinhardt Raabe in his
Coroner costume in 2002*

*Al Hirschfeld was the greatest
theatrical cartoonist of all time.
His distinctive line drawings
capture the history and the
flavor of American theater of
the last century and the
beginning of this one.*

WHO IS REALLY BEHIND THE TERROR DOROTHY AND HER PALS SEEM TO FEAR?

A SKULKING SHADOWY FIGURE IS UNUSUALLY FRIGHTFUL AND CREEPY. DOROTHY WORRIES OVER WHO IT MIGHT POSS- IBLY BE. THOUGH SCARED, SHE REFUSES TO BROOD OVER IT, THUS REASSURING HER SHAKEN CHUMS.

Al Jaffee

One thing I've noticed about *The Wizard of Oz* is that it has a fan-base following similar to that of *The Rocky Horror Picture Show* with activities that are just as fun and most entertaining.

AL JAFFEE

Al Jaffee began his comic career in 1941 and has contributed to MAD *magazine for many years. He invented the famous* MAD *Fold-In in 1964, and he is the creator, writer, and artist of the feature Snappy Answers to Stupid Questions. He lives in New York.*

Michael Wm. Kaluta

My first recollections of *The Wizard of Oz* were from my youth, being taken to the theater to see it in revival in the 1950s. The images I was left with weren't of the characters or the story. What I recalled strongly were the dreamlike backgrounds, especially behind the Scarecrow scenes. Those distant, almost breadlike bluffs spoke to me of a land over the rainbow—a place I'd never get to but that my heart yearned for.

In doing the art for this book, I let my mind draw closer, rolling into the Munchkin village with the Coroner on his needful journey. My imagination is still captured by the distant buildings, the inner lives behind the shutters. It was quite fun to be able to visit the scene as if I were inside the story!

MICHAEL WM. KALUTA

Michael Wm. Kaluta has been a popular illustrator since the 1960s, working on science fiction art, books and graphic novels, and comics. Among his most admired projects are the illustrated edition of Metropolis *and Edgar Rice Burroughs's* Minidoka. *He lives in New York.*

Sebastian Krüger

Some random thoughts about *The Wizard of Oz*:

• The movie shows a fantastic empire of surrealism.

• The Lion reminds me of James Hetfield of Metallica. I am
convinced that the figure inspired his band outfit and style.

• *The Wizard of Oz* must have been a major influence on
Peter Jackson's *Lord of the Rings*.

• The movie offers a wonderful and powerful nostalgic trip
back to childhood.

SEBASTIAN KRÜGER

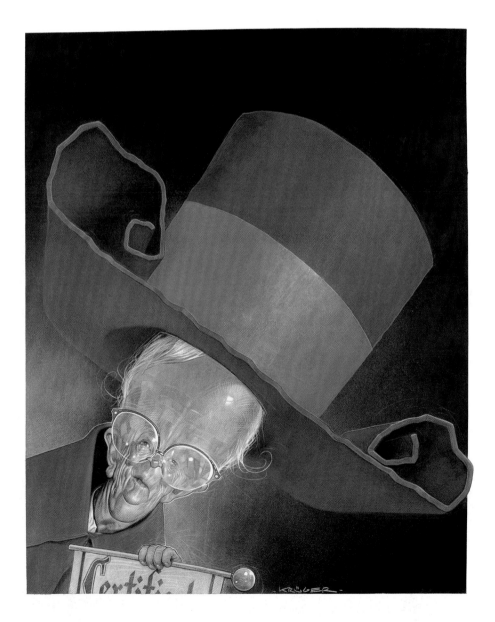

*Sebastian Krüger is
known for his remarkable
caricatures and portraits,
which are both humorous
and insightful. He "has a
genius for capturing the
essence of his subjects
through caricature," said
The* Times *of London.
Krüger lives in Germany.*

Anita Kunz

I don't think there's a film as quintessentially American as *The Wizard of Oz*. Everyone has seen it, and everyone knows the story and characters intimately. All of us have childhood memories of having seen the film and how the various situations within the movie affected us. Vividly imaginative, it's become legendary. So it was with great pleasure that I accepted the invitation to paint a picture for this tribute. And I'm thrilled to be in the company of so many artists I also consider to be legendary.

ANITA KUNZ

Anita Kunz has created art for Time, Rolling Stone, The New York Times, GQ, *Sony Music, and many others. Her distinctive watercolor-and-gouache work is featured in the permanent collections of the Library of Congress and the Musèe Militaire de France in Paris. She lives in Toronto.*

Peter Kuper

Growing up, watching *The Wizard of Oz* on television was an important annual family event. I remember how vivid and glorious the world of Oz seemed compared to Dorothy's Kansas. The funny thing was, my parents only had a black-and-white TV, and I was stunned as an adult to discover that the movie actually had color!

PETER KUPER

Peter Kuper's illustrations and comics appear regularly in Time, Newsweek, *and* MAD, *where he writes and illustrates* Spy vs. Spy *every month. He has many books to his credit, including* Comics Trips, *a journal of his journey through Africa and Southeast Asia, and a graphic adaptation of Franz Kafka's* The Metamorphosis. *He lives in New York.*

Liz Lomax

Creating a sculpture of Munchkinland was a dreamy experience for me. As a child, I was convinced it really existed and wanted to visit that magical little village tucked between the rolling hills and dotted with fantastically oversized flowers. I was infatuated with the little thatched huts and the swirling yellow brick road, the witch's striped legs sticking out from under the fallen house wearing the glittery ruby slippers, and the wicked witch who frightened the daylights out of me.

Rediscovering the film was a treat. I watched it several times in order to make a preliminary drawing of Munchkinland before starting the sculpture. Each time I noticed more whimsical details that made me appreciate this enchanting landscape.

LIZ LOMAX

Liz Lomax, a dimensional illustrator, is known for her remarkable 3-D figures of celebrities and their environments. One of her best-known works is Angelicow, commissioned for the New York Cow Parade and later purchased at charitable auction by Ringo Starr. Liz Lomax lives in New York.

Hermann Mejia

I grew up in Venezuela with a great curiosity for *The Wizard of Oz* (*El Mago de Oz*). Even though the movie was never shown on TV or available for video rental, the characters became part of our culture from some pictures in magazines, reviews, and posters in old-time movie theaters. It was not until my twenty-first birthday that I was finally able to watch the movie for first time; it was like opening a present that I had lost in my childhood.

HERMANN MEJIA

Hermann Mejia

Hermann Mejia began his career as an artist at fifteen, drawing "advertising graffiti" for concerts in his native Venezuela. At twenty-four, he was discovered by MAD magazine, where he quickly became a fan favorite, noted for his celebrity caricatures. He lives in New York.

Don Perlin

I was ten years old when I first saw *The Wizard of Oz*; that was in 1939. Since then I've grown old, and the movie has become a classic that will bring wholesome entertainment to many generations to come.

DON PERLIN

Don Perlin, a Reuben Award winner, has had a long career in comics. He has drawn Werewolf by Night, Ghost Rider, the Defenders, The Transformers, Spider-Man, Captain America, and many others in more than forty years in the field. In addition to this piece, he also contributed the Denslow-inspired chapter openers in Mr. Raabe's memoirs. Perlin lives in Florida.

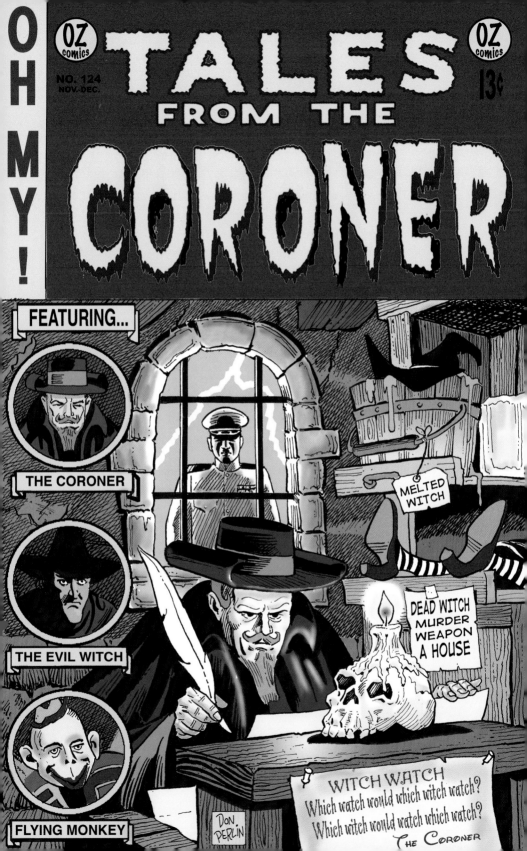

Tom Richmond

In the days before DVDs, VCRs, and Blockbuster, the only way to see *The Wizard of Oz* was to catch it when it was shown on TV once a year. This was a Big Annual Event for my family. We anxiously looked for the time and date to be announced, and that night was a popcorn, apple cider, and home-baked cookie extravaganza. *The Wizard of Oz* will always be associated with family and togetherness for me. And cookies, of course.

TOM RICHMOND

Tom Richmond, an illustrator for more than twenty years, specializes in caricatures and comics. His work is seen regularly in MAD *magazine. He lives in Minnesota.*

John Severin

I was eighteen when *The Wizard of Oz* first came out, and I remember taking my ten-year-old little sister, Marie, to see the film. We enjoyed seeing it on the big screen—and later on the little screen when it was shown on television. Every once in a while I get to enjoy it again with my grandkids. They sit in awe and watch the film with their mouths wide open—except to gulp down their Cokes—while I sit back and sip my Jack Daniels.

JOHN SEVERIN

John Severin is a legend of comic book art; his career began with cartoons for the Hobo News *in 1932. He was the writer and editor of* Prize Western *and also drew such strips as Lazo Kid, Black Bull, and American Eagle. In the 1950s, he began drawing for the whole range of Marvel comics, including The Hulk and Sgt. Fury. He lives in Colorado.*

Drew Struzan

A stranger in a strange land.

We are on the road to find where our heart is, for there's no place like home. Home is where are we comfortable, at peace and secure; we know we are loved. Oz seemed a wonderful place to visit, but all along her journey Dorothy's heart longed for the familiar, for home and friends. She preferred the comfort of her black-and-white world. I know how it feels to be a stranger in a strange land. My road has always led me somewhere over the rainbow to that place called Oz. While it is surely a place for the few, the odd, and the strange, Oz has always seemed to be calling me home.

DREW STRUZAN

Drew Struzan has created art for more than a hundred movie campaigns, including the Indiana Jones movies, the Back to the Future movies, the rerelease of the Star Wars trilogy, and Star Wars: Attack of the Clones. *Album covers, book covers, magazine covers, and advertisements have featured his distinctive work. He lives in California.*

Certificate of Death

Jack Syracuse

It was my great honor and privilege to illustrate the mythical characters of the marvelous land of Oz, because I have always thought I had a great deal in common with them.

Jack Syracuse

A longtime freelance illustrator for MAD *magazine, Jack Syracuse is often lauded as the magazine's best "idea man." He lives on a 27-foot sailboat and is seldom in one place for long. This seafarer fares well with his artwork, though the bottles he sends it in do not always make deadlines.*

Angelo Torres

It could easily be called the perfect movie. I first saw it at the age of ten, and in later years I would go see it in theaters whenever it appeared. Later I would catch the annual showing on television, replete with interruptions and commercials. Now, of course, I own it.

The movie is timeless. I watch it now and find it hard to believe it was made over sixty years ago. The wonderful acting and the music are as new and fresh and full of charm today as they were then. And when Dorothy steps through that door into the Technicolor land of the Munchkins, it is pure movie magic and you are captivated again.

ANGELO TORRES

Angelo Torres, a mainstay of MAD *magazine for more than three decades, has created caricatures and movie parodies that have been favorites for generations of readers. An ongoing contributor to* MAD, *he lives in New York.*

Rick Tulka

Having proudly collaborated on this book, my illustration and name in some magical, mysterious way are now connected to Dorothy, the Scarecrow, the Tin Man, the Lion, and one wonderful Munchkin—and Toto, too!

RICK TULKA

Rick Tulka's watercolors, pencil illustrations, and humorous caricatures have appeared in many magazines, including MAD, People, Reader's Digest, New York, *and* Rolling Stone. *He lives in Paris.*

Gillik
Count

Winkie
Country

Quadling
Country

N

W E

S

Sally Vitsky

From burying my head in my mother's lap each time the Wicked Witch appeared, to the first time I saw the movie on a large campus screen (and discovered—surprise!—Munchkinland is in COLOR!), to seeing it with an "Oz virgin" exchange student, to watching it with my own children—through all these moments, *The Wizard of Oz* has been a thread of continuity through my life, a bridge that spans cultures, and a common bond among friends old and new.

SALLY VITSKY

Sally Vitsky has been a freelance illustrator for more than twenty years, with clients running the gamut from MAD *magazine to* IBM. *She lives in Virginia.*

As with pretty much anyone born in this country in the past seventy years, *The Wizard of Oz* has been an integral part of my life. I grew up with the annual black-and-white television showings in the fifties and sixties (which were often oddly and unnecessarily "hosted" by TV stars such as Dick Van Dyke), and didn't experience the full-blown Technicolor effect of the film until I went to college in the seventies. While others found it a hoot to "turn on" while watching *Oz* (and later synchronized it to Pink Floyd's "Dark Side of the Moon"), I used it as a way to pass an elective film course. (My paper contrasting the film with L. Frank Baum's original book is without doubt a classic that will be forever remembered by, er, well, by . . . me.) One of my great joys has come from introducing the Emerald City and its denizens to my daughter, Alicia. Sad to say, though, she will never know what it is like to have the movie introduced by Dick Van Dyke.

SAM VIVIANO

Sam Viviano is the art director of MAD *magazine. A professional illustrator for more than twenty years, he specializes in movie parodies and caricatures. He lives in New York.*

MEMORIES OF A MUNCHKIN

MONTE WOLVERTON '04

Monte Wolverton

In 1936 my father was living in Hollywood, trying to make it as a young caricaturist in a city of caricatures. Meanwhile, in another part of the same town, someone was making preliminary plans for *The Wizard of Oz*. Even though that's a less than direct connection, it somehow gives me an affinity for the movie. As a fan of fantasy and science fiction, I often tend to focus on the environment of films more than the plot. The world created in *The Wizard of Oz* is as compelling and timeless as anything offered in films of recent years, technological advances notwithstanding. It's a place to be revisited often.

MONTE WOLVERTON

Monte Wolverton, son of cartoonist Basil Wolverton, inherited his father's detailed, offbeat, tremendously influential style. A regular contributor to MAD *and the editor of* The Plain Truth*, he lives in California.*

The artist must ask himself or herself: What is the weiner a metaphor for? The obvious conclusion might be to equate a Munchkin driving a huge gas-powered wiener with a kind of mechanical virility symbol not unlike the typical movie moment of the train going into a tunnel or a giant doughnut being dropped over a skyscraper. An understandable conclusion, but a little bit off the metaphorical bull's-eye. Let us look for a deeper meaning. On the surface, Professor Marvel and Dorothy seem be waving an innocent good-bye to our author's Little Oscar persona, grateful for his nutritious gift of wieners. However, on closer examination, many visual clues points to a subtle rejection of Little Oscar's metaphorical attempt to mix genes with young Dorothy—the wiener impaled on the stick, the dog biting the wiener, and Dorothy ignoring the wieners in her basket. Finally, the moving storm representing a passing threat. Dorothy escapes danger yet again.

BILL WRAY

Bill Wray grew up reading comic books, watching cartoons, and collecting Monster Gum cards. These laid the foundation for his future career working in animation for Disney and other companies and producing comic books. The art director for the Ren and Stimpy *television show, he writes and draws for* Dark Horse *and* MAD *magazine. He lives in California.*

Bernie Wrightson

Bernie Wrightson has been known for his detailed, horrific art, dripping with gore, for more than thirty years. Perhaps best known for Swamp Thing *and his dramatic version of Mary Shelley's* Frankenstein, *he has worked on comic books, movies, and books. He lives in California.*

The End

Index

Bibliography

Arnold, John. "Hollywood Color Problems." *Minicam*, vol. 2, no. 12, August 1939.

Baum, L. Frank. *The Wonderful Wizard of Oz.* Chicago: George M. Hill, 1900.

Bodin, Walter, and Hershey Burnet. *It's a Small World: All About Midgets.* New York: Coward-McCann, Inc., 1934.

Denslow, W. W. *One Ring Circus and Other Stories.* Chicago: M.A. Donahue & Co., 1903.

Carroll, Willard. *I, Toto: The Autobiography of Terry, the Dog Who Was Toto.* New York: Stewart, Tabori & Chang, 2001.

Cox, Steve. *The Munchkins Remember the Wizard of Oz and Beyond.* New York: E. P. Dutton, 1989.

———. *The Munchkins of Oz.* Nashville: Cumberland House, 1996.

Ebsen, Buddy. *The Other Side of Oz.* Newport Beach, Ca., Donovan Publishing, 1993.

Evanier, Mark. *MAD Art: A Visual Celebration of the Art of MAD Magazine and the Idiots Who Create It.* New York: Watson-Guptill, 2002.

Fordin, Hugh. *The World of Entertainment! Hollywood's Greatest Musicals.* Garden City, N.Y.: Doubleday, 1975.

Fricke, John; Jay Scarfone, and William Stillman. *The Wizard of Oz: The Official 50th Anniversary Pictorial History.* New York: Warner Books, 1989.

Fricke, John. *Judy Garland: World's Greatest Entertainer.* New York: MJF Books, 1992.

———. *100 Years of Oz: A Century of Classic Images from The Wizard of Oz Collection of Willard Carroll.* New York: Steward, Tabori & Chang, 1999.

———. *Judy Garland: A Portrait in Art & Anecdote.* New York: Bulfinch, 2003.

Harmetz, Aljean. *The Making of The Wizard of Oz.* New York: Alfred A. Knopf, 1977.

Hay, Peter. *MGM When the Lion Roars.* Atlanta: Turner Publsihing, Inc., 1991.

Hearn, Michael Patrick. *The Annotated Wizard of Oz.* New York: Clarkson N. Potter, 1973.

Hearn, Michael Patrick, editor. *The Wizard of Oz: The Screenplay by Noel Langley, Florence Ryerson, and Edgar Allan Woolf.* New York: Delta, 1989.

Hirschfeld, Al. *The World of Hirschfeld.* New York: Harry N. Abrams, 1970.

———. *Hirschfeld.* New York: Mead, 1979.

———. *Show Business Is No Business.* New York: Da Capo Press, 1983.

———. *Hirschfeld: Art and Recollections from Eight Decades.* New York: Scribner, 1991.

———. *Hirschfeld on Line.* New York: Applause, 1998.

Lahr, John. *Notes on a Cowardly Lion.* New York: Alfred A. Knopf, 1989.

Leopold, David. *Hirschfeld's Hollywood: The Film Art of Al Hirschfeld.* Harry N. Abrams, 2001.

Marx, Harpo, with Rowland Barber. *Harpo Speaks!* New York: Avon Books, 1961.

McClelland, Doug. *Down the Yellow Brick Road: The Making of The Wizard of Oz.* New York: Pyramid Books, 1976.

Scarfone, Jay, and William Stillman. *The Wizard of Oz Collector's Treasury.* West Chester, Pa.: Schiffer, 1992.

———. *The Wizardry of Oz: The Artistry and Magic of the 1939 MGM Classic.* New York; Applause, 2004.

Swartz, Mark. *Oz Before the Rainbow: L. Frank Baum's The Wonderful Wizard of Oz on Stage and Screen to 1939.* Baltimore: The Johns Hopkins University Press, 2000.

Sunshine, Linda. *All Things Oz: The Wonder, Wit, and Wisdom of The Wizard of Oz.* New York, Clarkson Potter, 2003.

Credits

Acknowledgments

My first and foremost thanks must be extended to the United States Navy for indirectly providing me with my coauthor, Lieutenant Daniel Kinske. Daniel flew—even though he prefers to sail—thousands of miles back and forth across the country helping me to search, re-search, and research rare *Wizard of Oz* ephemera, along with interviewing surviving members of the film's cast and crew—many of them previously undiscovered by other Oz researchers. He dutifully and stoically stood his watch at the helm of this project—and not only steered it in the right direction, but stayed the course through some pretty rough weather. So, on behalf of all of the Munchkins—I salute you, lieutenant!

The visual whimsy and substance of this book would not have been possible were it not for the kindness of the President and Chief Operating Officer of Turner Entertainment Company, Roger L. Mayer, and the Director of Clip and Still Licensing at Warner Bros. Entertainment, Inc., Marlene Eastman. Their admiration, love, and respect for *The Wizard of Oz*—along with their generous waiving of all licensing fees—has made me a very happy Munchkin.

It was a thrill beyond words to have had our cover artwork painted by the legendary caricaturist Al Hirschfeld. Meeting and greeting Al in his Manhattan home and studio was one of the most enjoyable encounters of my life. We have tried to "lionize" this venerable and humble Line King by sharing other works he produced for *The Wizard of Oz*'s promotional campaign in 1939. He has our eternal thanks and respect, as does this lovely wife and muse, Louise-Kerz Hirschfeld.

Miss Margo Feiden deserves many Munchkin hugs for her tireless personal and professional support. She and all of the employees of the Margo Feiden Gallery, Ltd., continue to celebrate the artwork of Al Hirschfeld, as she has done for over three decades—and she graciously allowed us to publish many of his fantastic illustrations—of course, they are *all* fantastic.

We would like to give a hand to all of the artful illustrators whose skillful hands and genuine enthusiasm for the project's subject matter provided us with an amazing artistic visual splendor and verbal accompaniments: Ray Alma, Sergio Aragonès, Philo Barnhart, Tom Bunk, Bob Clarke, Paul Coker Jr., Sophie Crumb, Jack Davis, Ron Dias, Mort Drucker, Duck Edwing, Al Feldstein, Frank Frazetta, Frank Kelly Freas, Drew Friedman, Greg Hildebrandt, Al Jaffee, Michael Wm. Kaluta, Max Korn, Sebastian Krüger, Peter Kuper, Anita Kunz, Liz Lomax, Tom Luth, Hermann Mejia, Don Perlin, Tom Richmond, John Severin, Drew Struzan, Jack Syracuse, Angelo Torres, Rick Tulka, Sally Vitsky, Sam Viviano, Monte Wolverton, Bill Wray, and Bernie Wrightson.

We would also like to bestow testimonials to all of the fine people who have helped us.

The honorary degree of Th.D.—Doctor of Thinkology—is conferred to the following people whose words of wisdom and mental mentoring proved very helpful in keeping this project heading in the best possible direction: Irving Brecher, John Fricke, Willard Carroll, Carol Summers, Randy Malone, Lieutenant Jeremiah Teti, USN, and Jake E. Smith, Esq.

The triple-cross Legion of Courage award is presented to the following brave people who truly showed their medal by assisting us through the entire three-year publication process: Patricia Kinske, Norman Webster, and Kirby Hamilton.

Heart shaped-watches are endowed to those "good-deed-doers" whose unconditional kindness and selflessness have earned our eternal admiration: Buddy and Dorothy Ebsen, Mickey and Jan Rooney, Laura Freas, Jackie Ackerman, Jay Stillman, Bill Scarfone, Steve Cox, Woolsey Ackerman, Charles Schram, Grey Smith (Heritage Vintage Movie Posters), Anita Page, Kitty Carlisle Hart, Patty Andrews, Dorothy Barrett, Margaret O'Brien, Maria Menounous, Rory Thorsen, Wally Westler, Mike Schibs, Keven Undergero, Karl, Rebecca, and Lil-Estelle Eichberger, Lieutenant Joseph P. Chopek, USN, Loretta "Peg" Blankenship, the Thrift Family, Rita Dubas, Leslie Bohm, Daniel Barley, Allen Lawson, Guy Clark, and "Admiral."

I would also like to thank my family for humoring my long-standing affiliation with the film over the years with patience, grace, and humor: my lovely and caring little sister Marion and her husband, Clifford, my cousin Arlene Clouston and her husband, Robert, and my cousins from my hometown of Watertown, Wisconsin, Glen Rummler and his wife, Mary.

Thanks also to my fellow Munchkins, Lewis "Idaho" Croft, Clarence and Myrna Swensen, Ruth Duccini, Jerry and Elizabeth Maren, Margaret Pellegrini, Mickey Carroll, Olga Nardone, and Karl Slover—this book is as much yours as it is mine.

We also thank the following people who generously provided their opinions, time, pointers, and pictures without any reservations or thoughts of compensation: Ned Comstock (University of Southern California Cinema-TV Library Doheny), Galen Wilkes, Faye Thompson, and Matt Severson (Academy of Motion Picture Arts and Sciences, Margaret Herrick Library), Tom Lasante (Manager, Photograph Services and Permissions, The New York Public Library), Jeremy Megraw (Billy Rose Theatre Collection, The New York Public Library for the Performing Arts), David Karpeles and Cheryl Alleman (Karpeles Manuscript Library Museum), Sue Heim (Hollywood Poster Frames), Ira Resnick and Joe Burtis (Motion Picture Arts Gallery), Leo Klein and Cliff Meth (IDT Entertainment, Inc.), Joseph Maddalena and Lorna Hart (Profiles in History), Margaret Adamic (Disney Publishing Worldwide), Cynthia Harriss (President, Disneyland Resort), Ralph Cline (Disney Imagineering), Jeremy N. Williams (Senior Vice President, Warner Bros. Entertainment Inc.), Leith Adams (Warner Brothers Archives), Lisa Henson (Muppet Productions Inc.), Ricky Byrd (The Kobal Collection), Jean L. Scrocco (Spiderwebart Gallery), Dianne Nilsen (University of Arizona, Center for Creative Photography), Ronald Mandelbaum and Tom Toth (Photofest), Laura Harden (MastroNet Inc.), Hugh Fordin, Eric Daily, Cory Carson, Sari Levy (Levy Creative Management), Russell Whitacre (Mobile Marketing Manager, Oscar Mayer Foods), Charles Busch, Bob Fennell (The Publicity Office), Aimee Marshall (Chicago Historical Society), Julia Hendry (University of Illinois at Chicago, Special Collections), Frank H. Lieberman, Siegfried and Roy, Thomas M. Skallerup (United States Copyright Office, The Library of Congress), Melina LaMarche (Christie's Images Inc.), Beth Fagan (Brown Shoe Company, Inc.), Valerie-Anne Lutz (American Philosophical Society), Kristine Stone and Neal Adams (Continuity Studios), John Romita Sr., Will Eisner, Will Elder, Gary Vandenbergh, Dave Dorman, Steve Smith, Andrea Faustman (Faustman & Schoenebaum GBR, Germany), Florence Whidden, Ryan Flanders, and the Usual Gang of Idiots, staff, and writers at MAD magazine for "not worrying" that your artists would be forever humming my favorite song, "Ding-Dong! The Witch is Dead."

Miscellaneous Munchkin requitals go out to the representatives of the English Guild at Jacksonville University in Jacksonville, Florida—Julie Brannon, Raymond Clines, Patrick "Batman Pat" McLeod, and Bob Stanton; along with the cast and crew of the Broadway musical *Wicked*: Idina Menzel, Joel Grey, Kristin Chenoweth, Carole Shelley, Michelle Federer, and Christopher Fitzgerald.

And finally, Daniel Kinske and I gratefully thank our literary agent, Eric Myers of the Spieler Agency, for taking a chance on our "little" project, as well as fellow Hirschfeldphile and renowned caricaturist Ken Fallin, for introducing us to his friend Eric. And of course we would be remiss if we missed mentioning the fantastic and fun-loving people at Watson-Guptill Publications who dared to take a chance on this book, and in doing so made my dream come true! These eager and ebullient professionals include: our wonderful editors, Laaren Brown, Mark Glubke, and Michele La Rue; our design wizard, Jay Anning; and the dynamic behind-the-scenes crew, Allison Devlin, Jason H. Maynard, Elizabeth Wright, Bob Nirkind, Sharon Kaplan, and Ellen Greene. Many Munchkin thanks to one and all!